Chicana Spiritual Activism

CHICANA SPIRITUAL ACTIVISM

Making Change, Making Soul

BRENDA SENDEJO

THE UNIVERSITY OF
ARIZONA PRESS
TUCSON

The University of Arizona Press
www.uapress.arizona.edu

We respectfully acknowledge the University of Arizona is on the land and territories of Indigenous peoples. Today, Arizona is home to twenty-two federally recognized tribes, with Tucson being home to the O'odham and the Yaqui. The university strives to build sustainable relationships with sovereign Native Nations and Indigenous communities through education offerings, partnerships, and community service.

ISBN-13: 978-0-8165-5407-2 (hardcover)
ISBN-13: 978-0-8165-5406-5 (paperback)
ISBN-13: 978-0-8165-5408-9 (ebook)

Cover design by Leigh McDonald
Cover art: *Guadalupe Cuando Joven* by Santa C. Barraza
Typeset by Sara Thaxton in 10.5/14 Warnock Pro with Helvetica Neue LT Std, Alize, and Remely WF

Publication of this book is made possible in part by the proceeds of a permanent endowment created with the assistance of a Challenge Grant from the National Endowment for the Humanities, a federal agency.

Library of Congress Cataloging-in-Publication Data
Names: Sendejo, Brenda, 1971– author
Title: Chicana spiritual activism : making change, making soul / Brenda Sendejo.
Description: Tucson : University of Arizona Press, 2026. | Includes bibliographical references and index.
Identifiers: LCCN 2026010063 (print) | LCCN 2026010064 (ebook) | ISBN 9780816554072 hardcover | ISBN 9780816554065 paperback | ISBN 9780816554089 ebook
Subjects: LCSH: Feminist spirituality—Texas | Mexican American women—Political activity—Texas | Women social reformers—Texas | Mexican American women—Texas—Social conditions—20th century | Mexican American women—Texas—Social conditions—21st century
Classification: LCC F395.M5 S46 2026 (print) | LCC F395.M5 (ebook) | DDC 976.4004/6872073—dc23/eng/20260511
LC record available at https://lccn.loc.gov/2026010063
LC ebook record available at https://lccn.loc.gov/2026010064

Printed in the United States of America
♾ This paper meets the requirements of ANSI/NISO Z39.48-1992 (Permanence of Paper).

The movement taught me I could change the world.

—MARÍA ELENA MARTÍNEZ, TEXAS RAZA UNIDA PARTY STATE CHAIR (1976–1978), EDUCATOR, AND *CHAMANA* (SHAMAN)

CONTENTS

PREFACE

"The Movement Taught Me I Could Change the World": Chicana Feminism, Activism, and Spiritual Encuentros

A single encounter over twenty years ago changed my life forever. It was the day I met María Elena Martínez. María Elena's life path illuminated so much, including my own path, which she helped me to see, understand, and step into—hence, this is where the story begins. That was my entry into the world of spiritual activism. That is the lens through which I write this book.

Had I not met María Elena in 2004, in the context of women's participation in the Chicana and Chicano civil rights movement in Texas, this book would not exist. From María Elena and her contemporaries, I learned a core teaching that forms the foundation of this work: that living out our individual purpose—rooted in an insistence on the full humanity, dignity, and right of all people to live out their purpose—paired with doing our own inner work, embracing our *medicina*, and sharing it with others are actions powerful enough to fuel a movement.[1] And as María Elena told me, "The movement taught me I could change the world."[2] I bring forth this message here, to our present moment, as a call to action. It is a gift from our elders, wisdom keepers who practice spiritual activism by extending the inner work of healing to our outer work of change.

A Surprising Turn: The Movement Continues in 2026

This story is many years in the making. And the social and historical context in which it is written has changed immensely over the course of the past twenty-two years since that initial encounter with María Elena. Nothing could compare, however, to the current moment. As of the writing of this introduction, we are midway through 2026. A wraith of fascism has unleashed an unfathomable degree of hate and violence against Latinx and Muslim immigrants, Black, Brown, and LGBTQIA+ communities, women, and children; has targeted research and historical recovery projects like this very book; and efforts are underway to dismantle research and ethnic studies centers women in this book helped to build. Never in my lifetime—and perhaps in those of the women I write about here—has it felt more pressing to share the stories, wisdom, and coping and survival strategies we have developed, among them, a profound and fierce love for humanity and insistence upon liberation.[3] This book is my humble contribution to today's movement—our movement. It is a movement of revolutionary love, generosity of spirit, uncompromising insistence on uplifting the dignity of those whose lives have been threatened and humanity questioned, and working for their survival and joy.[4] Through their historical movement activism and since that time, María Elena and the other women in this book—along with their contemporaries from the movement era across the country—worked tirelessly to produce vast knowledge and effective strategies that will serve us in responding to this moment.[5] It is not a twist I could have foreseen when the seeds of this project were planted on that spring day in 2004.

That encounter would lead me to a new way of understanding feminism and social activism, one that blends a commitment to transforming external material inequalities with the work of inner healing and liberation. In the face of today's stark social and political challenges and ongoing warfare against recovered histories and stories of lives like the ones in this book, the storytellers in the pages that follow offer guidance and hope on the path ahead. We can learn from their unwavering commitment to fostering love, community, belonging, healing, and wholeness—and we can use that as fuel to continue the work.[6]

The *Encuentro*

María Elena entered our graduate seminar at University of Texas at Austin to speak to our class as part of her participation in the Women of La Raza

Unida Oral History Project.[7] The project involved students interviewing women prominent in the Mexican American civil rights movement from the 1960s on. One of the central goals of the course was to teach students about "important themes of gender relations and a feminist critique of patriarchy in the Mexican American social movement of Texas during the 1970s."[8] The day María Elena arrived in 2004, she wore a colorful huipil (a traditional woven blouse) and a small beaded pouch around her neck.[9] She approached my classmates and me with a warm smile, intent on making eye contact with each one of us as she shook our hands. There was something about that intentional connection that stayed with me long after. In retrospect, I came to realize that in that moment I felt seen. Seen in a university setting—a space not originally intended for first-gen women and other people of color such as myself. Many of us came to such graduate programs and fields of study like Mexican American studies at UT Austin only through the arduous and tenacious activism of Chicanas and Chicanos in the late 1960s and 1970s including María Elena, the author and activist Martha P. Cotera, and the professor who developed and taught our course, historian Emilio Zamora.[10]

In that classroom, we shared being Tejanas. Our Tejana bodies held the generational histories of systemic injustices, like the racial segregation and discrimination held in place through Jim Crow laws in the late nineteenth and early twentieth centuries and the gender oppression facilitated by organized religion and other institutions. But on that day, something shifted.[11]

That initial meeting with María Elena marked the first of many encounters to come. Far from just encounters, I consider them *encuentros.* I draw on María Eugenia Cotera's use of *encuentros* as meaning active engagements with the past that have transformative effects in the present. Encuentros with María Elena and the other women, as I'll share in the coming chapters, have the potential to move us through *conocimiento,* a process of spiritual inquiry by which we come closer to our true selves, a central theme of this book that was originally theorized by Gloria Anzaldúa.[12]

That first encuentro, a spiritual encuentro, would be the catalyst for many more encuentros with several of María Elena's peers, igniting a charge and change within me that inspired not only this project but also my ongoing thinking about the power of encuentros, community, and connection to transform systems of oppression by working at the level of the spirit. María Elena visited our class to speak about her role as Texas state chair of the Raza Unida Party (RUP) and movement activist.[13] Our class had read about women's contributions to the party, so María Elena's reputation preceded her. The political narrative she shared that day was enormously engaging—she was active with the Mexican American Youth Organization (MAYO) at UT Austin, became the first woman to lead a political party in Texas, and cofounded RUP's women's caucus, Mujeres Por La Raza, which advanced women's political issues by asserting gender equality; affirming the importance of *la mujer* and *la familia*; and addressing concrete concerns such as access to quality childcare, job training, and reproductive rights. This active caucus brought together Chicana feminism and Chicano nationalism. Mujeres advocated for greater representation of women in public office and challenged patriarchal dynamics within both the party and its broader organizational structures, as well as the white supremacist systems they encountered within the mainstream women's movement. Mujeres Por La Raza emerged alongside the rise of the Chicana feminist movement in Texas, and several of its members were actively involved in both, including María Elena.[14] She was devoted to the educational advancement of Mexican Americans and education reform as well, working diligently alongside her comrades to bring attention to the need for effective bilingual and bicultural education, which resulted in bilingual and dual-language programs in schools around the state—a monumental feat in itself.[15]

María Elena's roles and commitments were deeply intertwined with her North Texas upbringing and lived experiences connected to her gender, racial, socioeconomic class, and religious identities. Her activism also revealed a profound love for her family, upbringing, and community.

I was in awe of all of the women participants in the oral history project with whom our class had the privilege to meet and work.[16] The rare opportunity to meet these women in person was life-changing. Women shared the sources of their activism during the public roundtables organized outside of class, and María Elena and Martha Cotera made classroom visits as well, to tell our class about the lived experiences that informed their politics and feminist consciousness. It was then that a distinctive element emerged in the story of María Elena's life journey. It caught my attention. Despite having just met her, a sense of familiarity

FIGURE 1 Women of La Raza Unida Party Oral History Project panel presentation, University of Texas at Austin, 2004. Left to right: Martha Cotera, Evey Chapa, Luz Bazán Gutiérrez, and María Elena Martínez. Brenda Sendejo.

enveloped me in her presence. Yet I couldn't quite pinpoint what resonated with me about her narrative.

The Politics of Spirit Emerge

The unique aspect of María Elena's life narrative that came into focus—one that wasn't as prominently featured in the political biographies of the other women in the oral history project—was that her political journey was interwoven with her spiritual evolution. In her life story, the realms of politics and spirituality intersected. I felt my own early questioning and constant search for a deeper spiritual connection in her words in a way I'd never felt before.

The impact of all this was overwhelming, a wave of emotions sweeping over me as I simply listened to her recount her journey. It was only later that I came to understand what had captivated me so deeply: Hers was a story that brought together gender oppression, racial discrimination, and religion within the context of a feminist critique. I recognized it but did not yet have the knowledge of such a framework. Nor, more profoundly, of what emerged at the intersection of those things: María Elena's deep sense of her truth. I found myself drawn to it, this energy and way of being that I couldn't quite put into words, yet recognized on a visceral level.

María Elena had experienced the effects of church patriarchy and racial and gender injustices growing up in a small farming community north of Dallas. She spoke of being raised Catholic, then sliding away from the church in the years following the movement. While once very involved in the church, she would come to question it, recalling experiences such as becoming physically ill in Catholic school when having to repress her voice around topics such as sexuality. This departure was followed by a period of what she calls "spiritual dormancy." During this period, the death of a dear friend left her questioning her spiritual direction and purpose. Shortly thereafter, she was introduced to the spiritual path that she embraced since her thirties, which included shamanistic *curanderismo*.[17] This path provided the spiritual fulfillment she was seeking.

Questioning: The Early Seeds of Borderlands and *Feminista* Thought

María Elena's period of spiritual dormancy and her eventual arrival at earth-based traditions and devotion to Our Lady of Guadalupe–Tonantzin (Guadalupe, the mestiza or Indigenous Marian mother figure, *and* Tonantzin, "our Mother" to the ancient Nahua) and the feminine divine were my first introduction to a Mexican American woman who practiced such things. She would later tell me, in reference to her transition, "The church no longer meets my spiritual needs." That statement struck a chord within me, aligning with my own upbringing in the Catholic Church and questioning of certain aspects of its doctrine, which I share with several women in this book. For me this intuition, sense of knowing, and familiarity were rooted in being a Texas Chicana on her journey of spiritual self-discovery in what I would come to see as the borderlands.

Chicana feminist scholars who are featured in this book, including Gloria Anzaldúa, Norma Cantú, Martha Cotera,[18] Inés Hernández-Ávila, and Yolanda Chávez Leyva provide us with the language for so many of our borderlands experiences characterized by cultural negotiations and identity formation[19]—which we can see as a path, a way of being. Anzaldúa's borderlands theory is particularly useful in explaining what in the women's lives led them to spiritual activism, as well as my own. Anzaldúa offers us a framework that illuminates Chicana life, derived from her lived experience growing up in the Texas Rio Grande Valley, navigating the social and cultural terrain of the Texas-U.S. Southwest/Mexican border. But beyond the physical and geographic borders, she offers that there exist metaphorical and conceptual borders.

"The psychological borderlands, the sexual borderlands, and the spiritual borderlands," she writes, "are not particular to the Southwest. In fact, the Borderlands are physically present wherever two or more cultures edge each other, where people of different races occupy the same territory, where under, lower, middle, and upper classes touch, where the space between two individuals shrinks with intimacy."[20]

Anzaldúa's borderlands theorizing—much like her other concepts and theories—acts as theory in the flesh. As Cherríe Moraga notes, "A theory in the flesh means one where the physical realities of our lives—our skin color, the land or concrete we grew up on, our sexual longings—all fuse to create a politic born of necessity."[21] This notion of "theory in the flesh," a way of knowing and being inspired by my own lived experiences, would be pivotal to my thinking around spiritualized activism and writing this book. María Elena's biography reflected how she navigated various structural inequalities in her geographic, educational, political, and religious borderlands. I now know that I too was navigating all kinds of borderlands and in the midst of conocimiento, on a path of transformation toward my truth—from that Catholic little girl to a grown Chicana feminist. This path led me to recognize the deep connection between my story and that of María Elena, one I do not think I would have or could have otherwise found. My and María Elena's stories intersected in those borderlands.

As someone who wondered from a young age why women could not be priests, I had many questions upon learning about María Elena's life. How and why did she leave Catholicism? How did she know this was the right move? What was that process like? What led her to her current path as a spiritual teacher and healer? The idea of religious remaking and spiritual transformation told within the context of a political movement signaled something very significant to me, something I felt in my heart and spirit, but did not yet know how to articulate intellectually. My mind, body, and spirit were very separate from one another then. I was fractured and fragmented trying to understand her story through "rational" Western conceptions of knowledge production, the only tools I had access to at the time. The tension within me was palpable, telling, and motivating.

Inner Work: A First Glimpse of Spiritual Activism

Over time, I realized that María Elena gave me a glimpse into something that I hadn't even known was missing: a feeling of connection and inner belonging in a space where I felt like an outsider. The uneasy feeling of misalignment was familiar—I first felt it in the Catholic Church growing up, then in the university. Little did I know how many parallels I would find between the two institutions. Upon coming to know María Elena and delving into her world, where spirituality was inseparable from a deep commitment to liberation, my mind, body, and spirit were reconnecting—a journey reflected in María Elena's own life. Listening to María Elena's story propelled me into what I would later learn were the early stages of conocimiento. Through that transformative encounter—a meeting with my own truth that launched me into deep inner work—I began to inch my way back toward the wholeness that I had all along, to re-membering, to home. That encuentro with María Elena and subsequent encuentros with several of her peers whom I would contact and interview for my doctoral research following the course were my first exposure to Chicana feminist thought in practice. That spiritual encuentro and the ones to follow opened a door to a new world filled with soul-activating stories and heart-opening rituals, ancestral wisdom and memory, possibilities for healing, community, and profound and powerful acts of love. It impacted me so deeply that it would become central to my life's work as well as a lived practice.

In the pages to follow, the reader will bear witness to my journey of moving through conocimiento, through stories of my relationships with

María Elena and the other mujeres I will introduce you to. My unwieldy journey—the essence of Anzaldúa's conception of conocimiento—is captured in the nonlinear storytelling and nontraditional format of this book. The ebb and flow between styles of academic writing and embodied writing, soul whispers and spirit stories, reveal a journey of making face and making soul: a journey of Chicana spiritual activism.

ACKNOWLEDGMENTS

It has been the honor of a lifetime to receive and weave together the wisdom of medicine keepers of the U.S.–Mexico borderlands. Susana Almanza, Santa Barraza, Norma E. Cantú, Rosie Castro, Martha P. Cotera, Carmen Lomas Garza, Inés Hernández-Ávila, Yolanda Chávez Leyva, María Elena Martínez, Mary Margaret Navar, Cynthia Pérez, and Rev. Virginia Marie Rincón: Thank you for your *coraje*, your time and trust in sharing your wisdom for this book, and for transforming lives, including my own. I also honor Gloria Anzaldúa, contemporary and comadre to many of the women, whose spirit guided this work and whose theory and practice of spiritual activism paved the way for it to be born.

A special thanks to University of Arizona Press Editor in Chief Kristen Buckles, who believed in telling *this* story from the start. She previously supported scholarship on spirituality and activism early on, before the topic had been generally taken up, by publishing *Fleshing the Spirit: Chicana, Latina, and Indigenous Women's Spirituality and Activism* in 2014. I contributed my first published piece to that anthology with the support of wonderful femtors and editors Irene Lara and Elisa Facio. My heart is full of gratitude for this profound, full-circle moment. The contract for this book arrived to me on December 12, the Feast Day of Our Lady of Guadalupe–Tonantzin, and on the same day two years later, the book's title was confirmed. That resonance is deeply meaningful, as Guadalupe-Tonantzin has been a divine guiding presence in my life, the lives of the women in this book, and this work since its earliest inception. The artwork on the cover of this book holds special significance. I am eternally grateful to Santa Barraza for granting permission to use her *Guadalupe Cuando Joven,* which I first saw in her studio in 2008. Santa would introduce me to South Texas folk religious sites and the possibilities for *milagros* when I needed them most.

My thanks also to Amanda Krause, Leigh McDonald, and the entire University of Arizona Press team for standing behind this work and nurturing it into being. During the production of this book, devastating revelations around sexual violence in the *movimiento* emerged, affecting the women in these pages and their *colegas* across the country deeply. The Press met those moments with integrity and humanity, pivoting where needed in production. Diana Rico tended to this manuscript and spirit stories with extraordinary care. I am grateful for the deep understanding of spiritual activism and respect for the women's stories that she poured into copyediting this book. Thank you as well to Kelly Lessard for supporting the manuscript at a pivotal time in its production.

The book is better for Irene Lara and Lara Medina's critical insights as reviewers and for their *corazones y espíritus* gracing its pages. Their leadership and guidance have strengthened not only this book but the field as a whole. Liliana Saldaña's spiritual activism inspires me, and I am so grateful for her support of this book. Aurora Chang's steady presence, spiritual grounding, and editorial brilliance helped carry this book and me through moments of deep transformation. Thank you for holding space for my true self to emerge on these pages.

My Austin community has sustained me deeply through all of the many stages of life. With a full heart, I thank María Elena Martínez—Meme—my spiritual *madrina, maestra,* and guide back home to myself. The seeds of this book were planted the day I met her. Meme lived spiritual activism, insisting that I carry this work forward, especially with youth, reminding me that I/we carry knowledge they need—knowledge often erased or silenced. The Martínez family generously shared their beloved Meme with her Austin family. They reviewed the manuscript with her and gave this book their blessing, which means everything. You are *familia—siempre.*

Martha Cotera's twenty years of femtorship left an indelible mark on my life and this work. Her brilliance, generosity, and unwavering commitment to liberation continue to guide me. In creating a "space in between" in the 1970s, she bridged university and community, as with her idea for a La Raza Unida women's oral history project that came to fruition through a collaboration with Professor Emilio Zamora, who brought students face to face with movimiento-era women to learn first-hand about their efforts to challenge patriarchy within the movement. That collaboration was a catalyst for this work, which I view as part of a legacy of Chicana feminist thought and community-rooted scholarship in Mexican American and Latino Studies at the University of Texas at Austin.

Alma de Mujer Center for Social Change has been a sacred foundation for this book, for my path as a spiritual activist, and for my becoming a mother. Deep gratitude goes to the board of the Indigenous Women's Network (IWN) and to Genevieve Vaughn for gifting the land to the IWN. The IWN, as stewards of the land for Alma de Mujer, make it possible to commune with the beauty, spirits, and creatures of Mother Earth and to connect with the ancestors. To the entire Alma community: Thank you for your love, your teachings, and your contributions to Alma. The lessons, relationships, and memories formed there with you and my students over the years continue to guide and inspire me. I thank Yvette Mendez, Cynthia Pérez, Rev. Virginia Marie Rincón, Velia Sánchez, Modesta Treviño, Gloria Quesada, Beth Ebbing, Margie (Mary Margaret Navar), Alicia Encisco-Litsche, and Naya Jones for their *comunidad,* wisdom, and love. Thank you to Mary Margaret for her careful review of the manuscript and for the many soul-nurturing conversations and *consejos* that helped birth this book. The spirit of Marsha Gomez is with us always, and her role in the creation of Alma is forever etched in its history and our hearts. Thanks as well to all of the directors of Alma and members of the Women's Council for their leadership over the years. I share a deep connection to Alma de Mujer with Alicia Encisco-Litschi, who has written extensively about Alma. Thank you, *hermana del alma,* for your heart-centered consejos and limitless wisdom throughout the journey of writing this book and the reminder to tell this story from my heart. Your *medicina* is potent.

It was through UT's Center for Mexican American Studies (CMAS) that I met some of my dearest friends in graduate school. Maria and Cruz and Elvira Prieto, my "sunshine sisters," are brilliant *poderosas* who taught me to never dim my light—that my power resides within it. I thank Jennifer Najera, fellow Chicana feminist anthropologist, for being a steady, loving presence in my life and for her guidance and support over the years and during the writing of this book. My Corpus *comadre* Jackie Cuevas is a brilliant activist-scholar who forever has my back. Her steadfast insistence that my spirit stories are needed helped bring this book to life. Along with Jackie, her spouse, my friend Jen Margulies, and their amazing Avital have been there for me and my family through thick and thin. I see and appreciate you all so much.

María Cotera and Linda Garcia taught me the urgency in documenting women's stories and the integrity that must go into it. They and their trailblazing Chicana por Mi Raza Digital Memory Project and Archive inspire this work. Thank you for paving the way and for your love and support, amigas. Thank you to Carla Alvarez, Latino studies archivist at the Benson Latin American Collection, for her valuable support with this project and for creating the conditions for life-changing *encuentros* to take place for our students.

Rebeca Burciaga, a healer with her art and powerful consejos, has brought much to my life in a short time. Thank you for supporting this work and for your creative brilliance in seeing the many possibilities for taking it out into the world. Aída Hurtado provided mentorship on this project and beyond on numerous occasions. Gracias, fellow Tejana.

Deep gratitude goes to my former students at Southwestern University (SU) in the Latina History Project and Latinx Spiritualities and Chicana Feminisms courses. They listened to me tell these stories and helped to document them over the years, receiving them in a way that showed me that the stories are medicine and that I have a responsibility to share them. My dear faculty colleagues, a group of kind, fierce, and brilliant souls, helped me to remember the why of it all and to keep shining my light. I am grateful to colleagues who became teachers and family: Alicia Moore, Maria Lowe, Ken Mello, Elaine Craddock, Sequoia Maner, Jethro Hernández Berrones, and Meagan Solomon. Alison Kafer read many drafts of this work over the years and supported bringing some of the women in this book to SU. Her constant faith in me and this work made this book possible, as did her feminist praxis, which is healing to the core. Lamiyah Bahrainwala has believed in me and my work to a degree I didn't know possible. Her spiritual activism has shaped me and my work in profound ways. Melissa Johnson, my anthropology colleague and friend, insisted on the value of this work and showed me that I had a way of putting it into practice and building community around it early on. We had many talks, and she reviewed many iterations of this work, constantly reminding me to share these stories my way, *this* way. María de los Ángeles Rodríguez Cadena's presence at SU reminded me that healers do exist within academia. Her generous *palabras* about my path post-SU helped put its importance into focus for me. *Mil gracias, querida amiga.*

Beloved friends and their families have sustained me and my Chicana feminist spirit work for decades. The love and support of Miriam Carrillo, Clary Ramos Sukkar, and Joedy Yglesias continue to carry me. Somos Tejanx, and I could not be more proud. I also thank Parisa Fatehi-Weeks, Bridget Barrow, Dawn Callaway, and Jen Shields for their belief in me and my *feminista* dreams from the very beginning.

To my soul coaches, Paz, Risha, and Rosa, each of you have shared your unique medicina with me on this journey in ways that have supported my spiritual growth.

Now to my beloved *familia*. To my parents, Gloria and Jesse, thank you for your unwavering love and giving me the foundation to dream, to grow, and to become. My mother, Gloria, is the first Tejana I ever knew. Her Aries fire lives within me, and I aim to channel it into doing good in the world. A hardworking Tejana born and raised in Corpus Christi, her story is one of finding the joy in life and expressing it—in music, dancing, and through laughter. This is *your* soul medicina and part of your legacy, along with your unconditional love for *familia* and acceptance of us for who we are. My father, Jesse, prioritized education and caring for his children in enduring ways that have shaped who I am today. Our shared love for Our Lady of Guadalupe is a special bond. My father's relentless love for his *mijas* and sensitive soul give me strength and comfort.

My sisters, Polly and Priscilla, your love, humor, strength, and faith in me are constant sources of joy and grounding. I am proud of our Tejano and *mexicano* roots and carry them and you with me always. You are amazing mothers and *tías*, and you and your families bring so much meaning to my life and this work.

To the extended Ademski, Ledesma, and Sendejo families, whom I love dearly: Thank you for receiving me and this work with such love.

And finally, to Tommy, Jude, and Luna. This book unfolded alongside our lives and carries our story with it. Tommy, thank you for walking this winding path with me, for your patience, love, and support. Meme tears up when talking about you, for she always says you are special, with your sensitive energy and deep connection to the earth. That you are, my love.

Jude and Luna, your soul seeds were planted at Alma de Mujer, and so this book is, in many ways, your *herencia*. I love you with all that I am—*con todo mi corazón y alma*. You are my greatest teachers and guiding stars. I see in my children the future I and others envision for this world—one where a balance between the sacred masculine and the divine feminine prevails. Our spirit pup, Mojo, was a supportive writing partner, by my side for much of the writing of this book.

This book is a rebirth made possible by these and many other beautiful souls. To my ancestors and to all who will carry these stories forward, gracias.

Chicana Spiritual Activism

INTRODUCTION

MAKING FACE, MAKING SOUL

Our Medicina *as the Manifestation of Our Truth*

Little did I know in that first encuentro that I was feeling the effects of María Elena speaking her truth, which I would come to understand as connected to her *medicina*. Living that truth, through her purpose, involved listening to her soul, which I will explore further through the concept of making face/making soul, which comes from Gloria Anzaldúa:

> We women of color strip off the máscaras others have imposed on us, see through the disguises we hide behind and drop our personas so that we may become subjects in our own discourses. We rip out the stitches, expose the multi-layered "inner faces," attempting to confront and oust the internalized oppression embedded in them, and remake anew both inner and outer faces. . . . We begin to acquire the agency of making our own caras. "Making faces" is my metaphor for constructing one's identity. "[U]sted es el moldeador de su carne tanto como el de su alma." You are the shaper of your flesh as well as of your soul. According to the ancient nahuas, one was put on earth to create one's "face" (body) and "heart" (soul). To them, the soul was a speaker of words and the body a doer of deeds.[1]

María Elena's (re)construction of her religious identity, "making face," coincided with the outer expression of her soul, which was the embracing of her truth; this in turn led her to her purpose, or medicina, and toward a spiritualized activism. While she had left the political realm after her involvement in RUP, the work she would later take on was not completely separate from her political activism of the late 1960s through the '70s, during the movement era. She was still living her purpose and engaging with politics, but in a completely different way. She would engage in a "politics of spirit" and bridge seemingly opposing ideas of spirituality and activism, offering a glimpse into spiritual activism—"spirituality for social change, spirituality that posits a relational worldview and uses this holistic worldview to transform oneself and one's worlds."[2]

In that poignant encuentro, María Elena brought me into the fold of something she would illuminate more deeply in the years to come. A lifelong learner and teacher, she extended insights from her own journey of personal growth, healing, and self-love to us through her teachings and storytelling. Her efforts were now centered on healing and spirit work—a spiritualized activism. This work, her life's purpose, came into clear focus for her through the process of coming home to herself, her whole self. Her re-membering and activism converged, inspiring an unwavering

FIGURE 2 María Elena Martínez, ca. 2006. Brenda Sendejo.

commitment to justice and liberation, as well as an embrace of a radical inclusivity in practice.[3]

Las Tejanas/Las Mujeres del Alma

As I've said, that powerful encuentro with María Elena opened the door to this project and to the lives of many of her contemporaries, whose activism I would look at, and locate within, signs of the spiritual or internal world. I refer to the group of women in this book, all self-identified Chicanas and Tejanas, or Texas Mexicans, as *mujeres del alma*, women of the soul.

My purpose in using *mujeres del alma* is twofold. In chapter 4, I discuss Alma de Mujer Center for Social Change in the outskirts of Austin, Texas, as a key site of Chicana spiritual activism in Central Texas. Indeed, some women featured in this text have played an active part in the Alma de Mujer community over the years. While not all have been involved, I feel compelled to refer to the entire group as women of the soul, for this book is an offering—an offering of stories, stories of women making soul. Hence, mujeres del alma. It is important to note that one woman, Inés Hernández-Ávila, is Native and Tejana. Her Nez Percé identity is a vitally important part of her life and how she walks through the world. Consequently, I offer here that Inés, as a bridge between the two, lives a Native/Chicana spiritual activism that expresses her Chicana/Tejana and Nez Percé/Native identity and its lineages and histories.

Texas Chicanas Shifting the Terrain of Activism

Chicanas shifted the terrain and reshaped the landscape of activism by integrating a spiritual dimension, which I interpret as a form of Chicana feminist praxis. These trailblazing Chicanas confronted the enduring impacts and repercussions of colonial legacies in Texas, grappling with issues such as Jim Crow–era racism, "linguistic terrorism,"[4] the denial of educational opportunities, border violence, historical erasure, religious patriarchy, and gender discrimination. Indeed, this was the context for women's creation of and participation in RUP. Central to their efforts was attending to the "internal violence of the spirit,"[5] which bore the scars of colonization and ongoing violence in Texas during and since the Chicana and Chicano movement.

Chicanas have relentlessly worked toward the dismantling of such oppressive systems with spirituality firmly embedded in the core of their activism, rather than existing in separation from it. These women are thinkers, theorists, activists, artists, healers, caregivers, soul tenders, and more. By conceptualizing activism and feminism holistically, this book extends our understandings of Chicana activism post-*movimiento* and enriches our conceptions of feminism from that influential era.

The Storytellers: Las Tejanas

This book explores how María Elena Martinez and a group of her contemporaries—Texas Chicanas from the movimiento era and beyond—transformed their personal and collective lives by integrating spiritual activism into their feminist and social justice efforts. I argue that this transformation took place by extending activism that addressed external material inequalities to encompass profound inner healing and liberation from systemic and other forms of oppression. Through their lived experiences, spiritual practices, and creative expressions, these women demonstrate the power of storytelling, spiritual agency, and self-acceptance as tools for personal and societal transformation. The book positions their work as a blueprint for action and for fostering belonging, healing, and wholeness in the face of continued attacks on difference and human dignity. Far from an expansive overview of all women's contributions to the Texas movimiento, this humble offering presents stories chosen on the basis of themes I identified through interviews with women, in pláticas and community with them, in their writings, in archives, and in various communications over the years. The stories in this book were gathered between 2004 and 2025. I am committed to feminist praxis in my writing and collaboration with the women to ensure accurate representation. I therefore took care to invite all of the women written about here to review and offer feedback on their stories over the summer and fall of 2025. I incorporated any changes and additions they requested.

The women in this book were far more than contributors to this project, for this "project" is so much more than the word conveys. A project of the soul, a project of the heart, perhaps. Since I began exploring the spiritual and activist lives of Texas Chicanas in 2004, women granted me access to their lives, hearts, and recollections of the past, precious offerings that I included in my dissertation, publications in anthologies, and now this book. Their many contributions to social justice and intersectional feminist activism in academic, political, educational, feminist, labor, literary, and cultural arts movements and to the lives of many (such as myself) whom they are responsible for assisting obtain PhDs are vast and deserving of many books and other cultural productions.[6]

All of the women I originally approached for what I initially called interviews and will later unpack as "methodologies of the spirit"[7] and spirit stories graciously and wholeheartedly agreed to participate in my dissertation research about the relationship between Chicana spirituality and activism, the early seeds of this project. They are an accomplished group, having contributed to the formation of bilingual education and establishment of fields, programs, and departments of ethnic and feminist studies across Texas, to a thriving Chicana/o cultural arts movement, to a robust body of literary scholarship, to electoral politics, and to community-based organizing and institution building in ways that have had rippling effects and are still very much felt today.

I am fortunate to have had the opportunity to learn from seventeen notable activists and community leaders for my doctoral research. While not all of the seventeen women whose interviews I initially recorded in the early 2000s fit into the frame of this particular book, they are all vastly important for their contributions to the movement and continue to impact us today. For my dissertation I conducted one interview with scholar, poet, activist, and historian Teresa Palomo Acosta, who was involved in La Raza Unida and whose writings on Tejana life are foundational to Tejana studies.[8] I also met with Sylvia Orozco, cofounder and director of the Mexic-Arte Museum in Austin, artist, cultural advocate, and former RUP member from Mercedes, Texas, and learned of her pivotal role in the cultural arts. She told me about establishing an art center and gallery for Latinx and Latin American art and artists and the influence of her mother, a writer and RUP activist in Cuero, Texas, Aurora Estrada Orozco.[9] I had the good fortune to do a phone interview with feminist, activist, and community organizer María Jiménez, born in Coahuila, Mexico, and raised in Houston, a major political figure during and since the social movements of the 1960s and '70s. I learned about her perspectives on being an atheist and inspirations for her tireless activism and advocacy, which served as an important "source of empowerment for Texas Chicanas developing a gendered critique of protest struggles."[10] RUP activist Irma Mireles sat down with me for an interview in her hometown of San Antonio. An active member of Bexar County's La Raza Unida party, Irma was elected to a seat on the San Antonio River Authority and held office for six years. Austin native and student activist Hortensia Palomares was among the Mexican American Youth Organization (MAYO) students at the University of Texas at Austin who advocated for and succeeded in establishing Mexican American studies there in 1972.[11] Hortensia would continue her activism in Austin, working for the creation of what would become the city's Emma S. Barrientos Mexican American Cultural Center. I also had a phone interview with Luz Bazán Gutiérrez, originally from South Texas but based in Yakima, Washington, an RUP cofounder and the first Raza Unida Party county chair for the state of Texas. Modesta Barbina Treviño, from Austin, was involved with the RUP and education reform along with María Elena. She was also very involved in the cultural arts, organizing and curating exhibits with artists such as Santa Barraza and José Treviño, Modesta's husband. She was a lead organizer of the historic Conferencia Plástica Chicana in 1979. Velia Sanchez was not interviewed; however, she deserves mention as an important part of the story of Alma de Mujer and made valuable contributions to the movement, advocating along with María Elena Martínez and Modesta Barbina Treviño for the development of bilingual education and bicultural programs in Texas. Again, these influential women are worthy of recognition for their immense contributions to the movement and for continuing its founding principles of justice and liberation.[12]

To varying degrees, the following women have been part of my life for the past fifteen to twenty-two years and part of one another's for much, much longer. In addition to María Elena Martínez, their stories are featured in the pages to come.

I made decisions about whom to include in this book on the basis of the common themes in their stories; access to observe, meet with, and interview them; and ways that I saw spiritual activism playing out in their lives. Close proximity to those in Central and South Texas made interviews and observational time more feasible for me. Yet even when separated by distance, many women still actively supported me and this book. For instance, Inés Hernández-Ávila has resided in California for many years now; she provided an initial phone interview in 2005 and participated in pláticas with me in 2024 and 2025, in addition to engaging in email correspondence. In the case of Inés, to create her narrative on spiritual activism for this book, I could also rely on her scholarship, poetry, and other cultural productions, as well as opportunities to interact with her at Mujeres Activas en Letras y Cambio Social/Women Active in Letters and Social Change (MALCS)[13] conferences over the years.

Austin native Susana Almanza is a cofounder and executive director of People Organized in Defense of Earth and Her Resources (PODER), an environmental justice organization in Austin.[14] She was a member of the Xinachtli Danza group and active in the Austin chapter of the transnational movement to transform the lives of Mexican Americans through radical action, the Brown Berets.[15] Artists Santa Barraza and Carmen Lomas Garza grew up in Kingsville and attended what was then Texas A&I University (renamed Texas A&M University—Kingsville), a hub for Chicana/o artists in the 1970s. Both continue their art today, with Santa in Kingsville, where she has her own art gallery, and Carmen living and working in San Francisco, California. Originally from Laredo, Texas, Norma E. Cantú is a prolific scholar, former president of the American Folklore Society, and founder and director of the Society for the Study of Gloria Anzaldúa (SSGA).[16] San Antonio civil rights activist, educator, and feminist Rosie Castro was an active member of the Texas Chicano movement and a pivotal RUP member as former chair of the Bexar County RUP. She was also involved with the Mexican American Youth Organization (MAYO) and the Committee for Barrio Betterment, recently serving on San Antonio's city council.

Martha Cotera is a cofounder of RUP, Mujeres Por La Raza Unida, and the Center for Mexican American Studies and the Mexican American Library Program at the Benson Latin American Collection at UT Austin; an archivist and information specialist; and a scholar of seminal works on Chicana feminism.[17] Yolanda Chávez Leyva, Chicana borderlands historian from El Paso, attended UT Austin, where she was involved in Chicano and lesbian organizing, and was a founding member of CHISPA, the first Chicana/o lesbian and gay organization in Austin. Inés Hernández-Ávila, whom I have mentioned, is from Galveston, Texas, and was an RUP activist,[18] founder of Mexican American studies at the University of Houston, and advocate for bringing Native activists to Texas during the Chicano movement. Cynthia Pérez was involved with MAYO and RUP in Houston and Austin and would come to cofound La Peña, a Latino arts organization in Austin, and Las Manitas restaurant, a hub for local activism, politics, and culture with her sister, Lidia. Cynthia is the current steward of Alma de Mujer Center for Social Change. Both sisters have deep roots in social justice activism. The Episcopalian priest Rev. Virginia Marie Rincon was active in the Austin community as a healer and spiritual guide and served on the Alma Women's Council. Sister Teresa is a sister religious in the Catholic Church, an educator who has been involved in social justice and feminist causes since the movement era.[19]

The involvement of these women in movimiento activities spanned multiple arenas, including RUP, the cultural arts movement, the creation of Chicana studies and Mexican American/Chicano studies programs, and spiritual, literary, and historical productions that attended to unsilencing and decolonizing the past in order to facilitate liberation and healing in the present.[20] Of those I interviewed, María Jiménez and Irma Mireles, two pivotal RUP activists, have since passed away. Their spirits remain with their *colegas* and the lives they touched and changed.

The group also includes a peer and, in many cases, a close comrade of these women, fellow Tejana Gloria Anzaldúa.[21] While I did not have the opportunity to meet Anzaldúa during her lifetime, her theories, *autohistorias,* and concepts serve as a central and particularly relevant inspiration for this book and contribute to the narratives of lived experiences shared in this ethnography of Chicana spiritual activism in Texas.

Toward the end of my dissertation journey, I would meet Mary Margaret Navar, "Margie," who today lives in Oaxaca City, Oaxaca, which has ties to Alma de Mujer and several of the women through healers who have visited Alma and shared Indigenous knowledge with its community. A dear friend of María Elena and others in this project, Mary Margaret, fellow Tejana anthropologist, would become an *hermana del alma y maestra espiritual,* a spiritual teacher and mentor to me, helping shepherd me through many stages of my own conocimientos, including the final stage, which corresponded with the completion of this book: spiritual activism.[22]

Undoubtedly, many subject areas are underrepresented here in favor of discussing the more common themes, and those—along with individual lives of each of these women—would be rich areas for future research.

A Web of Interconnected Lives

Through their stories and often outside of them, I would come to learn about the web of geographic, ideological, experiential, political, and spiritual interconnectedness among the women. While I am not positioned to know these connections, they are many, and the affection and love many of the women have for each other runs deep. They have been through love and loss, pain and joy together. Some of the women in this study grew up together, like Carmen and Santa, who share memories of visits to Don Pedrito Jaramillo's religious shrine in Los Olmos, a tight-knit extended family, and the realities of living with "a sense of domination," as Santa once called it, that was the social reality for Mexicans growing up in Kingsville.[23] Others, like María Elena and Modesta, attended college together at UT Austin and later became bilingual educators in the Austin Independent School District. They crossed paths with Martha Cotera, Rosie Castro, Luz Bazán Gutiérrez, Carmen Lomas Garza, and María Jiménez through their involvement in the Texas state chapter of La Raza Unida Party. Modesta Treviño and Santa Barraza came to be dear friends through a common love of art and through their participation in the women's art collective Mujeres Artistas del Suroeste.[24] Yolanda Chávez Leyva was also part of the Austin community in the 1980s and knew many of the women during her time attending UT, including Inés Hernández-Ávila and Gloria Anzaldúa. Susana and Inés were active in the same danza[25] group in Austin in the 1970s, Xinachtli. Today several women continue to be involved in numerous spiritual, activist, and artist circles in the Austin area and other parts of the state and country.

I continue to discover new aspects of the deep interconnectedness between the women. Even up to the final stages of writing I would learn that, for instance, Cynthia Pérez was once a student of Inés Hernández-Ávila's at University of Houston, where they both advocated for Mexican American studies.

Women's spiritual trajectories have evolved over time and emerged out of specific historical and social conditions. My methodological approach is interdisciplinary in nature and provides a portrait of one aspect of Tejana spirituality today that is not limited to a geographic area but rather is rooted in a particular kind of political consciousness informed by the material circumstances of living as Tejanas—both as racialized and gendered subjects but also as active agents in their social circumstances. While women are linked in various ways, as in sharing life experiences, spiritual beliefs, and/or political perspectives, exerting a Chicana consciousness clearly connects these women. They are also connected in various ways through shared experiences of gender, racial, and class oppression, experiences that transcend feminist, religious, and political ideological borders.

On Love and "Research"

I grapple with using the word *research*, for one of the many gifts I received throughout the journey to this book was love. I never set out to create the various bonds I did with these women—it just happened. They answered a call from the universe, from Guadalupe-Tonantzin, perhaps even from their ancestors to support the telling of these stories and to make them available so others could benefit from them. How did they do that? As I will share in the coming pages, they invited me into their homes and communities, fed me nourishing meals as a graduate student, listened to my questions, offered insights not just on the research but on my own life as a woman in her thirties going through life. In the process they mentored, uplifted, and saw me. In doing so, in a multitude of ways the women in this book nurtured my own spiritual activism. And that, too, is part of this story—a story that shows the vast impact we can make on others just by being present and seeing them, as the women did for me. I had a strong and loving foundation in my family of origin, and later in life I was raised to be a Chicana feminist spiritual activist through my association with these women in community in Austin. In both instances, I have been so fortunate to share a connection to the importance of offering stories and histories, *consejos* (advice), vast wisdom, and intellectual and spiritual gifts.

This is not typical ethnography. Feelings and emotions—from loss to love—are in these pages. I use autoethnography, *autohistoria teoría,* and *testimonio* to describe the impact the women made on my life as a lens into the larger impact they would come to have—and will continue to have—on the lives of others as part of their feminist praxis and unwavering commitment to liberation. The possibilities and potential for carrying forward their legacy of love and liberation are vast and needed desperately right now.

Love as a Foundation

The theme of love underlies every story in this book and is captured by movement activist and poet-scholar Inés Hernández-Ávila, who describes the connection between feminist activism and love during the movement in the foreword to the 2014 anthology *Fleshing the Spirit: Spirituality and Activism in Chicana, Latina, and Indigenous Women's Lives.* It is, I offer, a love that persists today. As she notes:

> As many of the writers [in the anthology] have indicated, Chicana/Latina/Indigenous women's spirituality, the fleshing of the spirit and the spiriting of the flesh, are inclined intrinsically toward social, environment, and global justice, to the wellbeing of us as women, to our communities and all of life, to all of our relations. What is the creative impulse that drives this need, this search? Amoridolor, a term coined by some of us in the 1970s in Texas, a contemporization of the Nahuatl "difrasismos." Amoridolor. We love deeply so we feel pain from the suffering of our generations (as Berenice Dimas notes in her poem) and, I would add, the suffering of the Earth. And we feel pain because we love. They are inseparable. Amoridolor. This is what moves us to create, to write, to be, with "sabor a rebeldía."[26]

Alicia Enciso-Litschi, friend, colega, and wisdom keeper, did her doctoral work on Alma de Mujer and the mujeres of Alma. She is of my generation and is also an important part of this story, as a scholar, a healer, and mi hermana del alma. Her embodied spiritual and intellectual knowledge from her experience with the land, history, and mujeres of Alma bond us in a special way and greatly informs this book and my own medicine journey. Her insights on love are healing salve in and beyond academia:

> This connection [to the mujeres at Alma] had to be real—not a connection for the sake of a research product. As discussed by Dillard (cited in Chilisa, 2012), for research to serve liberating and healing intentions, there has to be love. This includes relating to "community members as people that the researcher loves" (Chilisa, 2012, p. 278). That word—love—is often spoken at Alma but rarely uttered in the context of academic discussions of research methodology. Yet that is the methodology taught to me by the women, and I believe it is important to be transparent about that dimension of this knowledge-seeking experience.[27]

Amoridolor—pain and love—was and continues to be a powerful catalyst for women's spiritual activism and a means through which generations are deeply intertwined within this lineage of spirit-inspired changemakers.

"The Face of God Has Changed"

At the heart of this project lies a central tenet, which I introduce through the words of San Antonio activist Rosie Castro: "The face of God has changed." This statement resounds as a poignant expression of women challenging the entrenched hierarchies of religious authority through various means of creative resistance, cultural reckoning, and remaking. It embodies a reshaping of Catholicism and the forging of new spiritual pathways these Chicanas embarked upon. This bold step can be seen as a harbinger of early spiritual activism at play, one that brings us a stride closer to women's truth.

While these Texas Chicanas worked to alleviate forms of oppression in the tangible realm of the "outer world" encompassing electoral, educational, employment, and other spheres—forms of oppression that plagued Mexican and Chicano communities for generations—they simultaneously turned their attention to their own and their communities' "inner worlds."[28] This book illustrates how, postmovement, women's teaching, writing, art, research, organizing, healing, and other justice-inspired efforts became infused with a profound spiritual dimension.

Women embraced spiritual practices as integral elements in their organizing initiatives, the establishment of writings, and their building of archives and institutions, striving for inclusion and combating alienation. They embarked on a journey to unearth and recover the histories of Chicana feminism, imbuing them with decolonial imaginaries that refuted colonial conceptions of gender, race, sexuality, and spirituality through a feminist lens.[29] For instance, Martha Cotera's writings from the 1970s stand as a testament to her introduction of the Aztec deity Tonantzin and feminist interpretations of Our Lady of Guadalupe to counter tainted and exclusive narratives. Confronting biased and exclusionary narratives, these writers integrated women and their anticolonial struggles into the narrative fabric of achieving liberation, justice, and equality across multiple generations. This transformative effort not only influenced their own sense of identity but also challenged the racist and gendered conceptions of Chicanx as perpetual "others."

Spiritual Activism: The Fight for Healing and Liberation

This work is inspired by and builds upon Gloria Anzaldúa's conception of the theory and practice of spiritual activism. As the foundational framework of the book, Anzaldúa's spiritual activism involves engaging in "internal work, coupled with an earnest compromiso to struggle for social change." She goes on to say that "internal work begins with the body: self-respect, self-acceptance, self-forgiveness, and self-love," which can change one's relationship to oneself, which in turn allows one to change the world.[30] AnaLouise Keating offers theoretical perspectives on spiritual activism important to this project as well: "Anzaldúa's spiritual activism intertwines 'inner works' with 'public acts,' private concerns with social issues. Indeed, this simultaneous attention to personal and collective issues/concerns is a vital component in spiritual activism."[31] I propose that the women in this book exemplify the interconnectedness of social transformation and personal, inner change in both their lives and their work. As such, they are spiritual activists.

I found myself, throughout the writing of this book and in conversations with the women, wondering if the spiritual activism I witnessed was about a relentless insistence on existing as our whole selves. Beyond resisting colonialism and systemic oppression, could spiritual activism be about fighting for ourselves and our communities? And could it include cultivating an internal sense of belonging, self-love, and self-respect, which then equip us to advocate for others, for their full humanity, and for our own right to exist?

Healing the Wounds of Colonization: The Spirit Story as Medicina

The women in this book, as well as our shared relationships, have shaped my own conception of spiritual activism. Building on Anzaldúa's theory and praxis, I extend her ideas by emphasizing the role of stories and storytelling in circulating wisdom, knowledge, and strategies that foster healing and liberation, including the healing of the lingering wounds of colonization. This book focuses on infusing activism and feminism with spirituality by showcasing how each woman's unique medicina transforms lives and brings them closer to their truth.[32]

Methodologies of the Spirit and the Emergence of the Spirit Story

I don't recall the first time I felt a tension from not having the tools to fully understand or frame María Elena's spiritual and political journeys. Something just felt off. I was taught to use "interview" to describe what I was supposed to be doing. But it was insufficient to describe the wisdom sharing and deep connections we established. This inspired me to develop a relational methodology informed by women of color feminisms and feminist anthropology—what I term "methodologies of the spirit."[33] Since then, both my perspective and approach to understanding women and their stories have evolved. Consequently, I have extended my concept of methodologies of the spirit to create what I now call "spirit stories."

At the heart of methodologies of the spirit lie the stories of women engaging in spiritual activism, as well as the narratives they share through creative expressions, feminist praxis, and activism—stories that move people on a deeply spiritual and soulful level. As I will elaborate upon in chapter 1, these spirit stories are stories with effects, stories that transform, and stories that come from a place of knowing oneself and living one's purpose.

That first encuentro with María Elena was a spirit story—it propelled me onto a path of conocimiento that ultimately led to my own journey with spiritual activism. That journey would not have been possible without that initial encuentro, along with the subsequent interviews, pláticas, and moments of deep connection with María Elena and her contemporaries, who graciously welcomed me into their lives, worlds, and spiritual activism.

Methodologies of the spirit is an epistemological perspective largely informed by Chicana/Latina feminist scholars, Black feminist scholars, other women of color feminisms, and decolonial scholars. My ways I came into knowing is central to how I arrived at these narratives. It includes the relationships I have built over the years with these women—observing them alongside my students in community settings, participating with them in various events—and the multitude of ways in which they have impacted my own life.

Methodologies of the spirit are inherently relational and embrace intimacy, love, spirituality, and healing. They encompass everyday ways of knowing that aren't explicitly intended to generate new knowledge—such as phone calls and visits—alongside practices like pláticas, autoethnography, testimonio, interviews, oral history, and participant observation.

Spirit stories are an extension of methodologies of the spirit. They are the outcome of using such methods and epistemological perspectives. I have found through the writing of this book and the events that have transpired in my life, our nation, and this world in recent years that stories have a profound impact on both the tellers and the recipients. As I mentioned previously, spirit stories are narratives with profound effects; they reach people at the soul level and inspire healing and transformation. They come from a place of the spirit—from a storyteller who shares while grounded in their own rootedness, in a knowing and living of their truth and walking their unique path.

Mujeres Making Soul: The Path Toward Purpose and Truth, the Path of Conocimiento

Over the course of their lives, women enacted agency in (re)constructing their identities—spiritual, feminist, activist, and others—as they achieved self-actualization and came into their power. I have learned, through researching and writing this book, that arriving at and living one's truth and purpose constitute a process. It is a process that can be captured in Anzaldúa's concept of a path of conocimiento. As they ventured through their journeys of conocimiento, they traversed to and from, back and forth through various stages. Conocimiento—coming into a new way of knowing; a deepening of consciousness—is far from linear.

The first stage, the rupture, *el arrebato,* involves events that cause a rupture, woundings, fragmentation of the mind, body, heart, and soul. It marks an ending, a beginning, and entrance into a new identity. The second stage, *nepantla,* the Nahuatl word for "in-between space," is when we are torn between multiple ways, wading through the discomfort of in-betweenness that feels as if it will never cease, but indeed we are moving toward the new.

The Coatlicue state—named after the earth goddess of life and death and mother of the gods in Aztec cosmology—is the state of despair, of *desconocimiento,* a resistance to new knowledge that brings on a process of self-reflection and contemplation. We go inward in search of a new meaning, understanding that inner struggle is inevitable for change to take place. Next is *el compromiso,* the call to action—the crossing. It is an uncomfortable space. Self-questioning and hopelessness are the marks of this stage. But making it through offers a deeper understanding of self and the world around us. Here we work with Coyolxauhqui, the Aztec goddess of the moon who was dismembered by her brother; new personal and collective stories come by putting Coyolxauhqui back together. It is at this stage that the re-membering occurs and the fragmentation brings about new ways of knowing and being in the world, other possible reconstructions of self, and healing. Finally, we reach the stage of spiritual activism: deep transformation, giving life to our personal vision for inner and outer change through creative acts, self-respect, and self-love. Spirituality for social change.[34]

I offer that this process that moves women from the arrebato—rupture/fragmentation of the heart, mind, and soul—then through putting themselves back together and creating their own stories, and finally into the arrival at spiritual activism is women's shaping of the flesh. It is accompanied by the making of their souls, a perpetual process of learning to listen to one's soul and then acting on those insights. I propose that this involves women coming into spiritual activism by fulfilling their purpose through the "creation" of their own "faces" (bodies) and "souls" (hearts) on their own terms. In addition to listening for guidance from within, this involves sharing their medicine and following and living their truth. The telling of spirit stories as spiritual activism involves stories told from the heart/soul coupled with "deeds"—action.

Themes of This Book

I was incredibly fortunate to have the opportunity to platicar (in person, on the phone, and virtually), share meals, and attend events that reflected their spiritual activism with seventeen women for my dissertation, my original research project.[35] Their contributions to the liberation of women and particularly women of color, the Chicanx movimiento, and other forms of activism are vast and worthy of many books, films, and more. For the purposes of this book, I narrowed down their stories to the main themes that have emerged in their lives around spiritual activism. Hence, as I mentioned earlier, not all of the women interviewed for the dissertation project, nor all of the themes represented in that project, are included here. I hope that future storytellers will take up the vast trove of themes and stories yet to be written and further extend our understanding of spiritual activism to include other gender, ethnic, and racial groups; these should be in community and conversation with each other.

Thirteen women in total are featured in this book. Four prevalent themes emerged from the numerous pláticas, participant observations, and other methods I employed to gain insight into women's experiences over the past fifteen years. Each theme is represented in a chapter: the healing potential of history, historical narratives, and historical recovery; Our Lady of Guadalupe–Tonantzin as a spiritual and feminist warrior; Austin's Alma de Mujer Center for Social Change as a space for communal spiritual activism and embracing and sharing our medicina; and the dreaming of new worlds with and for future generations.

A Tejana Autoethnography of Spiritual Activism

I have wrestled with how much of my story to include in this book. I've arrived at telling the stories I do with the intent of showing the power of spiritual activism to change us and then change the lives of others and the world, as María Elena and the other women did for me and so many other individuals, groups, and causes. It just so happened that, since that first encuentro with María Elena until the conclusion of my work on this book, I have navigated through many stages and paths of conocimiento. From the depths of personal loss to the liberation of rebirth, María Elena and the women have been there for me. Through small yet impactful gestures and via larger *movidas,* I not only wrote about and thought about their spiritual activism but have also been the recipient of it.

The women have played a vital role in my personal and spiritual healing and transformation. This is a central lens through which I see and walk through the world today. As such, I felt it essential to share their stories in a way that reflects the depth of connection to self and spirit that their teachings, lived feminism, and love have had on those around them. It is my hope that this offers us models for sharing knowledge, imparting wisdom, connecting our lives, and building communities that reflect the power of merging the spiritual (inner work) with activism (outer work).

Additionally, my completion of this book also marks a beginning. After fourteen years as a tenure-track, then tenured professor, I made the decision to leave academia and pursue a path that aligns more with my own truth—a decision that happened to correspond to twenty years to the month when I met María Elena. Today, I am on a journey of self-discovery and self-acceptance while simultaneously working with those in and beyond academia who seek to align their own truths with their purpose. I bring my storytelling to my work as a practitioner-scholar of spiritual activism, weaving together history and healing and centering reconnection with our medicina as pathways to collective liberation.

I find resonance between María Elena's choice to leave the political life to follow her path and my choice to leave academia to pursue mine, which gives me glimpses into processes of conocimiento and making soul that I explore and expand upon with this book.

Ultimately, the autoethnographic narratives interwoven throughout this volume are intended to highlight these themes, illustrate the stories of women's personal transformations as they intersect with their feminist and social activism, and show how their stories impact those around them, such as myself. My intent is that the autoethnographic aspect of the book offers deeper insight into how these women changed themselves, then changed the world through the lives they touched.

Why This Book? And Why Now?

Much has occurred in our lives and in the world over the course of producing this book: deep personal loss of family members and dear friends, including friends from the movement; raising of children and grandchildren; retirements; global violence; a pandemic; and ecological and environmental tragedies of massive proportions. Accounts of the heteropatriarchy and sexual violence that Chicana feminists fought against during the movement are revealed to a stunned nation. We are up against a literal reversal of the laws, policies, and programs many of the women in this book worked for and sacrificed a great deal to bring into being. Our liberation and civil rights are threatened. If I have learned anything from the privilege of coming to know these women and others of their generation across the country, it is even in times such as those that are upon us, there is light in the dark.[36] These women—and those who went before them—offer us stories, histories, and a legacy of radical love, feminist movidas, intellectual and spiritual gifts, and more. Not only does this book document some of that, from which we can learn and chart our own paths of spiritual activism, but it also encourages readers to embrace their own creativity as they work to change themselves, which can also result in changing the world. Doing so feels revolutionary, necessary, and possible.

A Movement Consejo for Our Times

I take inspiration from one of María Elena's many consejos, an exchange that stands out as I reflect on the relevance of her teachings in the current moment. It was February of 2019. I reached out to her for a much-needed *limpia,* a spiritual cleansing, which came with the comfort of her presence, her energy, her home, and the solace of her consejos.

When I called, we laughed as she called me a good *brujita* because she had been about to call me. I asked if I could come for a limpia, and she replied, "Yes—come anytime. This is your church!" We shared another giggle, knowing the profound nature and irony of that statement, given both of our departures from organized religion and subsequent life's work of building communities of healing.

She greeted me at the door with her signature smile and warm embrace, which embodied over seventy years of Texas-Mexican borderlands history, activism, and feminism. There was a politicized dimension to her home, one that met a deeply rooted spirituality. After she performed the limpia, we moved to the living room to sit, as we often did. There the present and past collided amid movement-era artwork by Carmen Lomas Garza, Amado Peña, and of Modesta Treviño and her daughter drawn by Santa Barraza. Political protest photos, including a black-and-white image of a protest at the UT Austin Student Union in the 1970s calling for more ethnic studies professors, hung on the wall next to a Wixárika (Huichol) yarn art mask. A home altar sat atop an antique table with a basket full of various rattles and small drums next to it. The altar included a *Madre del Mundo* sculpture by Chicana-Choctaw artist and friend Marsha Gómez, former director of Alma de Mujer Center for Social Change in Austin. It was surrounded by photos of loved ones and a white buffalo, sage bundles, candles, feathers, and sacred objects. Her bookshelves held texts on Mesoamerica, shamanism, Latin American, U.S. Latinx, Tejanx, and Chicanx histories, goddess traditions, natural medicine, herbology, and more. A photograph of Doña Enriqueta Contreras Contreras, master Zapotec healer and mentor to María Elena, rested among images of dear friends from the movimiento era, her beloved mother, siblings, nephews and nieces, and my own children. This was the home of the first woman to lead a political party in Texas as the final state chair of La Raza Unida political party, a founder of its women's caucus, a bilingual educator of over thirty years, and a spiritual activist.

Settled into her inviting couch and warm surroundings, she listened intently as I tried to make sense out of constant injustices I witnessed in my university and broader social settings. I asked her, "Meme, during the movement, how did you get through the difficulties of fighting for justice? Of being rejected, overlooked, gaslit? The really hard moments?"

She didn't think long on the question, and her answer surprised me. "You accept it," she said. "And then you realize everything happens for a reason. That there are people that are ignorant, sad, were treated badly as children . . . and you accept that. And you move on and do the work anyway. . . . You don't have to take it with your hands down either. You take the change, but then you get busy." Later, she added, "No hay mal que por bien no venga. . . . There is always good in the bad. It teaches us," reminding me that we may not always understand why injustice happens at the time, but that understanding would come later.

The idea of accepting without condoning and then "getting busy," was a profound epiphany—a spiritual conocimiento. Still, acceptance did not come easily. The sting of injustice can be visceral—an embodied heat that rises, replaying moments of exclusion, microaggressions, and harm. And yet, her words return, like a soothing balm: You have to accept it. Then make change where you can.

I have come to understand that acceptance of self is also essential—the inner work that makes the outer work of justice doable. Putting this exchange with María Elena into the context of 2026 is the kind of work I aim for this book to inspire: Chicana spiritual activism that makes change by making soul.

Situating the Book in the Field

Scholarship on Chicanas of the movement era has grown over the past fifteen years. Several works aptly tell those stories, such as the 2026 *Fleshing the Archive: An Intimate Genealogy of Chicana Knowledge Praxis*, the 2018 anthology *Chicana Movidas: New Narratives of Activism and Feminism in the Movement Era*, and the 2011 *¡Chicana Power! Contested Histories of Feminism in the Chicano Movement*. The Chicana por Mi Raza Digital Memory Project and Archive, a vast repository of oral histories and archival objects begun in 2009, is also an important resource.[37] The reader can expect a different perspective on women's histories, contributions, and geographic locales. This book is set in Texas, as that is where I am from, where I attended graduate school, and where I developed connections and community to conduct my fieldwork. Since I completed my dissertation research, literature on Tejanas has become more readily available in such works as Teresa Palomo Acosta's *Tejanaland* and anthologies like *¡Somos Tejanas! Chicana Identity and Culture in Texas* and *Entre Guadalupe y Malinche: Tejanas in Literature and Art.*[38]

It is important to note that this book is inspired by works that focus on spirituality and activism in Chicana, Latina, and Indigenous women's lives, most notably, *Fleshing the Spirit: Spirituality and Activism in Chicana, Latina, and Indigenous Women's Lives*, edited by Elisa Facio and Irene Lara, and *Voices from the Ancestors: Xicanx and Latinx Spiritual Expressions and Healing Practices*, edited by Lara Medina and Martha R. Gonzales.[39]

This book is unique in its ethnographic angle, its concentration on Texas, and its storytelling methodology, which focuses on the healing effects of and communal and personal transformation in story.

Background and Context

Most of the women in this book were of the generation of Mexican Americans who were the first in their families to attend college. Several of their fathers were World War II veterans, and education was of paramount importance for the World War II generation, who in many cases had been denied educational opportunities in their youth due to racial and class discrimination. As a result—as in the case of María Elena—these parents often relaxed the traditional strict gender roles and allowed their daughters to leave home, something that was otherwise not the norm.

Women's participation in the U.S. Chicano movement was widespread, from coast to coast, north to south. The Chicana movement emerged within the context of the larger Chicano movement, marked by a surge in writings, art, and other cultural productions that explored identity, gender, sexuality, and spirituality. Women wrote about their experiences in the male-dominated RUP, and subsequently, Chicana feminist thought and the field of Chicana studies emerged with a wave of feminist critiques of the 1960s and '70s.

Chicanas were committed to amplifying the voices, histories, and experiences of their *familias* and communities, responding to omissions of women's histories and experiences in movement and larger historical narratives, advocating for representation in college curricula, and organizing bilingual and bicultural education initiatives. Chicanas active in the Austin Chicana movement included some native Austinites. While originating from South, West, and North Texas, many of the women in this book would end up in Austin and be involved in the Austin movement after having attended the University of Texas at Austin. Some were in Austin for a short time and then moved on. Some took part in one movement initiative; others engaged in overlapping activist endeavors over the course of the late 1960s, 1970s, and even into the present day, as they continue on a path of seeking justice and liberation for themselves and others.

Structure of the Book

Chapter 1, "The Spirit Story: *Nepantlera Medicina* and Making Soul," provides the methodological and epistemological contours of the project, detailing methodologies of the spirit and an outcome of them, the spirit story—my most recent concept. Women share their medicina through spirit stories, which help heal the wounds and continued effects of colonization. This chapter demonstrates how, as *nepantleras*—caught in constant in-betweenness and multiplicity of worlds filled with painful negotiations—women express their truths and embrace their purpose through their spirit stories, inspiring others through their work and encuentros to engage in spiritual activism.

Chapter 2, "'Healing Histories and Border *Arte*: Tejana Practices of Re-membering," explores the potential of history to heal in the context of women's work in the realms of education, art, knowledge production, the creation of archives, and community organizing. I show how encuentros with stories of the past via Chicana memory praxis don't just document; they transform by helping to create new and more inclusive inner and outer worlds, the "gran limpia," or spiritual cleansing, that Inés Hernández-Ávila notes is possible through historical revisioning and unsilencing of the past. Through the border *arte* of Carmen Lomas Garza, Santa Barraza, and the pioneering Chicana Research and Learning Center, this chapter shows how the cultural and literary productions of this group and generation are not just about the past, but about how stories of the past inspire us in the present and help us to imagine new futures.

Chapter 3, "Our Lady of Guadalupe–Tonantzin: Spiritual Activist, Protectress, and *Feminista* of the Borderlands," shows how Our Lady of Guadalupe–Tonantzin has persisted as a constant companion and cultural form throughout the generations, imbued with power and meaning across class, political, and gender lines. Here, I discuss the effects of the *gran limpia* that was the historical revisioning of Guadalupe and the incorporation of Tonantzin. Guadalupe's malleability afforded women unconditional love in their relationships with Guadalupe-Tonantzin, through which we can more deeply understand their reconciliation of feminist, religious, and ethnic subjectivities, identity formation, and world-making.

Through their myriad forms of devotion, women transformed Our Lady of Guadalupe, la Virgen, from an icon of virginal purity to a potent symbol of feminism and female empowerment, seeing her as a social justice warrior, a healer, a powerful mother, and a liberated sexual being. She assists women in reconciling their Latina cultural heritage with feminist sensibilities as a mode of healing and liberation, a practice they extend in their spiritual activism to others. Guadalupe-Tonantzin offers us a nuanced and multidimensional lens into the history and legacy of Chicana feminism in the Texas-Mexico borderlands, playing a key role in helping Chicanas to dismantle the gender hierarchy promoted by the church and upheld by various sectors of society and their own communities since the movement era.

Chapter 4, "Alma de Mujer Center for Social Change: Embracing Our *Medicina en Comunidad*," is an overview of women's participation in Alma de Mujer Center for Social Change in Austin, which marks the continuity of Chicana feminist thought and practice in the Central Texas region as a model for inclusive and healing pedagogies and activism. It is a space where nature, traditional medicine, spirituality, feminism, environmental justice, and activism converge amid multiple generations. Over the years this occurred by way of women's leadership, women's circles, spiritual gatherings, ceremonies, youth camps, and other programming.

Alma is a model for a community rooted in spiritual activism, one that nurtures the internal work of connecting to our truth and medicina through attentive engagement with the land and nature and one that fosters community by teaching us how to then use our medicina in service of others. I recount how the women in this project introduced me to the healing potential of comunidad—a realization that was solidified during a significant period in my life and later deepened when I took my own students there. At Alma, Indigenous ways of knowing are both practiced and transmitted, furthering the decolonization of Western ways of knowing by integrating Indigenous and women of color feminist epistemologies. This unique space provides not just intellectual nourishment but also spiritual and communal sustenance, which can be traced back to the mid-1980s, linking it to the Zapotec healing pathways that originated in Oaxaca, Mexico, and that will reappear as part of a broader rebirth at the conclusion of this book.

The book concludes with: "Invoking *Sabiduría*: Dreaming New Worlds into Being," which opens with a reflection about how this book could not have been written at any other time but now: This moment aligns with my arrival at the final state of conocimiento—spiritual activism—and arises at a time in U.S. history when we desperately need ways to heal and inspire liberation together, in community, doing both the inner and outer work. I discuss the insight that came to me over the course of writing this book: that changing the world is an inside job—one of self-acceptance, self-love, connecting to one's truth, sharing one's medicina and light with the world. I illustrate this with an example of a limpia from my community that guided me into the last stage of spiritual activism, which I offer as a model for communal care and healing. The conclusion contemplates the path ahead by way of a return of sorts—to Oaxaca, which marks not an end but, rather, a rebirth, a new beginning.

This book is the culmination of a twenty-year-long journey, one of learning from and with a group of women who brought me into their fold and allowed me the privilege of witnessing, and then experiencing, radical feminists' love and the many possibilities for the "internal work, coupled with an earnest compromiso to struggle for social change," of which Gloria Anzaldúa writes. They are thinkers, artists, activists, creative beings, teachers, and healers. They are mujeres who have changed the world, both personally and collectively.

To this day, I am in awe that the universe entrusted me with these beloved relationships and the stories that emerged from them, and I feel called, with the *permiso* (permission) of las mujeres del alma, las Tejanas, las Chicanas, to share these *cuentos* (stories). It is a responsibility I do not take lightly. Perhaps that is because I know firsthand of the immense impact their stories and lives have had and their potential to do so for others in a time when we desperately need it.

In the heart of these pages lies a tale of Tejanas: Texas Mexican women who stood at the crossroads of the Chicana feminist movement and the sweeping Chicano civil rights movement of the 1960s and '70s. I delve into the lives of these women, their roots firmly embedded in Texas soil, whose formative upbringings and place-based historical consciousness inspired their movement-era activism and shaped their lives' purposes today.

As the narrative unfolds, I invite you into the journey I took with them and offer insight into the power of stories to heal, transform, and empower, to help us to see how when we "change ourselves, we change the world."[40]

My intention is to share cuentos and ideas and allow space for the reader to interact in their own way with the stories and histories presented here. I choose this form of radical openness, rather than making theoretical assertions, in order to remain in the energy of fluidity, an energy of the divine feminine, and to honor the women in this project, their lives and wisdom. Their lives offer opportunities for contemplation and inspiration in and beyond our current times.

I include my own stories of growing up and of my relationships with the women to show the vast impact the women and their spiritual activism have had. I speak from my experience, but they have touched the lives of many, many others and stand to continue to do so in their lives and through their work, cultural productions, and spirit stories.

When women embraced and lived their spiritual activism and their truth, sharing and enacting their medicina, they changed the world. María Elena taught me that I could change mine—and that when I started with changing myself, it would open me up to being of service to others in ways I never could have imagined.

María Elena has figured prominently in my life—and that of my family—over the past twenty years. She inspired me to see spiritual activism in her world and in my own, and for these reasons she is featured prominently throughout this book. María Elena's stories and those of her comrades, *comadres*, and contemporaries are interwoven in ways only they can truly and fully reveal.

I hold tender the stories shared here, as I do the memories of being with the women as I documented them. How I have seen, taken in, and been affected by their stories has changed over the years. I invite you to receive the stories recounted here as an offering, an ofrenda with depths of love and gratitude to the women in this book. May the stories, questions, and shifts the book elicits within you support you on your own path of conocimiento and those whose lives are touched by your much needed *energía* and medicina.[41]

CHAPTER 1

THE SPIRIT STORY

Nepantlera Medicina *and Making Soul*

I cannot make whole the stories. This is part of the soul wound, the susto, of that which was disappeared or was usurped by oppressors. But I can leave these offerings because, over the hundreds of years since these books were created, enough knowledge of the old ways remained to arrive to me. In doing so, some points of time/experience are made whole in a dynamic continuation; knowledge is experienced with the whole of our being. I look for medicine within the painted knowledge, for the medicine made of stories, dreams, and ceremonial sweepings. What story is created from plants, patterns of nature, and human deeds? The maguey's needle is also thread.

—PATRISIA GONZALES[1]

That initial encuentro with María Elena Martinez ignited something within me—so much so that it has stayed with me, is core to who I am becoming, and marks seeing myself, truly seeing myself, through the lens of spiritual activism for the first time. I carry both the embodied experience and the memory of that encuentro with me to this day. Its impact is evident in how it has shaped and continues to shape me as an educator, scholar, storyteller, and practitioner of spiritual activism. It is such stories and their tremendous power and effects that inspired my commitment to using storytelling as a liberatory praxis and pedagogical approach in the classroom, in community settings, in workshops and circles, and beyond.[2] Learning María Elena's life story and seeing myself and something in it I had not seen before give me firsthand knowledge of the power of stories to bring histories and identities out from the shadows, to transmit vital survival knowledge, and to heal.[3] This is the inspiration behind my conception of the spirit story as a gateway to our medicine and to engagement with spiritual activism.

When I think about the power of sharing our stories, something María Elena once said comes to mind. It was in regard to leaving the political life and turning to the spiritual path of shamanism that she has been on since the late 1980s. In 2004, in response to an oral history interviewer who alluded to María Elena that her spiritual path was another way she now was creating change, in addition to her political work, María Elena responded, "It is a different way of being a service to a community, is the way I see it. And it is an important one given where we are in our world today, I think it's an important piece that is missing."[4] Reading these words shortly after that interview, then hearing María Elena share the same sentiment many times and watching her live it, taught me something that would be central to women's spiritual activism. But it did more. She did more. She spoke to something within me that I could not yet give voice, form, or reason to. It was akin to a realignment of sorts, a reorientation back to a truth that I now know was within me, waiting for me to tap into all along. For María Elena, that shift from the political to the spiritual marked not solely personal growth but a change within herself that would result in changing the lives of many others—a move from doing outer work in the world to changing people's inner worlds.[5] As she said, it became a way of changing the world.

In this chapter I'll outline the conceptual framework of this book and the concepts that help me tell this larger story of Chicana spiritual activism in Texas: nepantlera medicina, spirit stories, and methodologies of the spirit. These concepts emerged as important to the book through my embodied experiences and personal interactions with the women and their work, signifying the passing down of feminist and spiritual knowledge.

The Movement Begins Within: Making Face, Making Soul

I'll never forget the following response from María Elena when I asked her one day what she took away from the movement. We were sitting together, as we often did, *platicando* on her couch. Without missing a beat, she responded, "The movement taught me I would change the world." The years-long journey with María Elena and to this book brought me to this interpretation of her powerful statement—one of the most profound lessons I learned from her: The movement taught her she could change the world, and she teaches us that, while this is important outer work, as in political activism, this change is also necessary within.[6]

Anzaldúa's concept of making face/making soul[7] is useful here to describe María Elena's response and also something I witnessed among women over the years: the creation of identity as both body and spirit being in concert with the workings and expression of the soul. In other words, connecting to and living from one's truth are core to the formation of their identities on their own terms.[8] Anzaldúa offers that making face/making soul is about putting ourselves as the "subjects in our own discourses. We rip out the stitches, expose the multi-layered 'inner faces,' attempting to confront and oust the internalized oppression embedded in them, and remake anew both inner and outer faces. We begin to displace the white and colored male typographers and become, ourselves, typographers, printing our own words on the surfaces, the plates, of our bodies. We begin to acquire the agency of making our own caras."[9] She goes on, drawing from the ancient Nahua's use of Moyocoyani, the one who invents/builds themselves: "Usted es el modeador de su carne tanto como el de su alma."[10] You are the shaper of your flesh as well as of your soul. According to the ancient Nahua (the ethnic group of which the Mexica/Aztecs are part), one was put on earth to create one's "face" (body) and "heart" (soul). To them, the soul was a speaker of words and the body a doer of deeds. Soul and body, words and actions are embodied in Moyocoyani, one of the names of the Creator in the Aztec framework, "the one who invents himself/herself . . . the Builder Kachina himself/herself."[11] Taking from this, I offer that women engaged in *haciendo caras*—asserting the agency to shape and affirm their identities—are in alignment with their deepest selves, at the level of the soul. Their individual expression of this identity, through the (re)writing of their stories of self and of the world around them, embodies the "doing of deeds," the making of soul, across various expressive forms.

For example, as Carmen Lomas Garza reflected when I interviewed her in 2008, the movement afforded her the "voice" to express herself about her life, upbringing, and community while also illuminating for her the injustices and violence of colonialism; this has shaped her agency and choice to follow a Mexica-based spiritual path over Catholicism and has inspired her work as an artist. Others in this project also shared their stories of haciendo caras and coming to embrace a Chicana politicized consciousness and a feminist sensibility, such as María Elena's choice to embrace shamanism and Rosie Castro's seeing the feminine face of God versus a patriarchal God. They took off their masks and asserted identities of their own making, which corresponded with their making soul-inspired, soul-doing deeds.

Anzaldúa offers us an entry into the process of making soul. For her, the hand of the creator and their use of pen, brush, or clay are "an extension of our will" and communicates our voice, our thoughts; without the hand and tool, they cannot be expressed. "When tongue and hand work together, they unite art and politics and attack the dominant ideology. For many of us, writing, painting, performing, and filming are acts of deliberate and desperate determination to subvert the status quo. Creative acts are forms of political activism employing definite aesthetic strategies for resisting dominant cultural norms and are not merely aesthetic exercises. We build culture as we inscribe in these various forms."[12]

She goes on to say that "inherent in the creative act is a spiritual, psychic component—one of spiritual excavation, of (ad)venturing into the inner void, extrapolating meaning from it and sending it out into the world. To do this kind of work requires the total person—body, soul, mind, and spirit."[13] I propose that all of the women in this book, including Anzaldúa, have done this work. They have engaged in making face/making soul with their whole selves—body, soul, mind, and spirit. They have confronted the masks they have worn and practiced making soul through various forms of spiritual activism.

Nepantlera Medicina: Changing the World from Within

As nepantleras these women have navigated the world from the in-between spaces, living "opposing realities"[14] as they created their own identities. My experience of walking alongside and learning from them has shown me that these nepantleras possess a strong medicina. It is nepantlera medicina of the borderlands that functions, as Patrisia Gonzales states in the quote that opens this chapter, to address soul loss, land loss, and cultural and spiritual fragmentation brought on by the *susto* "of the soul wound, . . . that which was disappeared or was usurped by oppressors." Like Gonzales, the women offer us ways to rethink knowledge that is important for us in these times, times that demand the sharing of all kinds of wisdom. She notes that "enough knowledge of the old ways remained to arrive to me." What is the knowledge handed down to us by women such as those in this book—our elders whom we can learn knowledges from that can be "experienced with the whole of our being," not just in a politically oriented way?[15] I see this as a process of making face and making soul that leads women to come into their medicine. Several of the stories women shared over the years suggest that the movement afforded them a voice—a way to express themselves through language—and a newfound awareness of and appreciation for their history, culture, and identity. The movement offered them opportunities to reflect upon and share, even amplify, their lived experiences at the intersections of race, gender, socioeconomic class, and religion. They did so through participation in danza, the cultural arts, and the RUP, as well as through recovering their feminist histories and stories of the borderlands. This would come to shape the work they would eventually put out into the world. In these ways the movement was a pivotal personal catalyst for women.

In terms of expressions of inner worlds, as Carmen notes, "I think that [the] Chicano movement gave me not only the voice to express myself about my childhood, my life, my community, [but] it also pointed out a lot of the injustices of the colonialism . . . of the oppression and the genocide of the Indigenous, all of that history that was not taught to us [and] was suppressed by the Catholic Church and the government of Mexico and South America *and* the United States. . . . That was the beginning of my final decision to just leave the Catholic Church eventually."[16]

Like Carmen, María Elena shared with me that learning about the history of Indigenous peoples and colonization, as well as about goddesses such as Tonantzin and the feminine divine, allowed her to create a continuity in her relationship to the Catholic Guadalupe rather than making a complete rupture. That history supported and inspired María Elena in her work as a healer and guide to women. It also helped her overcome the trauma of being unable to speak all through first grade because she didn't know English and was put into an all-English-speaking class; she later would use her voice in her career in bilingual education and as RUP state chair. Santa Barraza was similarly shaped by learning unsilenced histories of the horrific treatment of Indigenous people, among them her ancestors. This greatly inspired her own artistic renditions and other expressions of nepantla—being torn between ways—such as her representations of Mesoamerican iconography, including the hieroglyphics of the Mixtec, Zapotec, Maya, Aztec, and many other Indigenous groups.

Spirit Stories: Catalysts for Outer Change

These are the kinds of cuentos I call spirit stories. The pages to follow include more examples of how women would come into a new consciousness through spirit stories, the kind of consciousness that Anzaldúa calls conocimiento, the "form of spiritual inquiry" reached through "creative acts—writing, art-making, dancing, healing, teaching, meditation, and spiritual activism." Women, as Anzaldúa writes, connect their "personal struggles with those of other beings on the planet, with the struggles of the Earth itself."[17]

Spirit stories are narratives that are circulated orally and in writing, through autohistoria, oral histories, testimonio, art, literature, pláticas, and archives, as well as in communion with nature. They are expressed through women's lived experiences, spiritual practices, and creativity. In this chapter, I propose that spirit stories hold knowledge and wisdom that have deep effects on people's lives and understandings of self. Thus spirit stories are a form of spiritual activism, helping people navigate the outer world.

Healing Through Autohistoria

The story that María Elena shared during our first encuentro was more and did more than the political biography I was expecting—it was, in fact, her autohistoria, a personal narrative that she came to after "reworking her story": "Tu Autohistoría is not carved in stone but drawn on sand and subject to shifting winds. Forced to rework your story, you invent new notions of yourself and reality, increasingly multidimensional versions where body, mind, and spirit interpenetrate in more complex ways." As noted in *Light in the Dark*, "Personal experiences—revised and in other ways redrawn—become a lens with which to reread and rewrite the cultural stories into which we are born."[18]

Such a cuento puts us on a path of healing splits among mind, body, and spirit, making it a spirit story. María Elena also told of how she was impacted by learning histories of the degradation of Indigenous people and how she came to question hierarchies of power—a story of how she rewrote the cultural script in which she was born, which is the core of autohistoria.

María Elena's autohistoria revealed a story about coming into herself and connecting with her truth, a truth that is reflected in her spiritual activism on the level of the personal—the "internal work" of self-love, self-acceptance, self-respect, and self-forgiveness that begins with the body,[19] that can change one's relationship to oneself, and that can equip one to change the world. Like that first story I heard of María Elena's, the women's autohistorias in this book are spirit stories. By rewriting their own stories, these women have shown that transformation is possible. By sharing their autohistorias, women have greatly impacted many others throughout their lives. My own conocimiento brought on by meeting María Elena and coming to know the women lasted for years and in the process helped me understand my own experiences as a nepantlera.

Shifting Power Within and Without: Integrating One's Truth into Activism and Feminism

When I look at the trajectory of María Elena's life, I notice that her truth has been evident throughout, anchored in what I saw and experienced as a radical inclusivity that shaped her views on justice, liberation, and love of self, others, the earth, and all of her beings. Whether it be her ability to identify racism from a very young age (even without the language to describe it); being keenly aware of injustice and becoming politicized during the movement to fight for Chicana/o rights; working as an activist and teacher for bilingual education to give students an equal and culturally relevant education; coming into her feminist consciousness and questioning, denouncing, and fighting against patriarchy; or leaving Catholicism to walk an egalitarian spiritual path, María Elena's truth-inspired actions would shift power dynamics in the material, outer world within educational spheres, electoral politics, and women's rights.

María Elena incorporated her spirituality into her activism and feminism—inner work that shows us how to shift power within. She did so through invoking her medicina, the gifts and knowledge that she put into the world in service of others to disrupt the soul wounds referred to by Gonzales.[20] These included practicing curanderismo and shamanism, sharing of her spirit wisdom and consejos, and creating inclusive communities of belonging and healing. In these contexts, María Elena supported women and other groups to connect to, (re)claim, and own their power. By living her life on her own terms, she modeled holding our power sacred and not giving it away, practicing that which she advocated for in her women's groups and when she spoke to groups of college students and in workshops and sessions at Alma de Mujer Center for Social Change. She was a woman who never compromised her principles; she would engage in a full moon ceremony one day and the next day explain, in no uncertain terms and with historical and empirical data to back it up, that we must not support politicians who degrade the rights of people, deny women reproductive rights, and stand for profit over caring for and protecting Mother Earth. I see all this is emerging from her internal work of spiritual activism. In this sense, I ask: Can we understand spiritual activism as changing the world from inside out?

In this chapter, I show how I came to see, feel, and know this, in an embodied and spiritual sense, through the use of methodologies of the spirit, which center stories and storytelling as tools for powerful personal and societal transformation.

Methodologies of the Spirit

I conceived of "methodologies of the spirit"[21] as a result of a search for a way to think, talk, and write about the profound and transformational experiences I had with the women, encuentros and connections that extended beyond what I knew at the time as "research." I originally set out to use ethnographic, feminist, and decolonial research methods. The unexpected turn was that I needed something that went even further: I needed something to account for and validate the kind of knowing that emerged between the women and myself. It was a knowing that arose unexpectedly by way of a traumatic personal loss over the course of my fieldwork. I was propelled into conocimiento as a result of that, and I needed something that would help me to understand the importance of that process and the relationships I formed with many of the women.

Chicana/Latina, Black feminist, and other women of color theories are foundational to the creation of methodologies of the spirit and the book's theoretical framework, with their attention to relational methodologies, power, and creative forms of resistance. I also incorporate influences from the anthropology of religion to show the effects of religious and spiritual practices on devotees, which is central to understanding the impact of spirit stories. I can apply this framework, for example, to understanding how the incorporation of the Nahua earth deity Tonantzin into Guadalupe devotion so deeply impacted Chicana feminists as a form of liberation.

Methodologies of the spirit are intersectional, decolonial, holistic, and relational methodologies that rely on ways of knowing that emerge through connection, intimacy, and love. I therefore emphasize women of color feminist methodologies that center the relationships established in these partnerships, collaborations, and "research." These methodologies attend to interrogating power in the "research" project; consideration of the body as a site of knowledge; research as relational, not top down; and research as a potential space for healing and vulnerability. Reflexivity is central, as is attention to spirit work and knowledge production as healing processes whereby the reconnecting of mind-body-spirit occurs.

These methodologies still hold up today. They draw on research methods and epistemological perspectives that attend to and validate ancestral, embodied, spiritual, feminist, and other forms of knowing. They document these forms of knowing through oral history, testimonio, plática, and other methods. While still a relevant concept, many years have passed since its original conception. And in that time my perspectives have broadened in various ways. The epistemological networks from which I draw and how they enable me to hear, witness, listen, and ultimately share women's cuentos and consejos have also expanded. For example, just as my worldview shifted during my initial fieldwork, it transformed once again at the conclusion of this project. As I describe in depth in the final chapter, all of the years of thinking about, witnessing, and embodying spiritual activism would culminate with my departure from academia and with my identity as an academic. After twenty years enmeshed in academia, I was no longer a graduate student or tenured faculty member working within the context of an institution. In what felt sacred and even as a ceremonial passage, my closest *gente* held space for me to express and live my truth, much as the women in this book did for one another. It marked a very important moment in the movement from one identity to the next. My community shepherded me into the next stage of my life, a stage that would involve coming into a different way of being in the world—being fully and wholly myself.

The Evolution of Methodologies of the Spirit

As I've described, María Elena's spiritual and political journeys inspired me to develop a relational methodology that could get to the depths of spiritual and other forms of knowledge. The concept of methodologies of the spirit allows for spiritual, intimate, and other forms of knowledge to arise and for those to be understood as valid sources of knowing. I extended methodologies of the spirit and conceived of spirit stories, the use of which more fully captures the nuances and complexities of how we can find, learn, and feel stories. Knowledge and wisdom can emerge in moments of connection, of shared loss, and of love. Spirit storytelling involves the impact and even transformation that occur as a result of the circulation of such knowledge and wisdom. They are stories curated and circulated in various ways: through archives, in oral histories, through art and literature, by way of recovered histories, and more.

The notion of spirit stories captures not only the power of the encuentro to propel one into conocimiento but the potential for the encuentro to inspire re-membering, the moving *back* toward wholeness. Central to this process is the internal work that results from the transmission, whether that transmission be in the form of recollections from the past, revised histories, or stories of identity, family, migration, love, and more, and whether that transmission come through an interaction with an archive or through stories relayed in visual art, literature, or orally. All these encuentros are encounters with stories that elicit effects in the present.

Employing methodologies of the spirit has the potential to foster belonging, facilitate healing, and reconvene us with the wholeness that has always resided within us, with our truth.

The Healing Power of Storytelling

Storytelling is and has been a powerful mode of communicating cultural, survival, and other forms of knowledge across the world for centuries. However, stories have other purposes as well. "How [stories] are told, who tells them, when they're told, how many stories are told are really dependent on power," observes Chimamanda Ngozi Adichie. "Stories matter. Many stories matter. Stories have been used to dispossess and to malign. But stories can also be used to empower and to humanize. Stories can break the dignity of a people but stories can also repair that broken dignity."[22]

The women in this project challenged traditional gender roles and power structures, aiming to rewrite stories. Those in RUP were often relegated to the kitchen during party meetings to cook or clean. They were rarely asked to run for key offices in the party, the result of which was María Elena deciding to run for RUP state chair. Many of them were often called "*vendidas*," or sellouts, advocating for women's issues and chastised for being vocal about sexual violence in the movement. Because they spoke up against and spoke truth to power, women, through their feminist practices and orientations, were seen as dividing the movement.[23]

Nepantlera Stories

These women were shaped by early life experiences in which they had to navigate pejorative narratives that surrounded new immigrants to the United States, speaking Spanish and/or limited English, eating taco lunches, and being lesbians.[24] Their nepantlera stories fueled the fire of their activism, including their feminism, and today offer healing and a kind of resistance that, as Nancy "Rusty" Barceló states, comes from the soul.[25] It is a spiritual activism that helps others to re-member, that is, to connect the "disparate parts of information from a new perspective . . . in a new composition, temporarily restoring your balance and wounded psyche."[26]

Entry into Women's Worlds: A Web of Interconnections and the Generative Nature of the Spirit Story

As I've described, I initially bore witness to women's spiritual activism, and the impact of their medicina as circulated through their spirit stories, for my doctoral research from 2004 to 2010. I have continued to document and reflect upon their lives up to the writing of this book in 2025. Sometimes our encounters took the form of one-on-one interactions in interviews or in visits over *cafecito*. Women would also offer me entry into their communities, as when María Elena invited me to a women's weekend at Alma de Mujer Center for Social Change in February 2008 and introduced me to a place that would become central to my life, spiritual community, feminist and spiritual development, and healing.

That first weekend at Alma was pivotal both for me and for this project. I met several of the women and found community, a deep respect for the land at Alma, and parts of myself. At her invitation, I joined Carmen Lomas Garza at Day of the Dead/Animas event in the San Francisco Mission District. I visited the Healing Tree and Don Pedrito Jaramillo's shrine, popular South Texas folk religious sites, with Santa Barraza. I marched with Modesta Treviño and María Elena and listened to Susana Almanza, cofounder of People Organized in Defense of Earth and Her Resources (PODER), former Brown Beret, and danzante, speak at an annual PODER Cesar Chavez Day event in downtown Austin in 2010. At every turn, they invited me into their worlds, much as they have done over the years in numerous contexts for many others seeking to (re)connect to themselves and find community. Martha Cotera and María Elena must have sat through over a hundred hours of interviews, chats, and pláticas-turned-mentoring/healing sessions. Today, the women continue to, as Martha once shared, "live their spirituality" by putting their feminism into practice.

I also read their writings and writings others have produced about them, sifted through archives, and attended events with them. Sometimes the knowledge came by way of surprise in-person encounters or impromptu phone calls. In more recent years, I have had the honor to be a co-contributor with them in anthologies and to present with some of them at conferences, learning about their lives and stories in that context.

The University as a Microcosm: The Academic Borderlands

Another important source of knowledge about women's lives and the impact of their spirit stories came about through my role as a faculty member. Given how much meeting María Elena and the other women had impacted me, since graduate school I was intent on creating encuentros for my students as well. I witnessed these women interact with students in the context of the university setting. As a borderlands anthropologist, scholar, and practitioner of intersectional feminisms, I saw the complexities and intersections of power, race, class, gender, religion, sexuality, and more played out. Often. The university where I once worked, Southwestern University, is a small institution. Therefore, racial and gender dynamics and tensions were amplified. It is within these borderlands and the context of students and other individuals negotiating identities and in-betweenness on a daily basis that encuentros with the women in this study occurred. And their spirit stories had indelible effects.

Within these borderlands, for instance, Martha Cotera, borderlands historian and movement activist Yolanda Chávez Leyva, and María Elena Martínez presented Southwestern University's annual Jessie Daniel Ames Lecture in Feminist Studies in 2016, "Chicana Feminism in Texas: Histories of Social Justice, Scholarship, and Spiritual Activism." Susana Almanza visited our virtual classroom in the throes of COVID-19, and Norma Cantú presented a keynote for the borderlands annual symposium. Students' encuentros with the women and their lives took place in the pages of Martha Cotera's seminal writings on Chicana feminism, Yolanda Levya's writings on recovering our previously erased histories as a form of healing, and the stories I recounted about these women in class discussions.

In a twist of fate, Gloria Anzaldúa was present in an unexpected way. I discovered an archival recording of a talk she gave at our university in 1994, a finding that deeply shaped my teaching.[27] Incorporating her

FIGURE 3 Gloria Evangelina Anzaldúa. Annie F. Valva. Gloria Evangelina Anzaldúa Papers, Nettie Lee Benson Latin American Collection, University of Texas Libraries, The University of Texas at Austin.

words into my classes, I watched, semester after semester, as students lit up with awe—realizing that Anzaldúa had once stood on their very campus, speaking to issues that, twenty-five years later, remained profoundly relevant to their own lives.

Countless times, the unexpected would unfold and new insights and conocimientos would arise by way of the encuentros with women's spirit stories. Time and time again over the course of fourteen years at that university I witnessed women's impacts on hundreds of students in the psychological, spiritual, racial, and physical borderlands of a Predominantly White Institution (PWI) in Central Texas.

Theoretical and Methodological Contours

The theoretical contours of this project are largely comprised of theories and concepts developed by Gloria Anzaldúa. The reason for this is twofold. First, her writings and audio recordings serve as ethnographic data for this book. I use her work and life in this way as a testament to her spiritual activism. Second, her ideas are reflective of the Tejana experience and multiple borderlands that she navigated with so many of the women participants in this project, making her theories particularly relevant here.

For example, Anzaldúa's theory of the seven stages of the path of conocimiento, whereby one experiences a shift in both inner and outer ways of knowing and of self and others, is central to this book, which has a focus on the last stage of spiritual activism—the last stage that doesn't mean the end but only that our process of coming into ourselves is never-ending. I show women engaged in conocimiento over the course of their lives, eventually arriving at spiritual activism. I also use spiritual activism as a lens through which I view my own experiences with the women and which helps me to tell this story.

Deepened Insights and Connections, a New Path of Conocimiento, and Spiritual Activist Pedagogies

On this new path of conocimiento, my work in the world continues to involve supporting others in connecting to their truths, as I attempted to do with students and mentees I worked with in the institutional context. Today, I do so just on my own terms, guided by the people I work with and their intuition and aspirations. I have pondered the impact of women's wisdom, the various kinds of knowledge they amassed over the course of their lives and that they applied in poignant, impactful, spirit-infused, and justice-centered ways. Their teachings prepared me for this next stage.[28]

Today, I feel a sense of freedom from external institutional constraints and, importantly, have arrived at an internal sense of peace that has impacted this project. Inspired by a newfound liberation that included coming into my own truth, I found that my creativity soared. My ability to tap into my intuition was heightened, and my ability to see these spirit stories and their effects sharpened. The stories and contributions of these women teach us how to live our lives in a manner that aligns with our inner truths and keeps us moving toward wholeness, by negating the Western violence of the mind-body split and advocating for the wholeness of bodymindspirit, as emphasized by Irene Lara.[29] In this way, methodologies of the spirit are also about spiritual activist pedagogies, whereby women change the world by sharing their spirit stories in various contexts.

The Gloria Anzaldúa Archives: An Encuentro with the Past Becomes a Spirit Story in the Present

As I've said earlier, spirit stories are an outcome of spiritual activism and can take the form of artistic renditions, oral histories, written narratives, in-person meetings, and archives. In the following reflection, a former student from my Chicana Feminisms course reflects on the impact visiting the Gloria Anzaldúa archives at UT Austin had on her, illustrating the power of the spirit story:

> After our visit to the Benson [Latin American Collection] the other day, I immediately texted my friends and told them that it was one of the most spiritual academic experiences I've had. . . . I also liked reading some of her [Anzaldúa's] things that we hadn't had the chance to read before, like the talk that she gave at [our own university] many years ago. . . . It is often that I have imposter syndrome, feeling as though I am not Chicana enough, but she wrote in one of her pieces that we saw at the archives that she too had experienced that feeling and that is where her term nepantla comes in. It's that middle ground that many of us feel. I don't feel Chicana enough because I don't speak Spanish, but I don't speak Spanish because my ancestors did not teach their children to speak the language because they were taught they would get punished if they spoke it in school. They wanted us to have upward mobility and did not see that possible when we spoke Spanish. I appreciated that Anzaldúa also had this experience and created a term for it because it has given me a lot of healing and growth.[30]

Reading Anzaldúa's published works and writings on her lived experiences in the archive did something for and to the student. The student notes the impact: She was moved toward "healing and growth" by reading Anzaldúa's autohistoria about her own borderlands life and experiences of otherness. That, and Anzaldúa's language of nepantla, the in-betweenness of navigating multiple identities, helped the student to more holistically understand her own borderlands experience.

Spirit stories can and do impact lives in such profound ways. They reach us at the place of wounding, at the place of alienation, at the place of our deepest selves. They are stories, as the student said, that inspire healing and growth and promote self-acceptance. The specific genre/form each woman's spirit story takes—in the case of Anzaldúa, it was her autohistoria and theorizing in her published writings and in the archives—is their individual medicina, that which they are meant to put out into the world. This is the work of spiritual activism.

The stories in this book demonstrate how I came to know of women's work in the world as their medicina. Their medicina involves what women do with their knowledge, wisdom, and gifts to impact the lives of others, which inevitably impacts them as well.

All of the women in this book are spirit storytellers in some way, shape, or form. The stories they tell have led me to ask myself, *Do stories have an energy to them? A purpose? Are all of them meant to be told and circulated?*

Spirit Storytelling, Making Soul, and Conocimiento

What I have come to learn is that when one tells a story from their truth, it can be an expression of their soul—of making soul, to use Anzaldúa's phrase. It can reach both the teller and receiver at a deep spiritual level, engaging spiritual activism. For the receivers of the story, this can be understood as spiritual conocimiento,[31] whereby those of us who witness, hear, and otherwise take in the story are impacted at not only the level of mind and intellect but the level of the heart and spirit as well, those places where we feel both alienation and belonging, love and loss.

The tellers of spirit stories are also moved, even changed by the telling, as they are often sharing stories that emerged after they came into new knowledge through recovered histories, such as feminist resignification of goddesses like Tonantzin. They are stories of women's conocimiento. The process of creation does something for them:

> A form of spiritual inquiry, conocimiento is reached via creative acts—writing, art-making, dancing, healing, teaching, meditation, and spiritual activism—both mental and somatic (the body, too, is a form as well as a site of creativity). Through creative engagements, you embed your experiences in a larger frame of reference, connecting your personal struggles with those of other beings on the planet, with the struggles of the Earth itself. Breaking out of your mental and emotional prison and deepening the range of perception enables you to link inner reflection and vision—the mental, emotional, instinctive, imaginable, spiritual, and subtle bodily awareness—with social, political action and lived experiences to generate subversive knowledges. The conocimientos challenge official and conventional ways of looking at the world, ways set up by those benefiting from such constructions.[32]

Women's stories reflect their processes of conocimiento while simultaneously creating space for the emergence of new conocimientos for the receiver of the story to experience, for witness to their lives to occur. This creates its own kind of borderlands—of race, gender, and so much more.

In 2016, a student researcher, Tori, was involved in an intergenerational project wherein she and other students interviewed María Elena Martínez, Norma Cantú, Martha Cotera, Yolanda Leyva, and others. She reflected on how some of the Chicana movement participants being interviewed said they found it healing to share their stories, yet for Tori hearing their stories was incredibly powerful. In this way, spirit stories are also reciprocal and generative. They involve the soul speaking and the body acting as one expresses their truth out into the world. This is making soul.

The Legacy and Impact of the Intergenerational Encuentro: Origins of the Spirit Story

My interaction with María Elena and subsequent encuentros with her contemporaries led to the first incarnation of my notion of "spirit stories" and my real observation of the impact of women's spiritual activism on people other than myself.

This occurred by way of a student-faculty project I developed in my second year as a faculty member. It was 2011, and I took the opportunity to apply for faculty-student research funds. I called the project "Spirit Stories: Narratives of Spirituality and Social Justice." I envisioned working with a small group of local women to gather stories of the intersection of their social justice work and their spiritual lives. María Elena Martínez; Rev. Virginia Marie Rincon, the ordained Episcopal priest and curandera/healer; Yvette Mendez, movement activist and educator; and Velia Sanchez, bilingual education teacher and reformer, graciously agreed to take part in that first iteration of "Spirit Stories." I met them all through Alma de Mujer, where the students spent time and learned from the women and the land. The goal of my project was to document women's spiritual and activist biographies. The project would come to do much more.

Telling Our Stories in Our *Tradicíon: "Vamos a Platicar"*

During my time as a professor, a spirit story emerged as a result of embracing methodology of the spirit. It happened unexpectedly, the day a student named Connie and I approached the home of Rev. Virginia Marie Rincon in Austin in 2011 to interview her for the "Spirit Stories" project. It was an interview that would turn out to be much more. Rev. Virginia gifted us a powerful reminder: We must be able to tell our stories within our *tradiciones* for true recognition, *respeto,* and relationality to emerge—for us to connect on the level of the spirit.

FIGURE 4 Rev. Virginia Marie Rincon. Brandon Hill.

Rev. Virginia welcomed us into her ranch-style home and led us to the backyard, where we were introduced to the casita, a space for community members' healing. We approached the door, recorders and notepads in hand. She showed us around the inviting space and asked us to have a seat. Upon my thanking her for allowing us the opportunity to interview her, she responded with a smile, "No interviewing here, *vamos a platicar.*"[33] She said, "We tell our stories in our *tradición*." Our tradition is deeply relational—it extends far beyond the mere transmission of knowledge. It is rooted in *cariño,* respeto, and a generosity of spirit. In that moment in the casita, something profound unfolded for Connie, who shared multiple identities with Rev. Virginia. She realized she was not alone—that her experience growing up as a lesbian in the Episcopal Church in North Texas resonated with Rev. Virginia's own journey as a lesbian leader in the same faith tradition and region. Through platicando, as Rev. Virginia shared her spirit story, Connie entered conocimiento, recognizing herself in the narrative and deepening her understanding of her own path.

That important encuentro in 2011 is an example of the kinds of interactions I had with the women over the years that inspired a different way of "doing research," which I now know is less about this thing called research and more about how we share stories that can support others on their paths of healing and coming home to self.

An unexpected outcome from that project was how deeply affected students were by their encuentros with women and their autohistorias. Today, I resurrect the concept of spirit stories as a means of capturing the power and essence of connection within self and between others that can result from the making and telling of stories.

Intergenerational Encuentros

Both my own experience with the women and my students' encuentros with them showed me the importance of the intergenerational aspect of spiritual activism through the sharing of spirit stories. Healing histories along with spiritual, intellectual, and survival knowledges are transmitted in various ways between generations: to students gathering to interview movimiento participants for an oral history project (much like I had with my class back when I first met María Elena), in the archive experience, in pláticas, even at presentations and conferences. In each type of circumstance, I witnessed and students relayed transformative effects of engagements with the past.

While they are often encounters with the past, spirit story effects can also take place in moments of connection and in various formats. In addition to autohistoria, as in the story María Elena shared during our first encuentro or the archival writings my former student encountered, I'll also outline pláticas and place as potential sites for the emergence of spiritual activism and the spirit story.

Archival Encuentros

The encuentro the student experienced in the Anzaldúa archives reflects the power of the archive to inspire belonging and healing. The ability of archives to generate spirit stories lies in their active ability to "not only generate new historical interpretations but also open the way for new forms of consciousness."[34] For purposes of the spirit story, this new consciousness—the first step toward conocimiento—also includes a move toward wholeness and one's truth in the context of present-day social and political climates and various systems that marginalized groups face.

Spirit stories can emerge from encuentros with the past because of the potential transformation that can come from the healing of historical erasures that have left us wounded, fragmented, and disconnected from our truth. Instead, spirit stories reconnect us, lift us up, remind us who we are, and in doing so, inspire belonging—both internal and external—as I will discuss at length in chapter 2.

Another example of the power of the archive is when María Elena taught me about Tonantzin, which I will detail in chapter 3. That moment of feminist practice brought me closer to myself, to my truth. Such effects make it a spirit story.

Listening to the Spirit Stories of the Land: Alma de Mujer Center for Social Change

I'll never forget the look in sof's eyes that day when the students arrived to Alma de Mujer Center for Social Change for the first time. In awe at the beauty of nature on the sprawling twenty-two acres located twenty miles outside of Austin's city center, sof's words were: "You never said it was like this." Like the Anzaldúa archive, Alma de Mujer is a site of encuentros and the subsequent transmission of spirit stories. It is also a site that many call home, as they feel so connected to the land and its energy, a site of sacred ceremony and community. As I will detail in chapter 4, Alma de Mujer is a place of spiritual activism in Texas. There, spirit stories have taken the form of visitors (re)connecting to nature as a (re)connection to self. Students whom I took to Alma never ceased to amaze me—every time, they were astounded that such a place exists. Cynthia Pérez, current steward of Alma, director of La Peña Latino Arts Organization and former Chicana movement participant, and others there relayed teachings that impacted us at the level of the spirit and soul.

Writings and Art as Spirit Stories

Several women in this project have amassed a vast array of writings that can be understood as spirit stories, widely cited and taught not just for their intellectual innovations but because of their effects on readers. These writings include work around the Aztec pantheon of goddesses uncovered by Martha Cotera and invoked in Anzaldúa's *Borderlands/ La Frontera: The New Mestiza.*[35] The stories relayed in art, as previously mentioned with regard to the artwork of Carmen Lomas Garza and in the incorporation of Guadalupe in Santa Barraza's art, as in *Guadalupe Cuando Joven,* her painting that is on this book's cover, are examples of the effect those recovered histories had on the artists, who grew up in what Santa has shared with me was a "culture of domination" in South Texas.

Spirit Stories as Feminist Activism

Spirit stories are a form of activism that extends beyond knowledge collected for purposes of research or scholarship. Spirit stories are examples of feminist praxis because of their effects as well, and in particular because of how they disrupt power dynamics and hierarchies of power by challenging colonized ways of writing, thinking, and knowing, whether through literature, archives, art, or testimonios.

As nepantleras, the women in this project see the world from various in-between, subaltern, and often shadowed spaces, from unexpected angles and through intersectional lenses. This is part of their power. For they take those stories and give them light; they give them life. In doing so, they offer us more possibilities for seeing ourselves. They have unsilenced and revised silenced and misrepresented histories; they have made visible experiences that are lesser known but nonetheless greatly impactful. We must continue their legacy.

Spirit stories elicit feelings we can't always put into words. I've used *home* to describe what this feels like. *Belonging, acceptance.* Things not everyone associates with home. This book offers us a way to conceive of home that includes the home we find, cultivate, and connect to within. It is the home we have agency over, unlike the "homes" we are often a part of outside of ourselves. The notion of home is indeed complex, as I write about in the following chapter.

Bearers of Spirit Stories

Are we all bearers of spirit stories, with the capacity to evoke home by connecting with our true selves? What does this mean for the nepantlera who, as Anzaldúa notes, carries home on her back? In this chapter, I have explored this question and examined the role of storytelling in the lives of nepantleras, honoring the creative ways of seeing, being, and expressing that emerge from our experiences as people of the borderlands.

This, I believe, allowed me to see the spirit story that María Elena carried and shared with me that spring day in 2004. And I, too, am a bearer of spirit stories, as evidenced by reactions from many students over the years upon learning about Chicana history. We possess a distinct way of seeing and recognizing truths of what is just, unjust, and deeply authentic—those we feel not just in our minds but in our hearts.

In the following chapter, I provide deeper insight into the healing power of histories through the historical recovery efforts that led to foundational works by Martha Cotera central to the creation of Chicana studies, as well as the healing histories put forth by borderlands historian Yolanda Chávez Leyva through the lens of Inés Hernández-Ávila's concept of the revisioning of history as a "gran limpia."

Stories that unsilence the past, such as María Elena's and her contemporaries' political biographies as movement leaders, and her questioning of organized religion that led her to a path that aligned with her truth, exist all around us. What I've come to know is that the initial story María Elena shared with my class in 2004 at UT Austin inspired within me an embodied knowing—the kind of knowing that is transmitted through an encuentro with a previously unknown story that resonates with the deepest part of ourselves. This was someone who made profound contributions to Chicana/o history, politics, education, feminism, and spirituality—someone who, ultimately, changed lives. Yet before taking that UT course, I had no idea she even existed. And still, she changed my life and played a pivotal role in my journey toward earning a PhD. How can these two realities coexist? This paradox speaks to the power of unsilencing the past and healing histories and the urgency to think creatively—and, if necessary, subversively—to recover, disseminate, and make possible opportunities for spirit stories, a theme that unfolds in the next chapter.

CHAPTER 2

HEALING HISTORIES AND BORDER *ARTE*

Tejana Practices of Re-membering

The revisioning of history es una gran limpia.

—INÉS HERNÁNDEZ-ÁVILA[1]

History is powerful, but a history that is confused, forgotten, or taken away hurts us, leaves us vulnerable, and keeps us living in the trauma of our past. The trauma of our past, historical trauma, is an historical event or process that shocks us out of our state of balance, as individuals or communities, often leaving us with long lasting emotional, physical, and mental effects. Historical *trauma, like a physical trauma, wounds us.* However, *just as history can be the weapon that wounds us, it can also be the medicine that heals us.*

—YOLANDA CHÁVEZ LEYVA[2]

A praxis of collecting and re-collecting, of membering and re-membering, Chi*cana practices of memory involve an active encuentro with the past to create new knowledges that engage the present in critical ways.* Neither *memorializing nor overly wedded to an idealized notion of historical facticity,* Chicana *memory practice uses the past to theorize the present and to move its practitioners through what* Anzaldúa *has called the path to conocimiento.*

—MARÍA EUGENIA COTERA[3]

Voicing our stories and recovering our histories as a means of (re)claiming our power and healing—for some, even surviving—feels more urgent than ever today. What is at stake in recovering our stories and revising our histories in times like these?

In 2024, as I considered how to frame this chapter in light of our current social, political, and environmental climates, the urgency of this question became much more salient in only a few short weeks, as the grim realities of the November 2024 presidential election began to set in and the urgency of (re)claiming our power and modes of healing unfolded. To deepen my exploration, I spoke again with some of the women in February 2025, focusing on the role of feminist and spiritual activism in this moment. I integrate the insights and reflections from those recent interviews, including Inés Hernández-Ávila, Rosie Castro, Santa Barraza, and Martha Cotera. Their words of wisdom offer not only solace in these times but also valuable models and ideas for forging a path forward. As we envision and enact creative forms of resistance, their insights provide guidance for supporting youth, families, educators, scholars, community organizers, creatives, and activists in their justice-oriented, intersectional feminist efforts to protect and restore dignity to those at the margins. These times call for radical love and community care. The efforts of these women and the ways in which they invoke healing histories as artists, writers, and activists offer us a framework for continuing their work today.

In this chapter, I explore how their historical revisions—which take the shape of border arte, archives, scholarship, recovery projects, and decolonial pedagogies—function as spirit stories by challenging mainstream exclusionary narratives, shifting power, and fostering agency among contemporary women and future generations.[4] These histories hold the potential to transform us at the level of mind, body, and spirit, shaping our sense of self and belonging in profound and necessary ways.

Patrisia Gonzales notes the importance of story as medicine: "Indigenous knowledge systems recognize the role of stories and storytelling as a medicinal practice and form of traditional knowledge."[5] She goes on to cite Inés Hernández-Ávila, who writes about our wombs "carrying stories of our oppression and pain." Gonzales references "the curandera who begins healing with a plática, a good talk," when she offers that "it is time to tell the stories that heal us and create medicine with stories. These birthing stories are medicine."[6]

Using stories to share our knowledge and wisdom, women "crafted a version of Texas history and culture that is inclusive of immigrant, female, queer, and other often silenced stories of the borderlands through their vast cultural productions." That transformation is evident in Gloria Anzaldúa's stages of conocimiento, which the women in this chapter and this book have journeyed through, and their "use of re-membering as a radical act of resistance: both the recalling and the re-membering of a formerly fragmented self."[7]

In terms of the impact of archives and artistic narratives I share in this chapter, I want to hone in for a moment on the quote from María Cotera that I cited at the top: "A praxis of collecting and re-collecting, of membering and re-membering, Chicana practices of memory involve an active encuentro with the past to create new knowledges that engage the present in critical ways." The "present ways" are crucial here for their effects, as I offer through the forthcoming narratives, in alignment with Cotera, that such practices from the past can move us through conocimiento in the present and toward spiritual activism. They offer us a model for creating opportunities in the present that draw from the past to promote healing and liberation.

"La Gran Limpia" of a Chicano/a Studies Class

My encuentro with María Elena in graduate school was not my first encounter with the past and glimpse into my inner truth and purpose by way of conocimiento. I had experienced another impactful encuentro at UT some ten years prior. Both experiences illuminate a key theme in this book that is relevant to the times in which we find ourselves: Unsilenced and recovered histories, told through story, have the power to counter the harm of erasure and alienation.

Both encuentros with the past frame my telling of the stories in this book and my perspectives—including embodied knowledge—about historical processes and their effects, historical processes that impacted my own students some twenty years later, showing that erasures, and their effects, can remain intact if not countered by historical recovery and the (re)writing and owning of our own stories. The experiences I share here are not mine alone but those shared by so many whose lives have been transformed by learning histories and identities previously silenced—histories and identities often connected to their own.[8]

It was 1995. I took my first Mexican American studies course as an undergraduate, an anthropology class titled Mexican American Culture. It was my first in-depth encounter with Mexican American history and culture in an educational context. It was so powerful that it sparked something within me that led me on a path of conocimiento, to pursue my doctorate and, ultimately, to the writing of this book. It also reflected a moment of cleansing, healing—a limpia.[9]

That encuentro opened my eyes to a history that made me feel seen. Made me feel proud. It countered an internalized racism I had felt growing up, one that was no fault of my parents but, rather, a culmination of social forces and histories, such as anti-Mexican racism. I had no idea that knowledge was a political project and that unsilencing the past[10] had the power to heal. As my story and those of so many others across the United States indicate, a society void of certain histories will feel the impact on those silenced. So, I ask in this book and at this time, what is the power and potential in amplifying the stories and histories of the marginalized? Of the most vulnerable in our society? What impact could that have at the individual and societal levels? The autohistoria and stories to follow are intended to demonstrate how social and historical processes, including both historical silencing and recovery, shape lives in the borderlands. While it is my autohistoria, elements of the following story will likely be familiar to many readers, as it represents a larger pattern of silencing and its effects.

Keeping the Flame Alive: Planting the Seeds for the Reclaiming of *Tejanidad*

Growing up, I learned a little about the Battle of the Alamo in seventh-grade Texas history class, but that was the extent of my knowledge of Texas Mexican history. The majority of what I learned did not feel relevant to me nor put into a context that spoke to me.

My history and that of my *antepasados* (ancestors) were silenced in school settings, in many cases nonexistent, as was—and remains—the case for marginalized groups across the United States. Again, like many other parents, mine were not to blame, for social forces coupled with teenage angst is a tricky combination when it comes to identity and culture. On the contrary, my parents' unwavering love for Tejano music kept the flame of my inner Tejana alive. They played it relentlessly, even as we kids in the back seat begged for '90s rock. They tuned in to *The*

Johnny Canales Show on TV every Sunday morning at Grandma's house, filling the room with its familiar sounds as we gathered over pan dulce and barbacoa after church. And they brought our large Tejano extended familia together for weekend BBQs and beach trips to Padre Island, ensuring that our culture would be not just a memory but a living, breathing presence in our lives.

Today I am grateful to them for their persistence, because it allowed me to reconnect to and reclaim my beloved culture and identity. Access to Chicana/o and Mexican American studies, helped me to do so on my own terms and in ways that shaped me profoundly.

My experience in that Mexican American Culture course powerfully countered my early educational experiences. In fact, what I learned from the course set the stage for my desire to learn more about Chicano/a and Mexican American histories and, eventually, Chicana feminism, as well as to pursue a doctorate.[11] That initial and profound encuentro with a past previously unknown to me deeply impacted the rest of my life.[12]

Unsilencing the Past: Historical Revisioning as a Challenge to Power

My road to becoming a Chicana feminist and cultural anthropologist of the U.S.-Mexican borderlands was paved with silences.[13] And those silences and their effects drive my work as a feminist and borderlands storyteller today. In this section, I map out the historical processes by which silencing occurred in order to offer insight into the ways that we can recover our stories and seize our power and right to tell them.

Silences occur in stories unheard that can result in connections to self unrealized. Hidden were the histories of my maternal grandmother, Victoria Rodriguez Ledesma, as a young woman pecan sheller in San Antonio during the time of civil rights activist Emma Tenayuca's leadership in the pecan sheller's strike; that of my paternal grandmother, María Castañon Sendejo, as an aircraft builder at Naval Air Station Corpus Christi during World War II;[14] and my cousin Roger Barrera's involvement in the Chicano movement and RUP. Power and politics surrounding Texas public school curricula and historical processes that excluded certain groups' access to academia—namely, people of color, and particularly women—had everything to do with those and other erasures. Through embodied ways of knowing and unknowing that took place within and outside of my educational and career trajectories, I came into a deeper understanding of the topic of this chapter: the healing and liberatory potential of Chicana feminist historical revisions told through story.

The Seed of Healing Histories Having Been Planted, Conocimiento Emerges

I have come to realize that I was primed to meet María Elena and the other women in this project at precisely the right time. The seed of my Chicana feminist consciousness had been planted nearly a decade before meeting them, with that first encuentro with the past. This was the first stage of my conocimiento: what Anzaldúa calls an arrebato, or a rupture that prompted a shift within. Stories of the movimiento marked a shift in my understandings of self, challenged my sense of identity, and sparked my truth within. This would catapult me into further conocimiento and years of inhabiting nepantla, the in-between space of two cultures or identities, which can be difficult as one transitions between states. A sense of self comes into question, as it did for me.

I now also know that my experience of nepantla deepened my understanding of the profound impact that uncovering their own histories had on women during the Chicano and Chicana feminist movements. These were, I believe, quite possibly arrebatos that prompted women into conocimiento.

For many of the mujeres, knowing their history has been a driving force behind their creative acts of spiritual remaking, allowing them to reposition themselves, their communities, and their families within the broader landscape of Tejana and Tejano history, experiences, and social relations.

Yolanda Leyva's contention that "history can be the weapon that wounds us as well as the medicine that heals us"[15] captures the essence of this chapter and raises questions of relevance to this project: How does such wounding arise? What kinds of medicine lead to healing? What could the "revisioning of history [as] una gran limpia" look like? Feel like? And what does history as healing, in the context of historical silencing and erasure, look like? How does that play into potentials for liberation and healing? I will explore these questions within the context of women's spiritual activism.[16]

In the following vignette, I share how my experiences with the women inspired me to bring them together with students when I became a faculty member at a small private liberal arts college. I wanted to provide my students with the opportunity that I received upon meeting María Elena and the other women all of those years ago. This passing on of the spirit story is indicative of the generative nature of Chicana/Latina feminisms. I connected the generations via two intergenerational archival projects based on the women's lives and activism, by creating courses where I taught their work and shared stories from my fieldwork, and by inviting women to speak to my classes and the larger university community over the years.

The Latina History Project and the Power of Unsilencing the Past

It was 2013. I was a faculty member at a Central Texas PWI. Tori, a Latin American and border studies major, student activist, and honor student, was one of the two first student researchers on our grant-funded Latina History Project (LHP) digital humanities collective that collected oral histories of women active in the Texas Chicano movement and beyond.[17] Like many of the students in my Latinx Spiritualities class over the years, Tori would come into a new understanding of self as she started engaging in encuentros with the past, first through course readings by Gloria Anzaldúa, Irene Lara, Lara Medina, Norma Cantú, Martha Cotera, and other notable Chicana feminist scholars. Next, Tori's encuentros came in the form of personal encounters with the women themselves, including Martha Cotera, María Elena Martínez, and Yolanda Leyva. We would come to cowrite an essay about our experiences with the project in which Tori reflected what it meant to her to interview the women: "Some Chicana movimiento participants stated that it was healing for them to share their experiences of fighting for gender and racial equality, yet I don't think they realized what it meant to me to hear their stories. Generations that preceded student activists like myself went through similar struggles to create change. This knowledge allowed me to heal and in this process I finally realized I belong."[18]

Tori's reflection and related conversations with me throughout her time with the LHP indicated something powerful was happening to and brewing within her.[19] Her encuentros with the women and their pasts felt very similar to my own encuentro with María Elena years prior. Both experiences resonate with Anzaldúa's take on seeking conocimiento and purpose: "Your story's one of la búsqueda de conocimiento, of seeking experiences that'll give you purpose, give your life meaning, give you a sense of belonging. It's a quest story of ordeal and distress, cyclic life stages, identity transformation."[20] It seemed that Tori was, as Anzaldúa notes, "connecting the disparate parts of information from a new perspective," composing herself anew through her emerging Chicana consciousness and beginning to temporarily restore her "balance and wounded psyche." From then on, Tori wrote her own version of herself and her histories, doing the inner work of belonging that women's outer work of social change, including through story, elicited.

Spirit Stories as Medicina, Movidas, and the Inspiration for Imagining New Futures

Underlying both my and Tori's experiences as Texas Chicanas are histories—silenced, erased, intentionally and unintentionally—that have both shaped and alienated us, just as they have countless others over time. I propose that this historical erasure forms the context for the "wounding" Leyva describes. Yet the stories and histories preserved in women's art, writings, and archives serve as the medicina that heals, offering restoration, resilience, and resistance. In this way, they are spirit stories.

Histories become spirit stories when they carry and circulate subversive knowledge and practices that inspire profound inner healing and liberation from systemic and personal oppressions. Through their lived experiences, spiritual practices, and creative expressions, women's lives offer examples of the power of storytelling, spiritual agency, and self-acceptance as tools for personal and societal transformation. Such encuentros with the past support women in helping to imagine and then create new inner and outer worlds. The work of this group of women and of their generation is not just about the past: It is about how stories of the past inspire in the present and help us to imagine new futures. Tori's story reflects the transformative effects of intergenerational encuentros—encounters with people, stories, and art that change people of multiple generations in ways that are often reciprocal.

In this section, I will explore healing histories through the context of movidas and the work of unsilencing the past. Movidas are strategic acts of resistance. As the editors of *Chicana Movidas: New Narratives of Activism and Feminism in the Movement Era* note, the word *movida*—in various contexts including institutional, home, and art—"often carries with it connotations of not only the strategic and tactical but also the undercover, the dissident, the illicit—that which is not part of approved and publicly acknowledged political strategies, histories, and economic and social relations. When understood as a mode of submerged and undercover activity, a movida operates as both the generative 'other' of what is visible, accredited, and sanctioned and as a strategy of subversion."[21] As I write elsewhere,[22] this subversion works in part to counter mainstream and often androcentric and Eurocentric historical narratives, which can have profound effects.

Rethinking Knowledge and Histories as Rethinking Self

For Anzaldúa, rethinking what counts as knowledge is key when it comes to reimagining histories and, hence, self. The goal for Anzaldúa is for the body to become a site of love, acceptance, and respect, thereby making possible the "inner work" that allows women to do "outer" and "public work" of social change. The final stage in the process of conocimiento is coming into self-transformation, self-love, and acceptance: A "form of spiritual inquiry, conocimiento is reached via creative acts—writing, art-making, dancing, healing, teaching, meditation, and spiritual activism—both mental and somatic (the body, too, is a form as well as a site of creativity)."[23]

Acts of unsilencing the past are movidas, that is, "maneuvers within and outside of the specular range of large-scale political and social relations" that function to create change and "shift power structures within social relations and ideologies."[24] The women frequently enact movidas, and they do so in ways that embody spiritual activism. As Chicana feminist practices of liberation, these acts nurture the mind, body, and spirit, fostering healing and wholeness. Through community building, ceremony, art, writing, mentoring, and other forms of creative and cultural expression, they cultivate resilience and transformation.

The histories and stories shared here are examples of women's movida praxis—the ability to subvert and shift power. They are spirit stories because of the effects they have on the bodymindspirit. As the following narratives will show, the Texas Chicanas I write about have resisted the effects of distorted narratives and silenced histories through their work, activism, and feminist practices. Rooted in the erasure of their own histories and those of their communities, their efforts have not only fueled personal and collective resistance but have also been a driving force behind the Chicana and Chicano movements and the establishment of Chicana/o and ethnic studies across the United States.

Ethnographic Vignettes: Cuentos of Re-membering as Movidas of Spiritual Activism

As the following examples demonstrate, women's movida praxis—subversive yet transformative acts of resistance—emerges in archives, border arte, community activism, literature, historical recovery, and spaces ranging from college classrooms to grassroots movements and beyond. As both the narratives I have shared and my own experiences illustrate, women engage in spiritual activism by guiding others in healing and re-membering. These movidas, conveyed through spirit stories, cultivate conocimiento and impact the bodymindspirit, bringing us into the realm of spiritual activism.

Cuentos of re-membering become movidas of spiritual activism when they carry wisdom and knowledge that inspire change, from a shift in thinking in some people to a transformation in being in others. Whether fostering a deepened sense of self-worth and pride (like with women who were moved by historical recovery in the Chicano/a movements and my own experience with the UT course that was the result of Chicana/o educational activism) or facilitating reconciliation and reclaiming of multiple identities, these stories resonate at the level of the soul, leaving lasting impact.

This is exemplified in the narratives that follow. Martha Cotera's historical recovery work of our feminist and spiritual heritage, alongside her research and written histories of the Aztec pantheon of goddesses, were developed and disseminated through the Chicana Research and Learning Center, which validates women's activist and feminist history. Carmen Lomas Garza's artwork and books counter histories of Mexican and Tejana/o exclusion and discrimination, celebrating South Texas life, family, and cultura by depicting pride and enduring love. Santa Barraza's paintings reclaim Tejanx-Indigenous history, offering a visual testament to ancestral resilience. Norma Cantú's border literature consists of transformative encuentros with students and others that validate experiences and, hence, lives.[25] And María Elena Martínez draws on histories and knowledge of the feminine divine to help women embrace decolonial, feminist spiritual practices that reflect their true selves and reconcile with their religious upbringings.

Through their activism, scholarship, art, archives, and teaching, the women crafted depictions, narratives, and stories and created communities and encuentros reflective of Tejana life in the borderlands. They put forth other ways of being and knowing that brought their family, community, and regional histories out from the shadows.[26] Through their vast cultural productions that reflect collective knowledge gathering, creativity, and agency in proposing other realities, they built a version of Texas history and culture that is inclusive of immigrant, women, queer, and other often-silenced stories of the borderlands.

Such historical limpias with effects in the present—born from women sharing their medicina with the world—have helped me and others heal from the fragmentation of bodymindspirit inflicted by colonization. They counter historical and generational trauma by fostering a (re)connection to and restoration of self.

The following stories of individual women are organized by themes that highlight the various ways in which unsilencing the past—an act of outer work—ultimately fosters inner transformation, healing, and belonging. The stories reflect histories that heal, movidas praxis as spiritual activism, and liberatory praxis. Some of their lives intertwine in various ways—through participation in RUP, for example, or in their work at

Alma de Mujer, or in their university attendance. They share the ability to invoke histories and personal stories from the past that have immense impacts on those who take them in. However, as the stories will show, and as the reader may potentially feel, these effects are not stable and bounded. For inner and outer work are a dynamic process, a process of moving through the ebb and flow of conocimiento.

Feminist Historical Recovery, Spiritual Activist Pedagogies, and the Complexities of Home

In this section, I explore history as healing through the lens of feminist historical recovery and its incorporation into higher education pedagogy and development of the field of Chicana studies.

Historical revisioning by Chicana feminists include the research and writing of Gloria Anzaldúa in *Borderlands/La Frontera: The New Mestiza* and Martha Cotera's work of recovering Chicanas' feminist history and heritage. Their work was pivotal to the development of Chicana/Latina studies and feminist thought by way of a vast body of scholarship, courses, and curricula. Yolanda Leyva's efforts also made an important contribution in the realm of history, Chicana studies, and beyond, through her activism in her El Paso community, her curating of museum exhibits, and her writing of numerous articles on Chicana, lesbian, and border history.[27] These Tejanas incorporated these histories into their lives and work, resulting in spirit stories, those stories that by now we know are imbued with healing and liberatory effects.

Gloria Anzaldúa offers a rich ethnographic look into the borderlands through her insider lens. Her theory and praxis of spiritual activism emerged from her lived experiences in the Rio Grande Valley and negotiation of many borderlands as a nepantlera. She shares some experiences of navigating the spiritual, material, and conceptual borderlands with many of the women in this study, making her ideas, theories, historical recovery work, and methodologies applicable to their lives. In addition to the material conditions of the borderlands, Anzaldúa speaks to the importance of the inner conditions of borderlands inhabitants: That is, she speaks to the body, the site of wounding but also the site of healing, both of which are relevant to this chapter.

Martha Cotera and the Chicana Research and Learning Center: A Pivotal Site of Chicana Movidas, Memory Praxis, and Spiritual Activism

I interviewed Martha Cotera for several years before I learned of the significance of her contributions to the creation of Chicana studies and its connection to the Chicana Research and Learning Center (CRLC) in Austin, which she cofounded with Evey Chapa.[28] The context was research for my chapter for the anthology *Chicana Movidas: New Narratives of Activism and Feminism in the Movement Era,* on the emergence of Chicana feminist thought in Texas. It was then that I learned about CRLC, active in Austin from 1971 to 1987.

What I uncovered was that the CRLC had a crucial and rippling effect on the formation of Chicana feminist thought and the field of Chicana/Latina studies, impacting "the production of Chicana feminist thought through its focus on facilitating Chicana feminist thinking and theorizing that manifested in countless cultural productions—scholarly, spiritual, literary, artistic, and other—during the early 1970s and in the decades to follow."[29] The CRLC laid the groundwork for "a specific genealogy of feminist and political thought that helped to shape Chicana feminist praxis in Central Texas," influencing future generations of scholars and activists in Austin and around the nation.

Given this, I offer that the CRLC's works functioned as feminist and decolonial historical recovery efforts that contributed to healing the wounds of erasure and violence inherited from colonization. I will illustrate this by showing how the CRLC actively practiced Chicana feminist conocimiento—the production and transmission of knowledge that integrates theory and practice in the service of justice—in ways that fostered healing and re-membering.

The conocimiento work of the CRLC can be understood as spirit stories—narratives with transformative effects that contributed to making soul for the healing histories they uncovered and recovered, spiritual and beyond. The key example I will provide is one that has had a profound impact on Chicanx and Latinx lives and scholarship: Martha Cotera's historical recovery of Tonantzin and other Aztec goddesses, a decolonization act that was a pivotal tool for women in the movement era and others to follow who would employ this spiritual heritage as part of their own history and praxis. Knowledge of Tonantzin and other goddesses were key to women's work of decolonizing their bodies, minds, and spirits.

Cotera, whose leadership and legacy span local and statewide politics, demonstrates women's vast and multifaceted participation in political and activist realms. Through strategic efforts such as founding the Chicana Caucus of RUP, she worked to bring feminism into the political arena. Even as she engaged in electoral politics—evidenced by her feminist writings drafted on the backs of RUP event flyers preserved in archives—Cotera remained deeply committed to historical recovery. Her work with the CRLC, along with her roles as a librarian, archivist, and seminal feminist scholar, exemplifies how she seamlessly wove feminism into every facet of her activism and scholarship.[30]

Cotera shared the following with regard to her goal behind writing the first history of Chicanas, the groundbreaking *Diosa y Hembra: The History and Heritage of Chicanas in the U.S.*,[31] a movida that can be seen as a subversive tactic to support women in their feminist and activist endeavors. Regarding gathering sources for the book, she wrote,

> I was totally challenged. So we had to say, we're not doing anything different from what the women in our culture have always done, to be activists,

FIGURE 5 Martha P. Cotera. Texas Student Media/*The Daily Texan*.

> to be engaged politically and socially and in every way. *Diosa y Hembra* was our justification for the fact that we had a feminist tradition and that we were acting in that feminist tradition and with that feminist legacy that we had, so there was the documentation of that. So it was a way of opening up the curtain on the women that went to war and that were soldiers, the generales and all of that, in the War for Independence and the Revolution, et cetera. So these were little tidbits of things, then people could go and do the Virgen de Guadalupe or do La Malinche, do the Partido Liberal Mexicano and the women's participation in that. . . . The third purpose was the concienciación de la Mujer . . . to have a text to justify our feminism, to document for future scholars, and then to raise the consciousness of women within the civil rights movement and outside the movement to become active in the social justice movement and in the movement in general.[32]

As I state in my chapter "The Space in Between" in *Chicana Movidas*, the works of Martha Cotera were intended to provide resources not only for scholars in the emergent field of Chicana/o studies but also for wider audiences, particularly in the public schools. Fulfilling the arduous tasks of researching and compiling information for numerous of her early works were but a few of Cotera's many contributions to feminist thinking and studies.[33]

Cotera's scholarship, the archives she developed, and her political and community activism are rich with stories and strategies of resistance—knowledge she continues to share today, uplifting younger generations of activists and supporting future generations of scholars such as myself. Her movidas are abundant, spanning her scholarship, political and feminist activism, and deep engagement with both the classroom and the broader community. Over the years, she has delivered thousands of lectures and keynote addresses across the country, to audiences ranging from community groups to students in middle schools and on college campuses. Her discussion of feminism, political activism, and silenced histories has had transformative effects, something that I have witnessed firsthand with my own students and have also experienced personally. She is unwavering in her commitment to impart valuable strategies and insights on activism to younger generations, applying an experiential lens to today's social issues and political concerns.

I made a discovery in the Gloria Anzaldúa archives that speaks to Cotera's influence and her vast movidas.[34] Anzaldúa's archives show that Cotera spoke to a class Anzaldúa taught called La Chicana at UT Austin in 1977. Not only did a course syllabus indicate that Anzaldúa assigned Cotera's revolutionary text *Diosa y Hembra,* it includes notes penned by Anzaldúa from Cotera's lecture on the Aztec pantheon of goddesses, including "Coyolxauhqui-Mixcoatl, goddess of the stars and clouds" and "Coatlique, Mother of the Sun." This document further signals Anzaldúa's recognition of the importance of *Diosa y Hembra* as the first real history of Chicanas in the United States. For decades and through her many contributions as a prominent scholar-activist, Cotera has countered, and continues to counter, historical erasure. Her many movidas inspire inclusion and belonging, traversing geographic and generational borders.

LA CHICANA: A COURSE IN HEALING HISTORIES AND COMING INTO ONESELF

My initial exposure to the La Chicana course at UT Austin—the first course to be offered in Texas on Chicana history and culture—was as a graduate student. I was offered the opportunity to teach the course, one I'd not had the chance to take—much less know of its historical significance—as an undergraduate.

At the time, UT was acquiring the Anzaldúa archives, and my colega Olga was working with the Benson Latin American Collection to process the materials. It wasn't until I finished teaching the course that Olga shared that it had also been taught by Anzaldúa, as well as RUP activist and tenure-track faculty member Inés Hernández-Ávila and CRLC cofounder and RUP activist Evey Chapa, some thirty years prior.[35] According to Anzaldúa's archives, some of her materials for the course came from the Chicana Research and Learning Center; otherwise she had access to so few materials on Chicanas or women of color at the time. I was amazed by the centrality of the CRLC to developing Chicana studies at UT Austin and Anzaldúa's class as well as my own role in coming to teach the same course. Since then, in thinking about Chicana and Chicano studies in terms of healing past wounds of erasure,[36] I've wondered if and how it would have affected me to know that Anzaldúa, Inés, and Evey had taught versions of that very course—that I was continuing a part of Chicana history that preceded me and others who would come to teach the course and other courses on Chicana feminist thought at UT Austin.

The students in that UT course were mesmerized by the topic, just as my students were some ten years later when, inspired by that experience, I developed the first Chicana Feminisms course at Southwestern University. As a faculty member, I introduced students to the lives and work of Martha, Norma, Yolanda, María Elena, and others. In both instances—as had been the case for me in 1995, when I first learned of the depth of Mexican American history—the courses I taught were the first exposure the vast majority of students would have to anything related to "Chicano," much less to Chicana history and feminism. If not for the development and dissemination of materials on the history of Mexican and Chicana women by the Chicana Research and Learning Center—and other women of color as well—the La Chicana course could not have existed. Nor would we be the beneficiaries of the immense impact that it had on generations of students who would later come to see themselves anew, a demonstration of feminist knowledge creation and historical recovery as forms of spiritual activism.

Yolanda Chávez Leyva, Historian and Curandera of the Borderlands

Much like the CRLC's efforts to recover and uplift the writings of feminist, lesbian, and Chicana/Latina women of color in both community spaces and universities, Yolanda Chávez Leyva's work as a borderlands historian and writer within the fields of public history, Chicanx history, and border history also engages with narratives that foster healing.[37]

A native of El Paso and professor of history at the University of Texas at El Paso (UTEP), Yolanda has spent her life, as she says, "listening to and now documenting the lives of people who live on la frontera." Yolanda's spiritual path draws from the *huehuehtlahtolli,* the ancestral teachings of ancient Mexico, from which she learns and which she applies to her life. Yolanda says that her life calling is that of *temachtiani,* the teacher. Yolanda often speaks about her Indigenous and *mexicana* roots and how they shaped her desire to become a historian.[38]

Walking the Red Road, guided by Indigenous knowledge and healing and in alignment with ancestral teachings, she views historical work as a form of healing. She also shares her perspectives on how Tejanx, other

Latinx, and Indigenous peoples have lost parts of their histories through "linguistic terrorism," the degradation of the native language, which is a form of historical erasure.

Yolanda's story, along with those of other women, reveals that historical revision is both a communal and an individual endeavor—one that strengthens self-worth and empowers families and communities. Through her engagement with spirit stories, she shares knowledge of healing histories, ancestral foodways, and Indigenous traditions, demonstrating how history and historical knowledge can be sources of nourishment, restoring the body, mind, and spirit.[39]

FESTIVAL DE LAS PLANTAS AND SOUL NOURISHMENT

In the fall of 2007, People Organized in Defense of Earth and Her Resources[40] hosted their annual *Festival de las Plantas* in East Austin. Following a delicious and nutritious lunch of nopalitos (prickly pear cactus) and bean chalupas, black beans, fruit, and *agua de jamaica*, my dear graduate school friend María and I made our way to the area where Yolanda's plática would take place. Yolanda was introduced and began her lecture on history, healing, and the spiritual and medicinal uses of the nopal cactus.

María and I sat and listened intently. A blanket was spread out in front of Yolanda with an array of brightly colored vegetables, including squash and corn, as well as lentils, cilantro, basil, and nopales. Yolanda spoke to the predominantly Latinx audience about how as Mexicans, as Indigenous peoples of the Americas, our Indigenous blood requires certain kinds of food; our bodies are not made for cheese and processed foods. She went on to say that history runs through our blood and we must feed our bodies accordingly; otherwise we will suffer health problems such as diabetes and high blood pressure.

Several things struck me about Yolanda's talk that day at the festival, one of which was her statement "History is healing. To know your history is healing." She talked about healing historical trauma from the Spanish conquest onward, as well as various acts of psychological, physical, and spiritual violence that characterize Tejano and Tejana social and religious history. Hearing Yolanda's talk inspired me to want to learn more about her spiritual path. What I knew of her up until then made me suspect that she was a healer, for the work that she did as a historian, including

FIGURE 7 Yolanda Chávez Leyva at PODER's Festival de las Plantas, 2007. Courtesy of PODER.

there that day at the festival, was the work of one who heals. I would later come across a testimonio Yolanda wrote where she referenced imagining a "healing history" and discusses her commitment to telling untold or understood stories as a historian tied to her communities of origin: "I had been imagining a healing history for several years, inspired in part by historian, poet, and activist Aurora Levins Morales's essay, 'The Historian as Curandera.' Her advice to 'make absences visible,' to 'identify strategic pieces of misinformation and contradict them,' and to 'tell untold or undertold stories' spoke to my own sensibilities as a historian who consciously cultivated ties to my communities of origin."[41]

Yolanda demonstrates that historical recuperation is a form of spiritual healing—remedying erasures, reclaiming histories, and honoring lives. In this way, it becomes an act of spiritual activism. As her contemporary and friend Inés Hernández-Ávila has described, it is a gran limpia—a great cleansing.

LIVING SPIRITUAL ACTIVISM

Fast-forward two years, to the summer of 2009 in El Paso. Yolanda graciously agreed to meet me for an interview, where I came to learn more about the role of history as a means of healing and how to live it as practice of spiritual activism.

Yolanda arrived at the coffee shop where we agreed to meet in a bright pink Mexican dress. Her long salt and pepper hair was pulled back in two long trensas (braids), and she wore long seed-bead earrings. She greeted me, we hugged, and we sat down. She asked if it would be all right if her compadre Antonio joined us so he could say hello. "Of course!" I told her. Antonio López is a dear friend of Yolanda's of many years from Dallas. I initially met him the first time I went to Alma de Mujer, where he was working. He is a gentle soul and welcomed me to Alma with open arms, sharing his knowledge and experiences of the place with me. Our talk that day at Alma turned to the topic of spiritual healing after the loss of loved ones, and I shared the story of my and Tommy's loss with him. He was incredibly compassionate at a very critical time for me. It is the kind of compassion one never forgets.

Both Antonio and Yolanda have histories at Alma de Mujer, like so many of the women in this study. Also from El Paso, Antonio went to UTEP in the late 1970s and has identified with his Mexican Indigenous ancestry for years. The two friends have shared practicing Indigenous teachings, principles, and ways of life of the southern Mesoamerican tradición for a number of years. Yolanda identifies as Mexican, American, and Indian. Her father was part Tarahumara—an Indigenous group of Northern Mexico—and her mother mexicana. While she grew up Catholic and her family attended church, Yolanda's parents did not receive all their sacraments but made her take them, "like many Catholics," she said. Yolanda described her current spiritual path to me as a "pan-Mexican indigenous path-Mexicayotl" (a movement to keep ancient Mexican Indigenous traditions alive), about which she said, "It's the first time I feel at home spiritually." She said perhaps it is because her grandmothers and grandfathers are from this continent. Again, this intuitive feeling that Yolanda described is one that I have heard of from other of las mujeres: When the right spiritual path came into their lives, they knew it was the path for them.

At the time of our interview, Yolanda was helping to raise her three grandchildren and living in her parents' house, the house in which she grew up. Her grandchildren were the fourth generation in that house, going back to 1960. She has written about her 2001 return to her childhood home: "Returning to the place where I could say, in the most profound way, 'I am who I am because I have been there,' meant that I would be confronting an often painful history—my own and, in a myriad of ways, that of my people—on a daily basis. It meant that, for my own survival, I had to continue my efforts to make sense of the painful stories and to find ways to create a healing history."[42]

One of the ways Yolanda attempted to find healing was through trying different religious paths—not only Catholicism but also interdenominational practices, charismatic (mostly Protestant) practices, and Santería. Yolanda's decision to leave Catholicism in her forties was less about how the Catholic Church or patriarchy had hurt her personally and more about its historical treatment of Indigenous peoples, a theme that runs through many of the narratives of las mujeres. She told me that she recalled images of the Virgin and Indigenous peoples around her church, Our Lady of Guadalupe in El Paso. These were portrayals of the spiritual conquest of the Indigenous by the Franciscans. She stated, "There were depictions of Our Lady of Guadalupe hovering over, almost conquering Coatlicue in a sense." It angered her deeply. When she decided to reject Catholicism, she told herself, "I'm never going to set foot in the Catholic church again!"

Segundo Barrio is an area in El Paso located between central downtown and the U.S.-Mexico border; it is currently being threatened by gentrification. When Yolanda started doing activist work to help save the historic area and keep its community from being displaced, it involved working with local priests. El Paso's City Council has been negotiating a plan with developers to destroy the area to make way for "downtown redevelopment." Yolanda has been fighting this plan for years, along with amplifying awareness of the barrio's gentrification, where the average household income is $10,000 a year.

Working with the priests on this social justice issue has opened her mind, she said. Her ability to work with the church and be involved with the church for purposes of her activist work mirrors the experiences of other activists, such as María Jiménez, a long-time social justice advocate and atheist who was based in Houston. The reality is that the church and priests are often involved in movements for social justice, so women like María and Yolanda must decide if and how they are going to negotiate their personal beliefs on religion and put them aside in order to engage in social justice work.

I asked Yolanda if she is a healer, and she said she felt uncomfortable calling herself one. But Antonio said that she has lots of *hierbas*, medicinal herbs, in her cabinets, and he knows because he organized them for her. Yolanda is also part of a calpulli, a group with Nahua origins centered on keeping intentional cultural communities bridging tradition and modern life. The women in it often call upon her for help, like to administer healings or to consult on certain life issues. She has done limpias for colleagues at UTEP who have requested them and appreciates UTEP for the fact that her dean and the school support her taking students to Mexico and taking part in ceremonia. Yolanda used to have a hard time negotiating the spiritual and the academic, but she told me she is better able to do so now.

Yolanda pointed out something about memory that I've heard several other women reference: "I believe we have ancestral memories in our bodies." Yolanda said, "There was something [in the Mexica tradition] that makes sense to me in a way that other paths do not. It does not all resonate, but some of it does, and that which does feels right, true." She says this in regard to participating in temazcals, for instance—the ritual sweat baths that are considered part of the southern Mesoamerican Indigenous tradition.[43] In a temazcal, she had the feeling that she had been there before. But it was not until her forties that Yolanda started embracing what she calls "her energies"—prior to that she was scared to do so. Drawing on traditional medicine and ancient healing practices, such as using the temazcal and hierbas, is very much connected to her idea of reconstructing and reclaiming history.

For Yolanda, history, memory, and healing are interconnected. Yolanda engages in a spiritual activism that takes several forms, including raising her grandchildren in the tradición and acting as a healer of community, historical, and spiritual traumas. Once again knowledge has positioned a Tejana where she can work to help reconstruct her history and that of her community and family, facilitating healing for both. Yolanda's current spiritual path is an anchor that helps her to accomplish this in her life and work while enabling her to remain connected to her ancestral heritage, to "feel at home spiritually."

Inés Hernández-Ávila: The Healing Potential of Danza, Leading with the Heart, and Feminist Historical Recovery

It was the first week of February 2025. Dr. Ińes Hernández-Ávila, Professor Emeritus of the University of California, Davis, had graciously agreed to meet with me for a plática, a follow-up to our 2007 interview and to another interview in December 2024. So much had transpired in our country in just a few short weeks, raising more questions for me about Inés's perspective on the current moment.[44]

A distinguished scholar, poet, artist, and pivotal movement activist, Ińes was a contemporary of many of the women in this project during her time in Austin as a tenure-track faculty member at UT Austin.

I opened up with the following: "Can you please reflect on your thoughts on the current moment?" To which Inés responded, "There's a lot of ways to think about it, but I'm daily reminded that I live in California. And that, in itself, is already troubling, as I have so much family in Texas. . . . Unfortunately, we're living in a moment that, in a way, had to come, because this country was founded on lies. And if you found something on lies, I guess you know the foundation is not stable."

Referencing the violence and traumas of colonization and demise of so many Native peoples, Inés went on to say, "So I think that the somber part of it is that, for example, for me as a Native woman, nothing that's happening is surprising. Nothing." As Nez Percé and Tejana, Inés holds as deeply personal the colonial violence and genocide against Native peoples and their residual effects, as well as the historical erasures and systems of oppression Native peoples and Tejanxs have faced.

Inés is not surprised at the state of things, though she is deeply saddened by them. And that history, along with the recovered histories that she learned about during and since the movement, have shaped her as a teacher, scholar, and activist. Her scholarship, prose, and poetry on Tejana-Indigenous life and spiritual activism offer rich and nuanced reflections on re-membering. Rooted in her love for her Nez Percé family and community and the broader communities in which she works as an academic and activist, Inés shows us what spiritual activism looks like from a heart-centered place of feminist praxis, one that is unique in her positionality as Native and Chicana/Tejana. While the form of spiritual activism I see in Inés's life is often lonely, as she noted, it is reflective of her role as a bridge between Chicanx and Native American studies. In her scholarship and teaching, Inés invokes Chicana and Indigenous feminist frameworks focused on women's healing and liberation, which she advocated for immensely during the movement. Her spirituality is rooted in her Indigenous practices and heritage, as demonstrated from her participation in *danza conchera* during the movement to the present.

DANZA AS AN OUTLET

I asked Inés about outlets she turned to when she was active in the movement, during the difficult, exhausting times. She recounted the joy that singing and dancing bring her now and how they sustained her during that time. With regard to danza, Inés recalls the draw of the practice that became an important aspect of her spiritual path and of Native and feminist identities that hold great meaning for her:

> I spent my time in Mexico City with the elders down there. That's where I learned more than from anyone up here about danza. And what I saw in danza was a tremendous respect for every single person, at moments when the community, the dance community, came together. The elders would say, would ask for the *palabra* [open the floor] by saying, "Dios," and then everybody [would] answer, "Dios," and then the elder says whatever they have to say, but if not, somebody—myself or someone else—could say something. And it would be listened to, whether it was a child or an elder or anyone. And so I realized that they had this incredible method of social organization and that they were organized by their values. There's no way that really in the United States we could do anything like that.[45]

The inclusivity of the danza community spoke to Inés's feminist sensibilities and the values of love and dignity she holds so dear.

Danza also holds an important aspect of historical recuperation and representation around one of the central figures in Chicana feminist historical recovery: that of the legendary La Malinche, also known as Malintzin or Doña Marina, a Nahua woman. Her relationship with Hernán

Cortés during the Spanish conquest of the Americas has caused her to become a symbol of the violated, raped, and dishonored woman. Chicanas have pushed back against narratives of her as a traitor, countering with a representation of La Malinche as one who used her tremendous powers of language as a translator and negotiator to ensure the survival of her people, an "honored ancestor"—a feminist interpretation[46] that can be seen in danza and that resonates with Inés:

> The hierarchy of danza is like a military hierarchy where the dancers are called *soldados* and then you have *capitanes* and *generales*. And on the one hand, that could be from the Spanish colonial project, but it probably has more ancient roots, and I know that the figure of the Malinche in danza conchera, it's one of the only places where she's actually honored as a path opener, as someone who not only opens the path, but cleanses and blesses it so that everyone else can come behind her. [In the danza line] she's up in front of the group. So, in that sense, danza was this outlet for many of us; for the women, it was like, wow. Because Chicana feminists have always defended La Malinche more than Mexican feminists have, actually. But the conchero dance tradition is the one that really says it all for me in terms of who she is and how they regard her, you know, as an honored ancestor.

FIGURE 7 Inés Hernández-Ávila (far right) as La Malinche. Pictured with Xinachtli Danza. Courtesy of Inés Hernández-Ávila.

Inés goes on to name other outlets that have been important to help her and others in the movement deal with challenges: "And the arts, of course, you know, the arts, and our poetry—we took on misogyny and sexual violation. Art and art artwork . . . there were . . . outlets like this, there still are."

Today, Inés is a prolific scholar and respected elder. She is often invited to offer prayers and blessings along with her scholarship at Chicana and Native/Indigenous conferences, and her literary works and poetry are included in all of the anthologies on Chicana/Latina/Indigenous spiritualities and beyond. Inés's writings are a vital contribution, as they center the uncovering of histories of colonization and the urgent need for healing these deep wounds—an effort that remains deeply intertwined with her own personal history. As noted by Patrisia Gonzales, this centering of such histories and healing address a return to the original relationships to land, place, and the natural world as a means of meaning making and healing.[47]

Inés's life illustrates the complexities of engaging with healing histories as a staunch Native/Chicana feminist who has spent decades writing about and addressing the wounds of colonization through both activism and scholarship. A largely silenced aspect of her personal history is one she has consistently addressed in her work and scholarship: speaking out against sexual violence within the Chicano movement. This painful, dark, and often overlooked reality has long been overshadowed by more dominant narratives, and it remains an unhealed wound in her own journey. Yet Inés is committed to breaking that silence and exposing the harm that has been buried for too long. Through her recent writings and public acknowledgment of this violence, Inés continues her activism—moving toward healing while also supporting others in reckoning with and healing from these historical experiences.

THE HEART SPEAKS, LOVE LEADS

Like so many of us, as I've described, Inés is on a healing path. In that and every other endeavor in her life, she leads, always, with her heart. It is a practice she says comes from her Nez Percé side, to be guided by love.

> I think that really, above and beyond everything else, in terms of my spirituality, that has been the constant, is that I know how to love. I have a love for humanity and a love for life and for the earth and for everything that

lives. There are different ways that I have chosen to express that. For example, connected to social movements, whenever I would give talks, when we had rallies and they pushed some of us up front to talk, I was always one of the ones they were always like, "Go ahead, Inés." I wish someone had taped one or two of these because I would speak from the heart. I often got standing ovations, and I had the sensation as I was speaking from the heart that I was listening to myself. Because I didn't know what I was going to say at the moment I opened my mouth, and yet I would be saying things and be talking. Like, I knew families who had people in prisons, so I'd talk about how I understood inequities that push our people to places where they end up being in prisons, where they end up being labeled for the rest of their lives and it being passed on through the generations, and we had to help to stop it. I don't remember how I would say it, but I remember I would think of those things. Even now, if you were to ask me, "What is the foundation of your spirituality?" it is the understanding of the need to love.

ON BEING BOLD: CONNECTION OF THE HEART TO THE SOUL

Inés offers a consejo on the wisdom of the heart: "It's about trusting your heart and being bold. Reflection is so important because the conversation with your heart, with your spirit, will let you know if your whole self is in agreement with what you're thinking as opposed to being possibly misled." Trusting in ourselves and relying on the heart are about making soul. This is the place from which the wisdom of our ancestors emerges, where our soul speaks. It is conocimiento, a way of knowing that is not a traditional way of thinking about knowledge. It is one that can serve us well if we learn to trust within, to do the inner work.

Love is at the root of Inés's spirituality, and she expresses it through her heart, voice, and body, as her soul speaks and her body acts. How she makes soul is deeply connected to her sense of justice and profound respect for human dignity. What I learned from Inés is what it means to embody a feminism that is spiritual and to enact a spirituality that is feminist.

Border Arte as Medicina: Nepantlera Artists Santa Barraza and Carmen Lomas Garza

My first introduction to the Chicano movement in that 1995 anthropology course I mentioned earlier would become the impetus for my long-awaited move to pursue graduate school. After seven years in the museum field—during which time I would come to work with Carmen Lomas Garza through an exhibit I helped develop on her artwork—in my thirties, with a Chicana consciousness looming, I applied to graduate school to study Tejana history and culture. Another seven years later, I presented my doctoral research on Carmen Lomas Garza and other Tejanas in the Union Building Chicano Culture Room at UT Austin. Through my doctoral research I found the melding of the spiritual and the political as a central theme among Chicana artists.

Having lived through racial and gender discrimination, classism, homophobia, and often their intersections, borderlands artists—much like their writer counterparts—have envisioned alternative ways of knowing and being. Through their art, they construct new futures, and in the spirit stories woven into their creative expressions, they communicate these possibilities. They engage in what Anzaldúa describes as the "fashioning of new narratives" through autohistoria, in art. She notes with regard to this border arte—as in the works of Carmen Lomas Garza and Santa Barraza, which she references—"Border artists inhabit the transitional space of nepantla. The border is the locus of resistance, of rupture, and of putting together the fragments." By "disrupting the neat separations between cultures," she writes, "Chicana artists create a new culture mix, una mestizada."[48] *Una mestizada* full of spirit stories.

This section will explore Tejana artists Santa Barraza and Carmen Lomas Garza in two contexts—as border artists who are "engaged in 'reading' that nepantla, that border . . . the source of creativity, dreams, fantasies, intuitions," and who, in that state of nepantla, are "at the threshold of transformation." Both artists offer that the Chicano movement had a significant role in ushering them into that state. As the following narratives will show, transformation awaited them both on the other side of nepantla and into new forms of consciousness that led them to honor their Indigenous and Tejano ancestors and ancestry.

As stated by Laura Pérez, Chicana art attends to the politics of the spiritual: That is, spiritual beliefs and practices generate social and political effects that count.[49] For Pérez, "in the work of Chicana artists making reference to the religious, whether through the use of elements of traditional or more hybrid spiritualities, what mattered most were the tangible effects of such beliefs and practices." These tangible effects are present for these nepantlera artists. As this chapter will show, for Carmen, these effects are reached through her practice of her Mexica spiritual path, and for Santa, through a deep connection to ritual and place.

Carmen Lomas Garza: Ancestral Recuperation and Reciprocal Healing

Resistance, rupture, and their healing effects are reflected in Carmen Lomas Garza's paintings, in her children's books, and in a spiritual path that is inspired by her family history, heritage, and the Chicano movement.[50] In her depictions of Mexican American life through "monito" paintings, "the spiritual is embodied in cultural practice and identity . . . to affirm that which is familiar to one, that which already constitutes a particular self, and from whose valiant alienation—through racist shaming—pain, loss, and disintegration ensue." To Pérez, Carmen's work is a testament to the "healing function of art and culture or, in the words of an expression dear to Chicana/o artists, to the truth that la cultura cura ('culture cures')." She goes on to point out the widespread attraction of audiences to Carmen's work, which depicts loving family and supportive community within traditional rural Mexican American culture and serves as a "balm" "against the dehumanizing assumptions and projections about Mexican American culture and values."[51]

Carmen's work is informed by her Catholic upbringing and the religious sacraments, traditions, and holidays with which she was raised, such as Easter and Christmas. Her family also celebrated the Day of the Dead, a popular religious holiday of Indigenous Mexica origins that Carmen would retain and practice as an adult through her Mexica practices.[52] The family also made regular visits to local curandero Don Pedrito Jaramillo's shrine, and Carmen's mother and grandmother were deeply devoted to Our Lady of Guadalupe, who sat upon both her mother and grandmother's home altars. Carmen states that the church was "the first museum I ever saw," that she was intrigued by its aesthetics, from reproductions of biblical scenes to artistic renditions of various saints and Jesus. But in her teens Carmen began questioning the institution, especially once the Pope relaxed numerous practices during the onset of the Vatican II Council in the mid-1960s: "Vatican II changed some of the rules—[they were] relaxed—Mass in Spanish [instead of Latin], women didn't have to wear veils anymore. . . . I read it in the Sunday paper when it came out about veils, so I showed my parents the article, and they still insisted I wear my veil, and I said I wasn't going to wear it. So as a protest I didn't wear it, and I was the only girl in the church who didn't wear a veil, and of course I got a lot of stares, but hey . . . the Pope says I don't have to wear it, I don't have to wear it!" She laughs.

Carmen describes herself as a very compliant daughter who respected her parents. However, she would continue to question the church:

> I was the oldest daughter and so was very dutiful. But I just wasn't happy with the Catholic Church. . . . It just didn't feel comfortable . . . I didn't feel like I needed to . . . be part of the whole ritual of the Catholic Church. And so when I was eighteen years of age I told my father and mother that I was not going to go to church anymore, because by the time you are eighteen you can make your own decisions. And of course we had a big disagreement about it, but I persisted. . . . I had been Catholic and now instead for the past fourteen years I've been doing *danza mexica.*

Carmen chose to dedicate her life to producing artwork as a tool for healing the wounds inflicted by the kinds of erasure and racism that she experienced growing up in Kingsville, Texas: "I think the paintings have served a tremendous function of doing the healing, not just for me but for whoever sees the work."[53] Garza credits the Chicano movement in large part for empowering her to speak out and act against injustices. It was through the movement, her university classes, and her participation in the Chicano cultural arts scene that she also learned about her history, following the same pattern other women and subsequent generations of Tejanas such as myself experienced. As stated in the earlier quote, the movement both gave her the voice to express herself about her childhood and pointed out injustices of colonialism.

Learning about the silenced history of an Indigenous past and the conquest of the Indigenous peoples and their ways of life also allowed Carmen to heal the wounds of inferiority caused by racial discrimination. She gained a sense of pride and belonging that the movement instilled in so many.[54] This pride translates to healing for those who see her works in museums, community centers, schools, public housing, airports, and other places. The brightly colored depictions narrate scenes of family barbecues and birthday parties with piñatas, scenes of conjunto dancing, a limpia being performed by a curandera, *tamaladas*, and quinceañeras—themes in Garza's work that reflect her personal experiences while addressing universal commonalities such as family, community, faith, and belonging. I witnessed this myself in 2002, at an opening of the exhibit I helped develop on her work, a testament to the fact that, as Garza says, "the art I was creating functioned in the same way as the salvia [aloe vera] plant when its cool liquid is applied to a burn. . . . It helped to heal the wounds inflicted by discrimination and racism."[55] Today, her artwork continues to be a healing salvia felt by thousands of people, Latinx and beyond, who see themselves represented in a museum exhibit or book of hers, often for the first time.

Carmen now lives in San Francisco, yet her tejanidad remains deeply present in her daily life. She expresses it through her paintings, which honor South Texas cultural traditions, and by wearing a danza *traje* (regalia) that includes feathers representing both her Texas roots and California home—intentional acts that affirm her identity and connection to her origins and current life path.

Stories have been central to her upbringing, her sense of self, and her work in the world today. Carmen shares that it was an uncle working on a family tree who brought stories forth from her grandparents: "That's when I started hearing the stories [and to] pay attention, actually, to the stories about the ancestors on my mother's side." She learned that her maternal grandfather came from New Mexico and that some of her ancestors were Native Americans who worked as vaqueros at the King Ranch, the largest ranch in the U.S., which is believed to have displaced Mexican and Tejano families when it was established. Carmen makes a direct connection between her current danza participation and this South Texas Indigenous heritage:

> Danza, danza mexica, danza azteca, gives me the opportunity to give thanks to the spirits of . . . all my ancestors for the sacrifices that they made to give us life, to give us energy, to give us ways of living, to give us the nourishment. One of things I like to do . . . when I talk about my artwork . . . like, for example, [the 1995 painting] *Nopalitos*,[56] is to point out that this [practice of cooking and eating nopal cactus] was a tradition that

> has been given to us by our Indian ancestors, and the tamales . . . those are [the] kinds of traditions that have been passed down through the generations by our Indian ancestors, and that we should be grateful for that. We aren't taught that in public school, we aren't taught that in our general education about Mexico and the Southwest, it's all about the [*Mayflower*] pilgrims, and so I take that opportunity when I am showing my artwork to talk about those things.

Once again the function of history in remaking Carmen's understanding of her social world emerges, as does how she uses the history she has gained to empower and to heal others. She goes on: "Who are we? Where have we come from? . . . To me [exploring] that was the beginning of my healing. . . . Going on with danza has given me another opportunity, another, different way of doing more self-healing and centering, centering myself and balancing myself." There is a reciprocity here in that Carmen's work produces a kind of healing of the soul wound brought on

FIGURE 8 María Elena Martínez (left) and Carmen Lomas Garza, Nettie Lee Benson Latin American Collection *¡A Viva Voz!* exhibit opening, University of Texas at Austin, 2009.

by colonization, and danza allows for Carmen's own "self-healing," which gives her the balance to do her work of healing history for others.

Like the other women I interviewed, Carmen is educated about the degradation of Indigenous peoples during the conquest of the Americas, which she learned about in part through her involvement in the Chicano movement. She is passionate about the violence that was perpetrated against Indigenous peoples and about the role the Catholic Church played in it: "Look at the tremendous cost. . . . It cost us dearly. . . . I feel an anger there that I just cannot forget from [what] the Spaniards did, [what] the Catholic Church did to the Indigenous people, to my ancestors, to the other half of my family."

This knowledge of colonialism influences Carmen's spirituality and shapes her spiritual path today, which, as mentioned earlier, is rooted in a Mexica tradition. The name of Carmen's group is Danza Azteca Xitlalli, and she has been with them since the 1990s. In terms of what needs being part of the group fulfills, Carmen says, "It'smostly to honor our ancestors. . . . It fits so well with my belief in remembering and appreciating all that our Indian ancestors gave to us. . . . It structures it in a way that I had not been able to do with my artwork. So the structuring, by participating with a group, it's a physical activity, it's a spiritual activity, a communal activity, it's familial—the whole family is involved . . . teens, babies, parents."

In 2008, Carmen invited me to participate in a Día de los Muertos event that brought together danza *grupos* from all over California for a beautiful ceremonia and honoring of ancestors. An all-night event, it gave me deep insight into Carmen's life and the draw of danza.[57]

Dia de los Muertos in the Mission

It is a cold and rainy night, and cars flood the Mission District on one of its most celebrated nights, November 2, Day of the Dead, or Día de los Muertos. We pull up to the church, and I reflect on the irony of holding a Mexica ceremonial event at a Catholic church. I locate the entrance to the church hall and enter to see hundreds of cempasúchil (marigolds, the traditional flower of Day of the Dead) arranged in vases, as well as photos, personal objects, and candles lined atop the *altar*; it is all about to begin.

I hear a little girl singing at the top of her lungs in what I soon realize is Nahuatl. She knows the song by heart. *More than just the words to a song, she knows the way, la tradición,* I think to myself. Copal smoke is heavy in the air. Children start to lie down, one by one, in their sleeping bags. Rattles, mandolin, thick energies, heightened drumming, more copal smoke. Communal sharing of food, giving thanks, taking only what you can eat. Reusing all plates and cups.

Carmen approaches the altar. It is her responsibility to blow the ceremonial conch, the *atecocolli.* She takes it seriously, does it at all of the appropriate times during the ceremony. She helps keep everyone in line who approaches the altar for a blessing, helps us all to follow form. Protocol is very important. Hours and hours pass. More song. More prayer. Sit, rest. Hot chocolate and pan dulce break . . .

Finally the morning beckons. I look out the window to the Mission in the early hours of the new day, touch the glass, so cold as the sun's rays begin to peek through the clouds. I hear scuffling, the *danzantes* preparing for the closing evet—the danza. People changing all around me, trajes, feathered head dresses, ankle rattles. Carmen changes into her traje—handmade, intricate. She shows me the two feathers on the

FIGURE 9 Carmen Lomas Garza and Brenda Sendejo on Día de los Muertos, San Francisco, California, 2009.

back of her crown. One from Brownsville, one from the ocean near San Francisco, feathers representing her dual and overlapping identities: her Tejanidad and her life in California. Over one hundred danzantes moving in unison, feathers, trajes of all colors, copal scent, drumbeats. I feel the drumbeat in my skin, in my heart, in my soul. Past the chipped windowsills I see the sun rising slowly to the east. Bright hues of orange, red, yellow; clouds of white and gray. Dancing ends. The danzantes take each others' hands, pray, and give thanks for a beautiful celebration. They greet the rest of us, and we give thanks for their blessing. Carmen and I say our goodbyes.[58]

While Carmen and Santa's artistic styles are very different, both capture the essence of the beauty, resilience, creativity, and possibilities inherent in living in the in-between. Santa Barraza's narrative, as explored in the following, highlights the importance of ritual and place in spiritual activism.

Santa Barraza, Homecomings, and Locating Self

It was a Saturday morning in 2009 when I headed out on FM 665 from Corpus Christi south toward Kingsville. I don't get back to Corpus as often as I would like to, so I used this research trip as an opportunity to visit some of my family while I was in the area. Just a few short miles outside of the city limits, I began to lose sight of the suburbs and came across that familiar landscape: the flat, dry land, the mesquite trees, the nopales, the acres of hoed fields, and the occasional railroad track. I remember thinking I would not have given a second thought to trading in the scorching South Texas summers and the murky, warm brown waters of the gulf for the blue of the Pacific Ocean and crisp 70 degree California weather I'd seen in the movies.

Today those same cacti, mesquite, the flat, flat land, and especially the gulf affect me in a very different and deep way, in a way that no other landscape in the state, country, or world ever has or ever will, a way that only someone with roots in South Texas who has left for a long period of time and then come back again can appreciate. Someone like Santa Barraza.

So I drove. Behind me, home; in front of me, my work. As I would come to learn that day, these two spheres are not so easily separated, in large part because of my cultural and collective memories that were activated in unexpected ways by the profound impact of being in South Texas;—the profound impact of place. And its ability to help us to reconnect to a part of ourselves, to re-member.

I arrived at Texas A&M University–Kingsville early for my 11:00 a.m. appointment. I spent a few extra minutes assessing the palm-tree-lined main entrance to the campus, formerly Texas A&I University, once a hotbed of political activity and an important site for the emergence of the Chicano cultural arts movement in the late 1960s and early 1970s. Many prominent Chicana and Chicano artists would come out of this institution, including Carmen Lomas Garza, Cesar Martinez, Jose Luis Rivera-Barrera, and the woman I was there to see that day, Santa Barraza.[59] Santa would return decades later to teach in their art department.

FIGURE 10 Santa Barraza painting her mural of Madre Julia Navarrette Guerrero, founder of the Missionary Daughters of the Most Pure Virgin Mary of Kingsville, Texas. Juan Lopez-Johnston.

Being in the vicinity of my own home and familiar religious practices—and experiencing this alongside Santa's similar experience and her interpretations of the events to follow—illuminated for me how place and memory inform issues of belonging, community, and identity. It gave me a deeper understanding of her works of border arte as forms of healing histories impacted by place.

Santa had invited me to sit in on a presentation she and her students were giving, after which we would have our interview. The presentation ended, and I waited for Santa in the art studio.

When she showed up, Santa, aware of my research interests, asked if I would like to see Don Pedrito Jaramillo's shrine and the Healing Tree while I was in the area. "Or maybe you don't have time and would rather just do the interview?" I needed no time to think it over: "I would love to."

"Great, Let me get Darin"—her colleague who would join us—"and we'll get going."

So we took off in my car down the highway toward Concepcion, Texas, Santa, Darin, and me. Established in 1873, Concepcion is one of the oldest cities in Duval County. There were not many cars on the road, considering it was a beautiful, cool Saturday afternoon in March. We approached

FIGURE 11 The Healing Tree, Concepcion, Texas. Brenda Sendejo.

a small house surrounded by a chain-link fence, passing the wooden sign with the words *arbol milagroso* (miracle tree) burned into it. Below was another sign that read, "Open 9:00–5:30." To the right of that was a light blue banner with the crucified Jesus in white, flowing in the wind. Dozens of plastic and wooden beaded rosaries of all colors and sizes lined the side of the metal fence that faced the road. Behind it stood a very tall tree: the Healing Tree.[60]

Estella Palacios Garcia, the woman who planted the tree in 2003 and in whose yard it stood, greeted Santa warmly, "Que gusto de verte! Hace mucho tiempo que no te veo." (What a pleasure to see you! It's been such a long time since I've seen you.) Estella would later tell Santa that three days prior, she'd had a vision that Santa would visit. "Pasale, pasale," she said, inviting us into the yard. After being introduced to her and thanking her, I approached the tree. "Put your ear up to the trunk," Santa told me. "Listen." I did as she said and heard the sound of running water flowing through the twenty-plus-foot-high tree, which, like the fence, was covered in rosaries. "They [the rosaries] used to be lower," Santa said, "but the tree has grown."

After a couple of minutes, I backed away from the tree, and as I did, Darin asked if I would like to hear his theory about the running water sound. I responded with a smile and shook my head. My purpose there was as an anthropologist and a Tejana learning more about the traditions of her heritage; such a phenomenon as this tree required no further explanation.[61]

We toured the grounds, which included a small chapel that had been erected by "two men who were called by Jesus to build it," the señora said. Inside, two walls were covered by hundreds of photos and letters of people in need of healing or whose lives had been touched by the Healing Tree. Another wall was lined with plastic and live floral arrangements, statues of Christ and the Virgins of Guadalupe and San Juan, and crucifixes, all donations from visitors. The daughter of the señora who owned the property showed us newspaper clippings about the tree and a black binder full of testimonies by people who had been healed by it, Santa's sister among them.

The testimonies spoke of Jesus Christ answering their prayers, as in the cases of women who had been told they were infertile and then bore children after visiting the tree and people claiming to be cured from cancer and other illnesses. In popular religious fashion, Christ and Catholicism were featured in this folk narrative, from the picture of Christ on the flag at the entrance to the presence of the saints and Christ in the chapel, and, most noticeably, in the photo of a priest blessing the Healing Tree. It was a priest who believed the Holy Spirit ran through the tree. While I stayed inside the chapel looking at photos and reading testimonies, Santa sat outside platicando with the señora.

Santa believes in the power of the Healing Tree. Her sister Frances experienced a miracle from the Healing Tree and is one of the people whose testimonies are kept in the black binder. Being there in South Texas at this shrine was meaningful to Santa. As she would later say, the ritual is important for her. As for me, returning to South Texas and visiting the Healing Tree provoked feelings that, yes, I was Tejana and familiar with the rituals as part of my ethnic heritage, but I had been severed from them in many ways. I came to understand the importance of place.

I began to wonder whether Santa and I—immersed in our Catholic heritage and its popular folkways, surrounded by a landscape rich with cultural memory—were experiencing something both deeply recognizable and, in some ways, recuperative. For me, it reversed a lingering sense of alienation I had felt since leaving Catholicism. Standing at the Healing Tree, and later visiting Don Pedrito Jaramillo's shrine just down the road, I felt a renewed sense of belonging. My Catholic and Tejana—specifically South Texas—identities granted me both familiarity and a point of entry into Santa's world.

There were also certain moments of connection with the South Texas land and landscape that, to this day, I feel link Santa and me in a palpable way. For Santa, returning to South Texas after years away was not just a homecoming but a reawakening of a belonging that only place itself can provide. A similar sense of belonging emerges in the classroom when I teach about the Healing Tree when students from the South Texas region recognize, or even live near, such popular religious sites. For many, it is the first time they see themselves and their homes represented in an academic space—a powerful moment for those whose families have historically been excluded from institutional settings through systemic racism and violence.

Santa has also made it her life's work to proudly share the history and culture of the borderlands of her Tejana-Indigenous heritage and a profound love of home. As Anzaldúa notes, Santa's pre-Columbian codices act as "reclamation of cultural and historical mestiza/o identity."[62]

FIGURE 12 Santa Barraza (left) and Brenda Sendejo, who holds a print of Barraza's *Nepantla* (1995). Raza Unida Reunion, San Antonio, Texas, 2022.

Anzaldúa goes on to say, "One of her [Santa's] devotional retablos is of La Malinche with maguey (the maguey cactus is Barraza's symbol of rebirth . . .). Like that of many Chicana artists, her work explores Indigenous Mexican 'symbols and myths in a historical and contemporary context as a mechanism of resistance to oppression and assimilation.'"[63] In *Santa Barraza: Artist of the Borderlands*, Santa notes, "My artwork is about resistance, de-colonization, self-definition, self-empowerment, and survival. I draw upon myths, family folklore, and indigenismo (a way of being)."[64] The border arte of Santa and Carmen attests to the possibilities of imagining borderland lives otherwise and facilitating healing through historical recovery and resistance both for the artists and for those who take in the art, cornerstones of Tejana re-membering.

Conocimiento and Re-membering: The Coyolxauhqui State

My experiences of conocimiento in my Tejana borderlands are the lenses through which I read and tell women's stories. Their own paths of conocimiento and acts of re-membering are radical acts of resistance: both the recalling of histories silenced and the re-membering of a formerly fragmented self.

I propose that women's work of unsilencing the past—in literature, in developing archives and resources, and in making art—has the capacity to propel us into conocimiento, particularly with regard to the fifth stage of coming into a new way of being: the Coyolxauhqui state. This is much like the experiences my student Tori and I had—along with those of hundreds, even thousands, of students over the decades—whose lives have been shaped by the historical recovery of the borderlands. As Anzaldúa notes, it is here that "after dismantling the body/self you re-compose it—the fifth stage of the journey, though reconstruction takes place in all stages. When creating a personal narrative you also co-create the group/cultural story."[65]

This state is one in which we develop new knowledge, deepen self-awareness, and write new stories. The women in this book have worked to unsilence histories—including their own—through the (re)construction of autohistorias, aptly described by Anzaldúa: "Connecting the disparate parts of information from a new perspective, you re-member Coyolxauhqui in a new composition, temporarily restoring your balance and wounded psyche. Like the heroine in a myth or fairy tale, after an arduous struggle in the dark woods, you return, bringing new knowledge to share with others in your communities."[66]

The rewriting of such stories and, as Anzaldúa states, the desire to repair and heal are not just for themselves but for their communities and society at large—creating healing histories in writings and border arte.

In this chapter, I have shown how archives and artistic and literary productions transmitted through movida praxis have the potential to heal wounds caused by historical erasure and historical trauma; as Yolanda Levya notes, "Just as history can be the weapon that wounds us, it can also be the medicine that heals us."[67] Histories that do so are spirit stories.

A central takeaway from this chapter is how the transmission of recovered histories is reflective of the generative nature of Chicana feminist thought and its legacy as liberatory praxis. When we converge with these stories that enable us to connect to our inner, true selves, we are empowered. That is, it not only inspires us to step into our power, it also causes a shift in power—in who carries the power to tell what stories and how. The legacies of the women in this project—and others whose stories are so vital to our spiritual sustenance, sense of belonging, and even sheer survival—are indicators that historically excluded and alienated groups no longer need to rely only on educational systems to show us we belong. Our own communities do so by helping shepherd us into conocimiento and amplifying our stories through art, writings, the classroom, and the archive.

In the next chapter, I discuss the transformative effects of healing histories, focusing on how Chicanas incorporating Guadalupe into an alternative Catholicism and recovering Tonantzin within their devotion to Guadalupe has shaped their ethnic, feminist, and gender identities. Through Guadalupe-Tonantzin, they engage in the profound acts of making face and making soul.

CHAPTER 3

OUR LADY OF GUADALUPE-TONANTZIN

Spiritual Activist, Protectress, and Feminista *of the Borderlands*

The Virgen de Guadalupe spoke very strong to me. . . . She has been the healing mother. . . . She inspires me and teaches me how to use my power for the good of all beings. Guadalupe-Tonantzin is an earth goddess. . . . We as women have to heal the collective unconscious of women, find our own feminine divine. We have to heal the memory of physical, sexual, psychological, spiritual abuse that has been suffered by women over the thousands of years and present in the world today.

—MARÍA ELENA MARTÍNEZ[1]

Guadalupe . . . the virgin mother who has not abandoned us.

—GLORIA ANZALDÚA[2]

Tonantzin opened up a whole new world.

—INÉS HERNÁNDEZ-ÁVILA[3]

Our Lady of Guadalupe—la Virgen de Guadalupe, *la morenita* (the dark-skinned one), often described as the Goddess of the Americas—is a cultural and historical icon held with deep reverence among many U.S. Latinos and throughout Latin America. Her story is also entwined with the violence of Spanish colonization and, simultaneously, with decolonial feminist reclaimings that link her to the Nahua earth mother Tonantzin. She is a symbol of empowerment and of the feminine divine. As Irene Lara notes, the Guadalupe-Tonantzin relationship has remained central to Chicana/o cultural memory since the apparition of Guadalupe in 1531, an enduring connection that persists despite efforts to deny Tonantzin's Indigenous origins.

This chapter examines this sacred continuity and the ways it endures through Chicana feminist historical recovery efforts, which have tangible effects in the lives of Guadalupe-Tonantzin devotees and those seeking to maintain a connection to her while embodying a feminist sensibility.

Dancing with Tonantzin

In 2024, I asked Inés Hernandez-Ávila to elaborate on something she said to me in a 2006 interview: "Tonantzin opened up a whole new world." Having heard stories of women resignifying Guadalupe by incorporating Tonantzin, in 2025 I resonated with Inés's reflection. As I relistened to the interview today, I realized that for Inés, this "whole new world" symbolized a deeper connection to her Native and Chicana ancestry through Tonantzin. Inés shared with me a moment of profound connection with Tonantzin, the earth mother, that she had at the Basilica of Our Lady of Guadalupe in Mexico City. The basilica holds the shrine of Our Lady of Guadalupe–Tonantzin and is located near Tepeyac Hill, where she first revealed herself to a Nahua man, Juan Diego. Inés described how, in danza,

> One year we danced at the basilica, one of the many times that I danced there. And I actually, I was dancing on that day for her [Tonantzin], and I chose to dance her dance because to my surprise, nobody before me had chosen that dance and I was thinking, *But it's her day. Why aren't we dancing?* So I chose to dance her dance and entered the circle. And I felt her dancing with me, under my feet. I felt the earth dancing. So that's when I knew, you know, *This is it. It's real.* It ends, and she thanked me for offering her dance on her day. . . . And I realize . . . the songs in danza are for her as Guadalupe. But it's still OK because we know that she is the earth mother. . . . So when you think about how she appears everywhere, like on the farmworker's hat, and the Zapatistas have her present too, it's just an amazing thing, right? That, and she's called the Empress of the Americas, so she's recognized everywhere, right? This Indigenous version [of the Virgin Mary].[4]

Dance and song are among Inés's greatest gifts—but are our gifts also the portals to our souls? To our medicina? To our connection with the ancestors? Dance speaks to Inés's soul, so it is no surprise that it is through dance that she connects with Tonantzin and the earth. She has shared with me that when she leaves this plane and crosses over, "I'll be dancing." It is in dance that she finds herself, her beloved Tonantzin, and the deep, unbroken connection between them.

Guadalupe-Tonantzin: Supporting the Inner Work of Unconditional Love and Acceptance and Outer Work of Healing and Liberation

Guadalupe-Tonantzin's ability to connect with women in the incarnation that is most reflective of the women's souls and truths is one of the most powerful themes that ran through the stories selected for this chapter. That is, through Guadalupe-Tonantzin's unconditional love and acceptance of women as their true selves, she offers healing and protection to women and their bodymindspirits. By giving them this unconditional love and acceptance, Guadalupe-Tonantzin supports women such as Inés in claiming and stepping into their power. What follows is the embracing of their light, their gifts, and their medicina through inner work and outer work—soul work of activism and feminista praxis. As such, the soul of the woman acts as the doer of deeds—the executor of spiritual activism.

Inés's contemporaries Martha Cotera and Gloria Anzaldúa gifted us histories and frameworks to use for purposes of healing, belonging, and inclusion. These have been circulated intergenerationally since the 1970s, when Cotera first started compiling, writing, and disseminating recovered histories such as those of Tonantzin and others from the pantheon of Aztec goddesses. Through Cotera's historical recovery and Anzaldúa's historical revision, La Virgen de Guadalupe—or Coatlalopeuh, the original Nahuatl name for her—emerges as a fusion of Catholic and Indigenous traditions, embodying histories shaped by both resistance and colonization. Reclaimed as the ancient Aztec goddess Tonantzin, she has evolved into a powerful symbol of Chicana feminism.

Inés conveyed a deep affection for and strong connection to Tonantzin through this story, illustrating how healing histories are lived, practiced, and felt. This reflects the transformative power of the gran limpia of historical revisioning that Inés has spoken of—one that fosters healing, self-awareness, and empowerment. The impact of this process, particularly in relation to Guadalupe-Tonantzin, is the focus of this chapter.

Tonantzin as a Symbol of Intergenerational Transmission of Chicana Feminist Thought

Intergenerational transmission of wisdom is a cornerstone of Chicana feminist knowledge production. Whether through research dissemination—such as the work of the Chicana Research and Learning Center that I mentioned in chapter 2 or through publications, consejos, interviews, or oral history projects bridging university and community spaces—these exchanges occur in social justice–oriented organizations, classrooms, public forums, and personal relationships. This chapter explores how Chicana feminists have incorporated such histories—those of Guadalupe's original Nahua identity of Tonantzin—into their lives. I frame this as spiritual activism because the invocation and sharing of the history of Tonantzin not only supports their internal work but also extends to shaping their outer work—their contributions to community and classrooms and their cultural productions.

The following story illustrates my experience of coming to know about Tonantzin on a personal level, a transformative encuentro with the past that marked the beginning of a decades-long journey that also involved arriving at a deeper knowing of myself, and the impact of Tonantzin on women, through Chicana feminist praxis.

Reclaiming Guadalupe, Discovering Tonantzin: A Chicana/Indigenous Feminista and Decolonial Practice

It is December 12, 2022, the feast day of Our Lady of Guadalupe–Tonantzin. And on this day, every year since María Elena moved back home to Wiley, Texas, to live with her lovely family, I think of and miss María Elena. For she gifted me one of the most profound *regalos* a Chicana on a spiritual journey could ever receive, something I now pass along to others, as a teacher, mother, and mujer: the gift of a spirit story, the gift of re-membering. Re-membering and reclaiming our history is also about integrating it into our lives as a means of reconnecting our minds, bodies, and spirits from the severing effects of colonization and alienation.

During a formative period in my life, María Elena was there with the healing salve that I needed on my journey. Time and time again, through her words, actions, and spiritual activism she taught me how to come more closely into alignment with my truth and my soul's purpose. The following is one such teaching: the gift of story, a story that is part of our Chicana feminist and spiritual legacy, something passed down to me from Chicanas of the movement era. It was an act of spiritual activism and feminista praxis, it was spirit storytelling, and it propelled me into conocimiento, bringing me face to face with a reckoning and reconciliation—with a re-membering. Though it happened years ago, this exchange remains pivotal—an invitation that profoundly shaped me and continues to do so, affecting my mind, body, spirit, and heart. Its impact ripples outward, touching not only me but also the students with whom I have shared this story that will stay with me forever. A story of Guadalupe-Tonantzin devotion as Chicana feminist praxis.[5]

It took place during one of the many phone calls Meme (as I call her) and I shared over the years. At the time, I was deep in the process of writing my dissertation, but on that particular day, I had no intention of interviewing María Elena or documenting anything. I just knew I needed to talk to her. My spirit was drawn to her—to the comfort of belonging, the embrace of unconditional acceptance, and the love that defines her way. The María Elena way. A way not unlike the very essence of Guadalupe-Tonantzin herself.

As she and I share the experience of a Mexican American Catholic upbringing, my feelings about the Catholic Church came up in our conversation that day. I found issue with the politics and hierarchical structures of the church and its treatment of women, among other things. She explained in her intelligent, compassionate, and unassuming way that I could open my formerly closed heart to a greater spirit through the feminine face of God. I could do so through understanding Guadalupe on my own terms, separate from the institution of the Catholic Church. I could reject attempts by the church to subjugate women and still hold on to Guadalupe as a symbol of feminine power, strength, and liberation. She explained that the church does not have a monopoly on Guadalupe, that she was not originally connected to the church, and that she does not have to be now.

On that day, the universe planted a seed that would blossom into one of the most significant conocimientos of my life. Through her teachings, María Elena has educated me about many aspects of life, including feminism, motherhood, spirituality, the environment, health, and healing. On that day, she taught me something that shook me. In a powerful moment, she at once brought clarity to my research questions about women's spiritualities and led me to question my own spiritual path.

Over time, the profound impact of what María Elena explained about how she knows Guadalupe as Tonantzin would become apparent. I would understand that this newfound way of seeing Guadalupe aligned with my Chicana feminist sensibility. I could reestablish my relationship with Guadalupe—and hence my roots, ancestral heritage, and even myself—without compromising my feminist principles. That allowed for me to at once retain my Tejana identity and claim my budding Chicana consciousness, something that had been brewing for years. I could call upon Guadalupe in my own way, on my own terms, in my own space and time, and for my own needs. I no longer had to keep a distance from her. I was finally able to reconcile my feminist perspectives with my ethnic and cultural identity. The hegemonic power of the church—which I saw as suppressing my spiritual creativity, personal independence, sexuality, strong moral convictions, and relationship with Guadalupe—

FIGURE 13 María Elena Martínez's home altar. Brenda Sendejo.

lifted. With this epiphany, I began the long process of feeling whole once again and of healing my formerly fragmented spirit.

This decolonial, feminist process of reclaiming Guadalupe led me to Tonantzin.

Making Face, Making Soul with Tonantzin

My experience and María Elena's guidance speak to the process of making face and making soul, of tapping into an inner truth as part of our construction of self. This is a process that many Chicana/Latina/Indigenous women, including several of the women in this project, have gone through. Perhaps it is because we share a mestiza consciousness,[6] a fluid and fractured identity, that I can have this connection with women such as María Elena and others. Drawing upon this personal insight helps me to more deeply understand the making and remaking of Chicana life and identity, often encompassing lived experience characterized by a "tolerance for ambiguity"[7] and resulting internal conflicts caused by inhabiting spiritual, geographic, psychological, ethnic, and sexual borderlands.

Intuition and Ancestral Wisdom: The Path to Women's Truth

María Elena's teaching about Tonantzin exemplifies the power of spirit-storytelling. That interaction—an encuentro with a story about Our Lady of Guadalupe rooted in Chicana feminist historical revision and praxis—was, in itself, a limpia. It moved me into conocimiento, guiding me toward a truth I hadn't realized was already within me. Not a truth about the "validity" of Tonantzin's existence, but rather a deep-seated knowing: that hierarchical and patriarchal power was never the way.

As I write this chapter (the writing of which I realize has involved a process of conocimiento in its own right) I understand that coming into a new spiritual way of being in the world involves deep inner listening—tuning in to the whispers of our truth, the messages from our souls. This is something Western society neither teaches nor values. Yet, whether through intuition, ancestral guidance, or spirit messages like that which

Inés experienced on the Hill of Tepeyac with Tonantzin, this kind of knowing evokes feelings of love and liberation.

Spirit storytelling is a way for the storyteller to relay subversive conocimientos, to inspire the listener to enact spiritual agency, as well as to model self-acceptance as a tool for personal and societal transformation. I shared this spirit story about Guadalupe given to me by María Elena in the hope that the strength I gained from that transformative encuentro can serve as a model for practices that cultivate belonging, healing, and wholeness—especially in the face of ongoing social and political challenges that fracture the mind, body, and spirit.

In this chapter, I demonstrate the ways that women invoke, reimagine, and transmit knowledge and wisdom about Our Lady of Guadalupe, which often involves integrating a devotion to her Nahua representation, Tonantzin, so as to inspire transformation in their lives and those of others in their communities. This spiritual activism around Our Lady of Guadalupe and Guadalupe-Tonantzin shows the unconditional love she offers women as they work toward self-love, how she is a reflection of them and their moving through conocimiento, and how she helps them to carry out their life purpose.

Guadalupe-Tonantzin and the Chicana Movement: History and Context

Guadalupe-Tonantzin offers us a nuanced and multidimensional lens into the history and legacy of Chicana feminism in the Texas-Mexican borderlands, playing a key role in helping Chicanas to dismantle the gender hierarchy and heteropatriarchy promoted by the church and upheld by various sectors of society and their own communities since the movement era. Through their myriad forms of devotion and integration into their lives, women rejected the Marian standards and symbolism of virginal purity associated with the Virgin Mary, including her specific manifestation as La Virgen de Guadalupe. Rather, women reimagine and embrace Guadalupe as a loving and potent symbol of feminism and female empowerment. To the women in this book and in this chapter, she is a social justice warrior, a healer, a powerful mother, and a liberated sexual being, among other things. She assists women in reconciling their Mexican cultural heritage with feminist sensibilities as a mode of healing and liberation, a praxis they extend in their spiritual activism to others.

Decolonizing Guadalupe, Decolonizing Self

Scholars including Irene Lara address the decolonization of the spirit through the process of understanding Guadalupe as Tonantzin and seeing Guadalupe's Indigenous identity as symbolic of the postcolonial process of healing colonial wounds. Lara's concept of Tonalupanisma is a lens through which to interpret Chicana/o cultural productions that engage Guadalupe-Tonantzin and related Indigenous figures from a decolonial feminist perspective. As a decolonial theory and method, Tonanlupanisma offers a valuable framework for understanding how Tonanlupanisma artists invoke and reimagine feminist and Mesoamerican Indigenous thought and iconography.[8] Through their work, they challenge and heal the colonial and patriarchal misrepresentation of women's spirituality and sexuality, disrupting the rigid Christian construct of the "virtuous virgen / pagan puta dichotomy."[9]

Since the Mexican American civil rights movement, Chicana feminist scholars have invoked the mestiza Marian Virgin of Guadalupe from a decolonial feminist perspective, eliciting Indigenous deities such as Tonantzin, the "mother goddess." As the earlier reflection of the exchange between María Elena and me shows, Tonantzin allows them to engage in the process of decolonizing their spirits while maintaining a connection to their cultural and ethnic heritage.

Journeying Through Conocimiento with Guadalupe-Tonantzin

The following stories reflect the central theme that emerged in interviews with the women in regard to Guadalupe-Tonantzin. They note that she gives women unconditional love and acceptance of their true selves, which allows women in turn to step into their power and shine their light—that is, embrace their gifts, share their medicina, and live their life's purpose. This involves a process of conocimiento that takes women to the final stage of spiritual activism.

These vignettes demonstrate how incorporating Tonantzin impacted women's lives, affording them the space and permiso to both implement a feminist consciousness and remain connected to their ethnic and religious heritages and identities. Incorporating Tonantzin opened up possibilities for the women. As Inés Hernández-Ávila stated about Tonantzin, "she opened up a whole new world."

Whether they temporarily distanced themselves from the church, severed their relationship with it, or minimized their participation in organized Catholicism, women could remain connected to Guadalupe by incorporating Tonantzin. Even when women were questioning their relationships to the church at different times in their lives, much like my own experience, Tonantzin revealed the possibility that no matter what, she remained. She is, as Norma Cantú shared with me, "a constant companion."[10]

A Constant Companion: "She's Everywhere"

The first theme I will explore is that of Guadalupe-Tonantzin as a constant companion to women as they ventured through feminist and spiritual conocimientos to arrive at their sense of self. Consistent with many of the women's mothers' Guadalupe devotion, they noted always being able to count on La Virgen. While women and their mothers' conocimientos may have involved very different paths in different times, and they prayed to Guadalupe for different things, Guadalupe remained by their sides regardless of their needs.

Through the questioning of hierarchies of power, gendered social norms, and injustices that women noted throughout our interviews, the theme of Our Lady of Guadalupe as a constant companion in women's lives is at the forefront. Guadalupe has remained present in women's lives even as they have come into feminist consciousness—a testament to her flexibility, unconditional love, and the liberatory force of Tonantzin, who was the vehicle through which Chicanas doing historical recovery work reclaimed Guadalupe from the Marian ideal of virginal purity. Cotera's excavation of Tonantzin and other historically overlooked figures was instrumental in making these narratives accessible to Chicanas and Latinas. Anzaldúa further contributed to the remaking of Guadalupe, paving the way for Tonantzin's reintegration into feminist thought. This pattern continues as women speak of Guadalupe-Tonantzin as a steady presence through their questioning of the Catholic Church, their evolving needs, and their feminist transformations.

Norma Cantú's Guadalupe-Tonantzin

I drove the short distance from Austin to San Antonio to meet with folklorist and educator-scholar Norma Cantú. As we sat in Norma's office, I glanced around at the many pieces of Chicana art that covered her walls: different depictions of the Virgin of Guadalupe, Sor Juana Inés de la Cruz, and Santa Teresa de Ávila; a collage piece featuring 1930s labor organizer Emma Tenayuca; and a painting of Norma done by Santa Barraza for Norma's *cincuentañera*. Referencing the representations of Our Lady of Guadalupe that adorned Norma's office walls, bookshelves, and windowsill, I asked if Guadalupe held a special place in her life, to which she responded without hesitation, "Absolutely, yes," then turned and motioned toward the various images of her that ranged from traditional religious

FIGURE 14 Norma Cantú in front of her home altar, 2010. Elsa Ruiz.

iconography to Chicana feminist portrayals. Norma smiled and said, with a hint of double meaning, "She's everywhere."

My interviews with Norma revealed a changing relationship she, like many of her contemporaries, had to the church and to Guadalupe as well. However, while the degree of women's connection to or dissolution of their relationships to the institution of Catholicism varied, in all cases women remained connected to Guadalupe. I asked Norma, "so you were going through this transition—when did that first start?" She responded, "I was in high school, early like fifteen, sixteen, when I started questioning and not really buying all the stuff that the church was doing and staying but always feeling that that was home. At one time, I did play around with Buddhism and some other things. . . . Actually, in grad school I thought, *I'm going to come back, but on my own terms*. . . . I think she's always been there, even through all those waves. It's a constant. And part of it, I think, has to do with my feminist awareness. I think she was very instrumental in my coming to that consciousness."

When I asked Norma if she thought the ways that women in her family prayed to Guadalupe—from her grandmother and mother's generations to her own—had changed, she said, "Definitely it's changed. One of the ways I think about this is through the images of Guadalupe created by Chicana artists—they reflect a very different understanding of that energy, one that returns to Tonantzin. I don't think my mother had that awareness, that [Guadalupe] was Indigenous; it wasn't a conscious understanding." Here, Norma points to a common pattern among the mothers of many women in this book: They were deeply devoted to Guadalupe, yet, like many Tejanas of their generation and those before them, they were unaware of her roots in Tonantzin. That awareness for Tejanas would come later, through the movement and the work of historical recovery.

I went on to ask Norma about those things she prays to Guadalupe for that her mother did not. To which Norma, ever the writer, responded with a smile, "I don't think my mother prayed for publications. And I don't have any children, so I don't pray to protect my children, but I do pray to protect my nephews and nieces, so it's kind of like a transference, I guess. Anytime I send a manuscript off I tell the Virgen to take care of it, and sometimes she tells me it's not going to be published, and I know it." Norma tells me that this feeling is not an intuition but rather a *facultad*, as Gloria Anzaldúa would call it, and she goes on to say, "a way of knowing that perhaps we have not acknowledged yet. We call it intuition but it's really something else, beyond intuition."

Norma says that that Guadalupe has always been a part of her life. For her, she is "the affirmation of that power of the earth . . . as *la tierra madre* . . . it's a female energy, definitely. By having power, by being a very powerful female, it's almost like [she's] a role model that's there."

In terms of how her feminism informs her spirituality, Norma shared:

> I think it goes hand in hand because it's that respect for your spirit, for being who you are . . . and that trust in the universe. . . . I think [in] some cases the religion can be a contradiction. I often hear people say, "How can you be Catholic and be a feminist?" And it's true because it is contradictory. But like I told you earlier, I think I've chosen the parts [of Catholicism] that I want to work with, and there are some very strong feminist Catholics—I mean, Sor Juana, Teresa de Ávila, you know, all these precursors, and even now [Sister] Yolanda [Tarango, a Chicana feminist], all these women that are still doing it . . . Sister María Elena Gonzalez with [the Mexican American Catholic College] . . . strong, very efficient, able, and spiritual.

In an interview for the documentary film *The Road to Guadalupe*, Norma was asked about her belief in Guadalupe. She described the portrayal of Guadalupe that the Catholic Church constructed and propagated, a portrayal that conflicts with Norma's feminist politics: "She [Guadalupe] represents an aspect of Catholicism that is sometimes very oppressive to women. She is usually looking down, she has her hands folded. She is not an agent. . . . Just passively there. Because she represents a higher being, she can get away with it. But a brown woman can't. If you are submissive, downcast . . . that's how people are going to treat you, and that's what you become."

Here, Norma draws a distinct connection between Guadalupe's submissive image and the lived consequences that enacting such submissiveness can have on the "brown woman." She went on to say, "She's Indigenous but . . . she's European, so she embodies that, but at the same time she represents them, she's brown like we are. There is . . . an identification with her image that transcends the division of the colonizers and the colonized. . . . She made roses come out of nowhere so she would get what she wanted. The ways she is portrayed around the church have to do with women . . . not being very loud and forceful and not taking agency. But the way the church looks at it—I would not want to do that."

Norma consciously chose to invoke Guadalupe on her own terms, contrary to the Catholic Church's renderings. Norma's choice to remain a practicing Catholic speaks once again to Guadalupe's immense versatility in Tejana lives and her central role in identity formation—haciendo caras, or making face. This fluidity allows for a construction of self that aligns with the soul—a process of making soul.

Guadalupe is one way Catholics like Norma reconcile with the aspects of Catholicism with which they disagree or choose not to adhere to. Reconciling is always hard, says Norma. "With the pro-life movement, with the pope's total disregard for women's communities. The women in the convents, the nuns that I have known in the past are always at odds with what Rome is dictating, so yeah, that's a constant. But I don't think it is new. I think it goes back to the twelfth century, when there were women's groups who were not in favor or did not have the favor of Rome. It's a manmade institution, and I specify *manmade* with all its flaws and everything. It is what it is."

Norma drew a comparison between the Catholic Church and academia, stating that both require having to endure contradictions: "You know, it's the same struggle."

As did several of her contemporaries, Norma shared that she believed she came into a different way of knowing Guadalupe in graduate school, at a time when she was doing a lot of meditation: "I think when I was doing meditation and some of the [spiritual] work, it changed from my young Catholic upbringing, and I started seeing her as an energy and a force, not just as an image or just the mother or something to pray to. I think there was a change at that point, it was like a paradigm shift." As a conocimiento framework would suggest, this outer shift aligned with Norma's own inner questioning and transformation.

This paradigm shift holds deep significance for Norma and for many mujeres. It marks a transformation in how they relate to Guadalupe—moving beyond the way they saw her as young girls to new, more expansive understandings. And, I propose, it also reflects a shift in how they see themselves. Norma described going to Alma de Mujer Center for Social Change in Austin in the 1980s and experiencing the presence of

Tonantzin during a temazcal, a traditional sweat lodge ceremony: "I used to go to Alma de Mujer when the Indigenous Women's Network used to meet there. [I had] an awakening, if you will, during a temazcal, and I sensed her, I sensed Guadalupe-Tonantzin. It was very special, and I've had different occurrences."

Norma described numerous instances of sensing Guadalupe's presence, whether via the scent of roses where none existed or in knowing that a certain journal would accept her piece for publication. She described experiencing feelings that she instinctively connected to the Virgen, much like the connection to Tonantzin that Inés recounted. In this way, Tejanas' invocations of Guadalupe have evolved across generations—she transforms alongside them, adapting to their changing worlds.

Norma's spiritual beliefs and practices exist at the intersection of her feminism and faith. Her profound devotion to Our Lady of Guadalupe embodies her ability to blend Catholicism with Indigenous traditions, a fusion that defines her spiritual understanding. She practices what she calls "alternative Catholicism," which doesn't fall strictly within the traditional religious context and which attracted her to the matachines, a traditional religious dance group that blends European and Indigenous cultural influences[11] and where she has the flexibility to, as she says, take what is useful to her and leave the rest. Norma's ability to selectively embrace aspects of Catholicism allows her to maintain both a Catholic identity and her ties to the church. For Catholics like Norma, this alternative Catholicism is an act of creative agency—one that enables them to shape a faith that meets their spiritual needs while aligning with their feminist and activist consciousness.

Norma described periods of questioning Catholicism and, at times, refraining from participating in Mass and the sacraments during certain periods throughout her spiritual development. But when I asked her what Guadalupe meant to her, she said, she is "indígena, más que nada" (Indigenous, more than anything).

"The Face of God Has Changed": Rosie Castro and the Feminine Face of God

Rosie Castro, a longtime San Antonio activist and important Raza Unida Party participant, was a member of a community of like-minded Catholic

FIGURE 15 Rosie Castro. Brenda Sendejo.

women who engaged in readings and discussions of *mujerista* theology. This theology denounces patriarchy and sexism within the Catholic Church and strives for a model inspired by a philosophy of social justice that advocates for liberation from oppression for all, including women. The mujerista framework has provided Rosie a mechanism for challenging Catholic hierarchy and patriarchy. She referenced the work of Sister Yolanda Tarango, who co-authored the seminal 1988 book *Hispanic Women Prophetic Voices* with Ada María Isasi-Díaz. Rosie shared with me how Sister Yolanda spoke about the feminine face of God—a perspective that Rosie found eye-opening. It allowed her to transcend traditional religious teachings in ways that deeply resonated with her feminist beliefs and strengthened her devotion to Guadalupe.

This moment marked a pivotal shift in Rosie's spiritual journey, prompting her to rethink the concept of "God." Like many other women, this transition signified stepping into a new stage of being—a deeper path of conocimiento. Rosie described this process as a re-inscription of her understanding of God, framed within a growing self-awareness. Her engagement with mujerista theology not only transformed her perception of the divine but also reshaped how she saw herself, illustrating the inner work that her feminist spirituality nurtured and sustained:

> What IS faith when you go through good things and bad things. . . . Faith is not just when things are great, there is God to give thanks. So I think much of my experience in the Chicano movement and just life experience made me think about what that faith was. But the changing face of God—or much of it as I grew up—was in seeing and understanding the role of women in the Catholic Church. The role or how we were seen by the male hierarchy and the understanding that that obviously did not make sense. If

> we are all God's children, then how is one aspect of God's children better than another part? I don't know if it was one thing, but if there is something it was probably Yolanda. That had a big impact on me. . . . I would say back in the '80s . . . there were several of us who would get together and sometimes we'd pray and sometimes—a lot of times—we'd discuss.

I was interested in how Rosie applied these ideas to her daily life and how they impacted her. She told me that the notion of looking at God as a woman "says to you that in life what you've been taught—that you are lesser . . . men are the powerful ones . . . that's not what God wanted. It was a question of, 'Was everything I taught basically a lie?'" In answer to her own question, she relayed that she did not see these things as lies but rather as part of "a broader view—an expansion of the child notions that you were taught, that it wasn't a God that . . . was going to kill you and be angry and take revenge, but the feminine character of a nurturing and loving and of a forgiving, not a warrior, God."

This statement aligns with Rosie's feelings about women being taught to be subservient to men. It explains how a mujerista theology would be attractive to Rosie, a philosophy and a mechanism she employs for reconciling with church patriarchy. "How we were taught that women were subservient to men," she says,

> . . . that just did not sit well with me, and that never did. Even as I was young, but especially as I got older. It just does not make sense that women should be subservient or not equal to men or could not do the same things. . . . I think that there was this prescribed role, and some of it was cultural, and some of it was attributed to the teachings of the church—being demure, respectful but overtly respectful, where you had to bow to authority. I think the overtly [part] came directly out of the church. I always rebelled against it. It is just inconceivable that one male, one female, because of different body parts, that one is more able than the other. I really felt that the church, with so many of its prescriptions, made it difficult for women to really enjoy their humanity—their full humanity. I don't know why I felt that way, but I felt that way from being very young. Maybe I was overly exposed—I went to church six days a week. . . . I've always felt that it did not make sense that a woman would be less than a man. And to me it's a fundamental thing that was taught by the institution of the church.

For Rosie, reconciling with Catholic patriarchy happened through her ability to selectively engage aspects of Catholicism, aligning with much of the alternative Catholicism of which Norma Cantú spoke. This occurred largely in private: by participating in a progressive Catholic women's community, through personal engagement with Catholic saints, in her daily prayers and working with her home altar, building a context within which she experienced an internal shift in her understanding of God and herself, and attaining a sense of equality that institutional Catholicism fails to fulfill.

Rosie's statement "The face of God has changed" encapsulates this reconciliation—one rooted in recognizing the feminine face of God, which she experiences largely through her relationship with La Virgen de Guadalupe. She speaks of an ethnic identification with Guadalupe as a Latina and emphasizes her significance during the Chicano movement, stating that "all of us who were involved with the movement saw her as a central figure." Rosie said she had always worn an image of the Virgen around her neck and that she was a prominent figure with whom Rosie has always had a relationship: "I prayed to the Virgen de Guadalupe in terms of her being the mother figure. A very strong relationship. To this day I have a picture of the Virgen in my home. I have seen her as a dominant female figure."

Beyond just helping Rosie (and others) to remain connected to Catholicism, I view the Virgen as serving another very distinct role: She allows women to do so while retaining their feminist sensibilities and engaging in power analysis. In Rosie's childhood, she said,

> males were the only ones that [could] be priests, have confessions, perform sacraments. Everything we learned in church has to do with males that communicated God's truth. The power therefore rests with males. Now fortunately with Catholic/Chicano/Latino upbringing there is a very prominent place with Mary, the Virgin of Guadalupe . . . and some of [the] saints, but . . . the Anglo Catholic liturgy—and all of that that we were taught in school—does not totally balance our Latino Catholic upbringing. Mary does not totally balance everything we learn in Catholic school in terms of male patriarchy.[12]

If not for the Virgen, Rosie might not have been able to overcome this imbalance. I asked if her understanding of Guadalupe had changed in any way over the course of her life. Her response reiterated the centrality and deep significance of the role of the Virgen in her reconciliation with Catholicism:

> I think that it's changed somewhat. But mainly the idea of the protector, of someone who is particularly . . . protective of and special to Chicanos, is kind of the way I've always seen her. And I think that that idea has grown over time for me . . . in that . . . in spite of all of the Anglo Catholic upbringing that I've had, she is a figure that probably has done more to keep my faith in the Catholic Church alive in that there is that potential of, . . . if not a female god, but a female role, close to a divine role, that you don't see in the Anglo Catholic tradition. At least for me she has grown more as . . . not just the mother of God but . . . the idea of God—a feminine God—and I think she portrays that as well.

I was interested in the specific ways in which the Virgen had helped Rosie to keep her faith alive. Rosie shared that it was not until she was older that she started to think about the rules and regulations, the actions of the church.

She shed light on a particularly relevant topic for Catholics, referencing reports of widespread sexual abuse within the Catholic Church that have been revealed over the past two decades. Rosie describes the current state of the church: "in the last several years the falling short of the clergy, for example, in things like the pedophilia, their inability to police themselves, to deal with their own shortcomings in an open way, in a way that had any common sense at all to it." For Rosie, the inherent contradiction was troubling:

> That [pedophilia cover-up] juxtaposed with how especially the male clergy put so many restrictions on a woman's body—morals, you know, what you were supposed to do, not do, what you can—prescribing for women what they can or cannot do and failing in their own right to deal with what priests were doing . . . to deal with things like battery by males with their wives. . . . All those kinds of things made it difficult at times . . . to go into a church. . . . It left a lot in terms of trying to find community in a church in a formal Catholic setting. There is a difficulty with reconciling the actions of the church many times with what the teachings are supposed to be and

> what your understanding of Christ's teachings were and looking at what the church fathers are doing . . . that became more and more of a struggle. I think that being able to hold onto a strong female figure has been a good thing, had been kind of a salvation or glue that keeps you still attached to the fundamentals of the Catholic faith.

Rosie remained unwavering in her critique of the church, particularly on social justice issues, an area where she believes the institution has failed. Her struggles with the church stem from teachings that shaped how she viewed her own body and from its increasing alignment with right-wing conservatism—especially on issues related to women's bodies, such as reproductive rights. Speaking with passion, she described the church's impact on her self-perception, echoing sentiments shared by many Chicanas: "From early years the whole idea that was ingrained with me was how sex was dirty, how aspects of our bodies were dirty."

Rosie struggled to reconcile the church's actions with the Christlike values she was raised to believe in. A devout Catholic, she remained frustrated that the church itself—not she or other Catholics—deviated from those values. For Rosie, the institution became something unrecognizable, making reconciliation difficult, except through her personal relationship with God and her devotion to Guadalupe.

Despite this disillusionment, many women have found solace in alternative expressions of faith, as I've mentioned—through Guadalupe, women's prayer groups, home altars, and personal prayer. These folk and popular religious practices become even more vital in sustaining their spiritual connection, offering spaces where their faith is not only maintained but also nurtured and strengthened. Such practices mirror an earlier historical moment when Tejanos, alienated from the institutional church in the mid-1800s, developed popular Catholicism, a tradition that continues to flourish today.[13]

In modern times, women's questioning of the church, their efforts to reconcile with it—or their decision to reject it entirely—and their creation of alternative spiritual spaces reflect the ongoing remaking of religion in response to social conditions that demand it. The face of God exists beyond the Catholic Church, taking feminine forms in many ways and for many reasons, shaped by the needs and lived experiences of the women who seek her.

This longtime civil rights and political activist, mother, and grandmother illuminated a critical component in the process by which the face of God has changed for her, which in turn led me to consider how this occurs in the lives of other women and under what conditions. As Rosie's and other women's narratives suggest, reconciling their religious pasts with their politics—such as their perspectives on gender, race, and class equality—is paramount. Guadalupe creates the possibility for reconciliation through an alternative Catholicism, one rooted in her flexibility, which can also be understood as unconditional love. This love allows women to discover themselves as they rediscover Tonantzin, shifting from narratives of virginity and submission to those of empowerment and self-acceptance.

Guadalupe-Tonantzin As a Reflection of Women and Their Developing Feminist Consciousness

Alternative Catholicism is one way that women reconcile with their feminist consciousness, and Guadalupe-Tonantzin plays a central role. They take what is meaningful to them and distance themselves from that which is not. In this way, Guadalupe-Tonantzin is not only a constant, she also meets women where they are. She offers unconditional love, supports them with their changing needs and developing feminist identities, and at the same time acts as a guide for the women in their roles and stages of life. The following sections provide examples of how Guadalupe remains ever-present in women's lives—as mothers, healers, activists, and advocates for the environment and Mother Earth.

Sister Teresa on the Reclaiming of Tejana Agency: Guadalupe as a Redeemer

Growing up, we saw religious sisters (also called women religious) infrequently, if at all. Laywomen taught our catechism classes, and sisters made rare appearances at Mass. I knew essentially nothing about them growing up and must admit that I never understood exactly who they were as individuals, beyond their roles as deeply religious devotees who had dedicated their lives to God. The role of the priest was more clear to me. Perhaps knowing what I did about priests—their power, visibility, and stature—was why I so often questioned why women couldn't be priests. The role of Catholic sisters was far less defined in my understanding or Catholic teachings and upbringing. Over time, I learned about the many social justice initiatives and movements across the U.S. and Latin America in which women religious—Latinas among them—have played a vital role for centuries, including organizations like Las Hermanas, a national religious-political organization of Chicanas and Latinas active in social justice causes and feminist theology, of which Sister Teresa was a member.[14]

That I grew up unaware of the activism of women religious is unsurprising; their contributions to social movements have historically received far less recognition than those of Catholic priests. This was on my mind as I sat in the lobby outside Sister Teresa's office, awaiting our meeting.

Sister Teresa emerged from her office and welcomed me. I explained my project to her, and she nodded, listening enthusiastically as I discussed the connections I was exploring between spirituality and social justice. We began the interview by Sister Teresa telling me what had attracted her to the sisterhood. She was driven to the service of God because she was drawn to church work and church service—"Service is sort of my bottom line"—and by joining the sisterhood, she could do both. Several times over the course of our interview, Sister Teresa would return to the fact that she was driven to the sisterhood largely by her desire to serve, indicating its centrality in her life and hence the melding of her religious and activist identities, or her inner and outer worlds—her spiritual activism.

Sister Teresa described her early childhood growing up in the 1950s and 1960s in West Texas. Like other women in this study, Sister Teresa had a sense of her ethnic and racial difference early on; she experienced being discriminated against in school. Another prevalent theme in women's narratives is the silencing of and shame projected upon the body. For Sister Teresa, this manifested itself in low self-esteem that she and other Tejanas she knows possess. She told me that she began invoking Our Lady of Guadalupe in order to redeem that aspect of her self-identity. Interestingly, Sister Teresa was not raised with Guadalupe devotion. In what she said was an attempt to assimilate as a result of racial oppression, her family did not practice Mexican Catholicism. She came to know Guadalupe later in life.

Sister Teresa's relationship with Guadalupe was linked to her self-perception and self-worth. For her, Guadalupe played a pivotal role in the redeeming of the Tejana body and soul. Sister Teresa, a Tejana, compared herself to her colleague Angela, a Latina who came to the United States as a young adult: "She [Angela] has a confidence that I will never have, because she grew up in an environment that accepted her personhood and did not see her as 'other.'" Sister Teresa noted that the real poverty is low self-worth. She pondered how this translated into religious self-understandings, the internal work, asking, "How do we experience God's love if we don't experience self-love? And so the bottom line is really self-love. . . . As Latinas we can be so impacted with the idea of our non-personhood and our sense of inferiority that we start believing it."

She discussed how Latinas were ashamed of themselves and their bodies, embodying internalized messages of not being good enough—not tall enough, thin enough, light-skinned enough, pure enough. In this sense, she saw Guadalupe as a redeemer who "redeems our bodies because Guadalupe is dark and people identify" with her. She asked me if I'd read Sandra Cisneros's essay "Guadalupe the Sex Goddess."[15] "Oh yes," I told her, "I teach it in my La Chicana course." Then she said, "OK, what she talks about is 'a woman like me.' I always use that [when I teach my classes] because it is such a fabulous piece. The whole sense of Guadalupe [is], 'I need you to believe that I'm a person. I need you to believe that I'm worthy.'" Sister Teresa appreciated Cisneros's piece because it is saying that "the God that we've been presented is not one whom we can connect with as women. Hence, only a God whom we can identify with can redeem us from our own shame. In that way it is then like the original sin."

I asked Sister if she approved of Chicana artists' various interpretations of Guadalupe, such as Alma Lopez's controversial digital print of the Virgin in a rose-clad bikini.[16] "Oh, absolutely." She had seen the work at the Museum of International Folk Art in Santa Fe. "Really what she is dealing with is, Can a Latina body be sacred? Or be considered holy or be considered even acceptable?" She told me she also loved the work of artist Yolanda Lopez and felt it was important for her students to be exposed to Lopez's famous Guadalupe series. "I think Guadalupe is just critical to the redemption of Latinas. We have to deconstruct Guadalupe in order to recognize ourselves. . . . This is not the Guadalupe with her eyes cast down." Here Sister Teresa reiterated what other women have said, that the image of Guadalupe typically associated with the church is not the Guadalupe that they think of, that they know. She cited strong Guadalupe images made by Chicana artists: "Enedina Casarez Vasquez has a great Guadalupe that I love because it's a Guadalupe with her eyes wide open. It's the Guadalupe of Ester Hernandez in the karate suit. It's Yolanda Lopez's Guadalupe with the strong legs ready to jump off her pedestal. And the Guadalupe saying, 'This is my body, and it is not vulgar.' I remember when Sandra wrote that piece on Guadalupe the sex goddess. She sent me a copy before it was published and she said, 'Oh, you're going to hate me.' And I said, 'No, I'm just so jealous, I wish I could have written this!'"

RELATIVIZING: A MEANS OF RECONCILIATION

Sister Teresa is among a group of Catholic nuns who possess a deep devotion to Christ and God but who experience some tension with the hierarchy of the Catholic Church. This is in large part due to the sisters' subversive beliefs and approaches to patriarchy within the church. As Sister Teresa explained, while sisters are able to have some freedoms—in terms of what to teach in their classes or the ability to write and be vocal about the importance of feminist theology—there is a limit to the degree to which they are allowed to express their views or exercise leadership in the church.

So women religious such as Sister Teresa must always be cautious and strategic about expressing their feminist beliefs publicly. Drawing on the ideas of mujerista theology is a means to reconcile women's role in the church and remain connected to the faith:

> Relating to the whole idea of relativizing the church, . . . I think what we mean by it is the sense that it's not our first authority. What it is, is that really our first authority is our faith, our community, the faith that is nourished by our community. . . . It's not an individualistic thing like saying, 'Well, I think I'm right, and the whole church is wrong,' but rather it's saying, . . . 'I'm a person of faith, in the community where I am there are people of faith, and together we will move along and won't be held back by institutional boundaries.' And at the same time we're not leaving it because we can't leave it, because it is who we are. We are the church.

Here, Sister Teresa illustrates how agency enacted through relativism allows her to do her social justice work without the constraints of "institutional boundaries." She makes an important distinction between faith and the institution of the church that resonates throughout the Catholic Tejanas' narratives in this book. She goes on to describe how sisters took service work into their own hands: "And so with Hermanas we stopped looking to the church and its institutional representatives to define what ministry could be, and we started defining it for ourselves and just doing it." Spiritual agency of feminists does not just happen with women who leave the church. Las Hermanas and feminist sisters demonstrate that this can happen within and through the context of organized Catholicism while maintaining a strong connection to Guadalupe-Tonantzin and to self.

NEGOTIATING THE FLAWED ISSUES WITH THE CATHOLIC CHURCH AS WOMEN RELIGIOUS DEDICATED TO SERVICE AND SOCIAL JUSTICE

Because Sister Teresa joined the sisterhood in order to serve, her spirituality and the material circumstances of life have been intimately intertwined, from her own early experiences of oppression to fighting the oppression of others. Religious social activism has been a significant part of the Tejana and Tejano religious experience and has included commitments to local communities by organizations such as Las Hermanas, PADRES,[17] and the Mexican American Cultural Center in San Antonio. However, examining religious activism within the context of a feminist Catholic's life raises unique questions about the complexities of participating in social justice work while interfacing with what Sister Teresa saw as flawed aspects of the institution of the church. Having to do so necessitated finding a framework that enabled Sister Teresa to reconcile the patriarchy and the submissive roles of women with her desire to engage in social justice work.

Themes of negotiating patriarchy and reconfiguring women's roles and their social positions within and outside of the church were present in Sister Teresa's interview. What we see here is how women religious negotiated such issues in their attempt to remain connected to the church. They employed similar mechanisms to women outside the church but did so from within the institution and from unique positions. As such, she possessed the social justice commitment apparent in the lives of other women in this book.

Sister Teresa shared that she once associated Our Lady of Guadalupe with virginal purity and submission. However, as she came to know her as versatile and as Tonantzin, her meaning transformed into one of female strength. This shift was mirrored in Sister's own self-perception—she felt empowered by her new understanding of Guadalupe-Tonantzin, which nurtured self-love and replaced the negative self-image she had carried since childhood. In this, and in many other ways, women's evolving spiritual needs have necessitated new forms of spiritual engagement and illustrated conocimiento.[18]

As women like Sister Teresa navigate patriarchy within the religious realm, strategies like mujerista theology and a deep and personal devotion to Our Lady of Guadalupe become important mechanisms to advance their dedication to service and social justice work, while exhibiting a deep faith and maintaining a relationship to God.

CHALLENGING STEREOTYPES OF WOMEN RELIGIOUS

Like my own preconceived and misguided notions of Catholic sisters, women religious are often stereotyped as lacking agency. However, Sister Teresa's life challenges such mainstream conceptions of Catholic women religious. It did mine. From her staunch feminist perspectives to her attraction to Chicana feminist reconfigurations of Our Lady of Guadalupe that help reverse negative perceptions of the Tejana body, her story provides deep insight into processes of conocimiento for Tejanas and women religious as they come into new knowledge that impacts them on the identity and soul levels—they are making face, making soul.

Furthermore, Sister Teresa's life expands and lends nuance to understandings of religious boundaries and categories as fixed and immutable. Her narrative moves us beyond traditional conceptions of institutional Catholicism to help us understand how it can function on the personal, individual, and personally political levels among those who have dedicated their lives to it. Through her devotion to Our Lady of Guadalupe–Tonantzin and her participation in mujerista theology and feminist theology and spirituality, Sister Teresa demonstrates the power of spiritual activism within the context of institutional religion and the hearts and souls of women religious.

Susana Almanza and Guadalupe-Tonantzin, Earth Mother and Activist

I vividly recall the silver pendant Susana Almanza wore around her neck the day of our interview at her office at Austin's People Organized in Defense of Earth and Her Resources (PODER) in March 2008. It was a beautiful pendant with an image of Guadalupe superimposed over a cross. I had not seen many silver pendants like that of the Virgen before, mostly smaller gold ones like what my grandmother used to wear. I complimented Susana on it and asked if she would tell me about it. Touching it and smiling, she said that her friend, PODER codirector Erika González, had given it to her. "It's really unique because you always see the sign of the cross but you usually see Jesus. But on this cross you see the Virgin, who represents the mother, Mother Earth. So to me it was . . . such a rare gift to get it." I asked Susana why it was significant that the Virgen be associated with the cross rather than Jesus. She responded, "To me it's really so important because . . . through my Indigenous teachings . . . the earth is the mother, she gives life; she's more like the female energy. . . . When I look at the earth mother it's a woman, so to have a woman that is amidst all the four directions, the four elements . . . to me, is very significant. . . . And so here it is, a woman . . . representing the four elements." Susana's earth-based spiritual practice is central to her life and activism. This includes honoring the elements (air, water, earth, fire) and the cardinal directions (east, west, north, south) to align with natural energies and to provide balance and protection, for the elements and directions represent spiritual, emotional, and physical forces.

By identifying with Our Lady of Guadalupe as an earth mother, Susana acknowledged Guadalupe's Indigenous counterpart, the Nahua earth goddess Tonantzin. Through Tonantzin Susana remained connected to both a Mexican and Indigenous heritage and to her own mother. Like María Elena, Susana drew upon something previous generations of Tejanas, including their mothers, did not. Seeing Guadalupe as an earth mother, Tonantzin, is of great importance to Susana, as her response to the question of whether she identified with Tonantzin illustrates: "Definitely. To me Tonantzin and the Virgen are the same, going even back as [far as] Coatlicue." Coalticue, she of the "serpent skirt," is the earliest of the Mesoamerican fertility and Earth goddesses. She was the creator goddess, mother of the celestial deities, and represented birth, death, and fertility. She's believed to be the oldest derivate of the ancient goddess Tonantzin.[19]

Like many of the women in this study, Susana Almanza's activism is rooted in the material conditions of her early life history. She was raised in East Austin in what she describes as the Mexican area that was next to the Black area in the Guadalupe neighborhood, only a short few blocks from what later became PODER's offices. Susana had both Mexican American and African American friends. She was brought up Catholic and attended Our Lady of Guadalupe Catholic Church. However, later in life, she came to question the church's teachings and history: "I learned how the Indigenous people had to transcend a lot of the Catholic symbols [and] the prayers and that a lot of the sacred sites were sacred before even the Catholic churches got there. [The Indigenous groups] already had a spiritual connection."

EARLY INSPIRATIONS FOR EARTH-BASED SPIRITUAL PRACTICES

Susana was raised in a home where they valued the importance of the earth and giving back to the earth. Her mother always had a garden and told her children, "You've got to massage Mother Earth because when you massage and work with her she'll give you things; she'll give you life. . . . She'll give you this food, these vegetables." In her own way, her mother very much had a spiritual connection to Mother Earth.

Susana told me that she did not really have a relationship with Christ; instead, her spirituality was deeply connected to the earth and its elements—an earth-based spirituality. This path aligned with her commitment to ending environmental racism and other injustices, a mission she carried out by cofounding PODER. As she explained, her spiritual practice was rooted in Indigenous philosophies that emphasized respect for the earth and its resources—values she embodied in both her daily life and her activism. She also expressed her spirituality through her relationship with Our Lady of Guadalupe–Tonantzin.

COMFORTING COMPANION TO WOMEN

As in the lives of so many other women, including my own grandmother and mother, Susana shared how her mother's connection to the Virgin was as a companion—they had a woman-to-woman connection. Susana relayed that La Virgen knew how to heal her mother of physical and other pains in a way only a woman can. Susana and her siblings felt the comfort La Virgen brought to their mother and thus saw her in a similar light: La Virgen "was a special woman who understood the pain and the sufferings of people that would somehow bring some kind of peace to us or make us feel good or help us in whatever things were going on in our lives, [such as] racial and class discrimination."

Attending a church named for Guadalupe further solidified her centrality: "And of course, when we went to church it was always about Jesus and God, but since it was Virgen de Guadalupe Church, the Virgen was the main [persona], and I think that [name] even confirmed to us, . . . 'This is the church of the Virgen, so she must be all-powerful if she had a church named after her.' So I think that really reinforced that not only at home but at church the Virgen was the . . . center." This idea of Guadalupe being at the center in ways normally considered unique to Christ is prevalent throughout Mexican American religious experiences.

I asked Susana how she thought her relationship was similar to or different from her mother's and she responded:

> I don't know if my mother ever said that the Virgen was Mother Earth, that she symbolized Mother Earth. And I think that that might be the difference there . . . that she's more than the Virgen, that she's . . . the creator and so she's the Mother Earth. . . . Yes, she is a woman, but she is also the main creator, she symbolizes what the world is all about. It's all about life and death and birth and death and rebirth, and so she symbolizes those things to me. . . . My mother never put it in those terms. She put it in the terms of a woman.

Here again, the difference between Susana and her mother's relationships with Guadalupe was evident—Susana saw her as the Earth Mother, while her mother viewed her primarily as a mother and woman, but not necessarily as a symbol of Mother Earth. That both Susana, who was no longer Catholic, and her mother, who remained Catholic, could each relate to the Virgen on her own terms speaks to the shifting spiritual needs of women across generations and to the Virgen's remarkable versatility. She offers each woman what she needs—whether it's a feminine figure who understands women's struggles or an earth goddess through whom

FIGURE 16 Members of Kalpulli Teokalli Teoyolotl, Danza Mexica Xochipilli and Danza de la Luna Huitzilmeztli: Alvaro Priego Segovia, Veronica Cruz, Abuela Jessica Tlazoltiani Zamarripa, Abuela Rosa Tupina Yaotonalcuauhtli founder of Kalpulli Teokalli Teoyolotl, Susana Almanza, Alejandro Quiahuitl Martínez, Irene Martínez, and Abuela Felisa Yolocuicapahtli Yzaguirre. Danzantes dance annually in tribute to Our Lady of Guadalupe-Tonantzin on her Feast Day. Our Lady of Guadalupe Church, December 12, 2017, in Austin, Texas.

women can stay connected to their Tejana and Mexican identities while reclaiming aspects of their Indigenous past, including an earth-based spiritual tradition and way of life.

REINTERPRETING RELIGION AND EMBRACING INDIGENOUS PERSPECTIVES: FORGING A CONNECTION BETWEEN INNER TRUTH AND FAMILY

Similarly to how Susana (and other women) incorporate Tonantzin into their Guadalupe devotion, Susana (re)interpreted the cross as a sacred symbol of the four elemental energies and the four directions of earth-based spiritual traditions: "When you look at the cross, what is the center point? It connects all of that [the four directions and what they symbolize], and that's love. You know it's love that connects them and the middle and keeps them together. . . . It was about the directions, and it was spirituality. Then you didn't have to be fighting with people about is this religion or that religion better . . . because it's just spirituality and . . . anybody can be spiritual."

Susana reiterated that spirituality for her was about recognizing the sacredness of the elements that give us life—that we cannot live without them. It is vital to honor our water and Mother Earth because "it's our spirit . . . it's our spiritual connection," she said. Susana differentiated this kind of spiritual connection from involvement with the church, an important distinction that underlies many of the lives and practices explored in this book: "[You] don't have to worry, is this person going to punish me for this? . . . In the church it was always about punishing and the saving, punishing and the saving . . . but in . . . spirituality it's just about the recognition . . . trying to make sure that you integrate yourself into these four elements so that you can sustain yourself. To me that's spirituality. To me it's about energies . . . keeping a balance inside of you and then outside of you." Here Susana was asking how to maintain this internal (i.e., spiritual) as well as external (i.e., material) condition, which she is adamant that every human has equal access to: "We [humans] really needed to be sure those elements were protected [from environmental harm] for the betterment of all the people."

This philosophy aligns with Susana's contention that her social justice work is "absolutely" intertwined with her spirituality. Her spiritual path allows her to maintain a connection to and to honor the earth, as her own mother instilled in her early on, while allowing her to remain on a path of justice, in relationship with an ancestral past that resonates with her truth and gives meaning to her life.

Martha Cotera: Guadalupe as Subversive Mother and Maker of Movidas

Political and community activist and feminist scholar Martha Cotera's relationship to Our Lady of Guadalupe is both historically rooted and a reflection of her feminista practice—what she has called and what I see as "living spirituality."

During one of our many interviews over the years, Martha recalled being "raised in a household of feminists," where politics was a constant topic of discussion. Feminist ideals and intellectual prowess were therefore early influences in Martha's life. Though her household was Protestant, she was raised in her early years with a lack of female religious figures. This would change later as she began developing her feminist sensibility.

Exposure to Martha Cotera's extensive body of scholarship, including foundational works in Chicana feminism from the 1970s, was formative for many Chicanas of the movement era and many since. In both instances, a lot of them were learning of the histories of their feminist and Indigenous ancestors and heritage for the first time.

As a Chicana feminist endeavor, the recovery and dissemination of the history of Tonantzin was an intentional act on Martha's part: She wanted to show that women had a long legacy of activism and feminism to counter the submissive, compliant version of Guadalupe propagated through religious narratives and gender expectations. As such, the historical recovery of Tonantzin as a strong earth mother would come to position the goddess in a manner that aligned with Martha's conviction that the political should be put back into spirituality. In Martha's personal application, she would invoke Guadalupe-Tonantzin as a subversive mother and maker of movidas.

Martha's works paved the way for new forms of spirituality and political activism that would impact future generations of Chicanas and inspire literary, spiritual, and various other Chicana cultural productions. Her life, and particularly her spiritual and activist development, provide insight into the ways in which spiritual and political transformation occurred within the movement generation.

(RE)IMAGINING RELIGION AND THE POLITICS OF SPIRITUALITY

Martha's life story speaks to Anzaldúa's assertion that the political (which I read as a kind of politics that overtly critiques social hierarchies and patriarchy) is missing in much of contemporary spirituality. We can see Martha's attempts to remedy this in her conversion from Protestantism and her search for a female role model. Conversely, Martha also shows how the spiritual is often absent in people's political lives. "In spirituality, the political connection is missing," she states. "Worse still, the spiritual is missing in the political connections." Martha is talking about an egalitarian, feminist-infused spirituality that would bring people from opposing views and political perspectives together and galvanize them in the service of social change. Martha shows not only how the spiritual is political, but also how political activism must be a spiritual endeavor.[20]

While Susana Almanza, María Elena Martínez, and Carmen Lomas Garza follow a pattern of growing up Tejana and Catholic and coming to spiritual transformation after their movement experiences, Martha converted *to* Catholicism rather than from it, a move that was inspired by her need for female role models on her spiritual path. The seeds of this transformation were planted early on in Martha's life. She was raised in a Protestant home in Mexico, where she recalls many a political discussion around the dinner table with her parents and grandparents. She was raised in a household of feminists, but she had no spiritual role models who were women, so she turned to Jesus Christ: "Considering the way that as a little bitty child I saw Christ, you know, . . . he was the only feminist in the spirit world; in the real world I had a lot of women and history around. . . . In my spirit world he represented these feminist values for me. . . . Christ was the one role model. . . . He represented the feminine to me, because his values are feminine."

THE DRAW OF FEMALE SPIRITUAL ROLE MODELS

In her twenties, Martha went through what she calls an "intellectual conversion" to Catholicism. She was driven to Catholicism in part by the respect, admiration, and reverence she had for Catholics for holding female figures such as the Virgin Mary in high regard. She conducted a lot of goddess research, during which time she learned of the wisdom goddess Sophia and the connection between Sophia and feminist values generally and values that were attributed to Christ. She stated that while Christ was endowed with feminine characteristics, he was invoked as a masculine model. Imagine, she told me, "a whole section of Protestant women with no female role model!" Ancestral history of goddess devotion is not just present in the histories of Mexicas that Martha has uncovered in her scholarship; it also manifested in her own spiritual and activist development. This became evident in her response when, after learning that she is a firm believer in the power of prayer, I asked whom she prays to: "When I have to think of something very specific, just to cover my odds, I pray to the grandmothers . . . because I think there's a connection, a direct connection from the grandmothers to the goddess. And I pray to Jesus Christ, because I think . . . he was a most fabulous prophet, I think he was just a fabulous representative of something very good."

Martha's intellectual conversion to Catholicism—her personal form of Christianity and practice of goddess devotion—took the shape of an alternative Catholicism, much like that of Norma and Rosie. For instance, she was adamantly opposed to what she viewed as the church's hierarchical structure, where women were held in subordinate positions to men. Raised with strong feminist values, which she considered human values, she was a staunch advocate for women's rights and for women's intellectual and personal development in all spheres of life. These same feminist values not only led her to seek out feminine spiritual role models and leave Protestantism but also shaped her approach to Catholicism—a faith she engaged with through negotiation but not compromise. Like Rosie and Norma, Martha chose to reject aspects of Catholicism that did not support her spiritual growth, align with her core values, or meet her needs. Instead, she retained and reinterpreted the elements that resonated with her beliefs on social justice, equality, and personal empowerment.

THE FEMALE ATTRIBUTES AND EMBRACING DIFFERENCE: CHRISTLIKE VALUES AS A GUIDING FORCE

Similarly to many Catholic and formerly Catholic women I encountered throughout my research, Martha was in the process of reevaluating her relationship to the Catholic Church when I interviewed her in 2012. In doing so, she was clear to note that it was the institution she questioned, not her relationship to the Christlike values that she said are at the core of her spiritual practice and fundamental to her understanding of what Christianity originally was and still should be. The life of Jesus Christ is a life that deeply inspired this passionate social justice advocate. The compendium of attributes embedded in Christ, as she said, were all female: "He's a beautiful model."

In this way, Martha attributed feminine—and I would suggest feminist—qualities to Christ. Her understanding of Christ aligned with her search for feminine spiritual role models. He was a Christ who championed equality and social justice—a Christ Martha deeply knew and loved. This simultaneous strong connection to both Christ and Guadalupe-Tonantzin was unique in my findings. While Our Lady of Guadalupe remained a constant presence in the lives of the women in this study, and many maintained a relationship with Christ, none engaged with him in quite the same way as Martha did.

Living these Christlike values is itself a form of spiritual activism that connects the metaphysical with life's material circumstances. However, it has not been easy for Martha to continue to enact such values within the context of institutional Catholicism, as shown in the distinction she makes between the social justice teachings of Christ and the institution of the Catholic Church: "We [Martha and her husband] are really rethinking our relationship to the church, but it's not our relationship to Christian values or to human values, because [Christ] was always speaking for human rights. His approach . . . to really embrace . . . difference and diversity and urging people to accept one another and to work and love one another . . . I really, really love that."[21]

It is evident here that Martha values the social justice orientation of Christianity, which she feels has gotten lost in the politics of the Catholic Church.

"IT'S NOT ALL ABOUT THE BOYS": PARALLELS IN POWER AND PATRIARCHY BETWEEN THE MOVEMENT AND THE CATHOLIC CHURCH

The core values that shaped Martha's religious and spiritual life extended into other aspects of her activism and advocacy. She openly discussed the sexism and gender politics she and other women in RUP encountered and were forced to navigate. Drawing a sharp parallel between the patriarchal structures of the Catholic Church and those within the Chicana/o movement, she reflected on her experience as an active participant in RUP. "La Raza Unida [Party] is like the Catholic Church: You don't have to like it all. You have to be able to see the real cause and issues—it's not about the boys."

This statement by Martha Cotera is a poignant commentary on parallels between religious and movement hierarchies of power, specifically heteropatriarchy. Her statement inspired me to consider how women like Martha have carried the same strategies they used to navigate gender hierarchies within the political sphere of the 1960s and 1970s forward into their approach to religious institutions today. In this ongoing negotiation, Guadalupe-Tonantzin and historical revisioning remain central to their efforts to reclaim space, authority, and self-determination.

Martha applied the same tools of political negotiation from her past to her present. I argue that Martha's spiritual activism entailed calling upon and refining the strategies she used during the Chicana/o movement to articulate and critique the ways racial, gender, and class inequalities operate. She combined this with her deep knowledge of Chicana/o and mexicana/o religious and cultural histories to once again challenge, navigate, and work toward dismantling patriarchy.

She continued this work in various arenas, including the religious sphere, through her critique of power structures within organized religion, particularly Catholicism. I contend that her critique was rooted in both a feminist sensibility and an active resistance to institutionalized religion. One way this manifested was in her decision to attend Mass less frequently than before. In saying, "It's not about the boys," Martha pointed to the larger purposes and struggles at stake—ones that should not be overshadowed by patriarchy.

For instance, she said, Jesus Christ's messages of social justice pointed to the "real causes and issues," and it was most important not to let that get overshadowed by sexism or gender oppression in the Catholic Church. This can also be likened to not letting the sexism that she and other RUP women experienced from male-centric leadership and efforts, and the necessity to keep in mind the larger goals of the Chicana/o movement and the fight for racial, gender, and class equality in mind. Compartmentalizing—staying focused on the bigger, deeper goals—allowed Martha and other Tejanas to stay within RUP at a time when women in other movimiento groups were leaving and creating their own groups, like the Brown Beret women in East Los Angeles who broke off and formed Las Adelitas de Aztlán. Instead of leaving RUP, women like Martha and María Elena founded the party's women's caucus, Mujeres Por La Raza.

In the following quote, Martha illustrates her contention that not only does the spiritual need to be critiqued from a political standpoint, but that political and activist positions should be informed by a strong spiritual foundation: "I think it would be very difficult to arrive at a feminist—an activist—position without a very strong spiritual and value space. . . . You have to have that to begin with." This contention aligns with Martha's idea of doing spirituality: the living those spiritual values, the doing of the "outer work" of which Anzaldúa speaks. Martha draws upon her Christ-based values to do so, as well as her devotion to the Virgin of Guadalupe, another symbol of the feminine divine and a role model for Martha in her spiritual and activist work:

> To me the Virgen represents the divine in women. . . . The way I see it is the way I see Jesus Christ—who, again, was the embodiment of the wisdom goddess, Sophia, and all these wonderful attributes . . . it's OK, I don't mind, I think it's good for men to have that role model. I think it's good to have a goddess as a role model. I incorporate goddess worship, and the way I incorporate those values is by living . . . and not necessarily by worshipping in an institutionalized setting. It's by living day to day, minute by minute, and by doing whatever I can do given my human resources and my human strength of all kinds. . . . I think it's just living, living to the best of your abilities and doing the best that you can with your resources and sharing those as much as possible.

Living spirituality requires spiritual resources to continue to move forward, gathering the strength to continue the work even in the face of adversity. This is a critical component of spiritual activism that Anzaldúa articulated and which Martha exhibits.

For Martha, converting to Catholicism was a feminist act, one she made in order to embrace the feminine face of God and a close relationship to Mary, particularly in her form as Our Lady of Guadalupe. Over the years, however, Martha would come to question the church. In her current questioning of a flawed Catholicism, Martha is actively critiquing patriarchy. As she did with RUP, Martha is focusing on the aspects of social justice that inspire her in her life. She withstood and contested the patriarchy within RUP to fight for the larger cause of social equality and is doing the same in her religious life today, embracing aspects of religion and spirituality that resonate with her feminist and humanist ethics and discarding the rest. Martha's spiritual journey is characterized by the challenging of religious hierarchies and a deep commitment to a Christ-centered social justice praxis by which she lives her life—the doing of spirituality that can be understood as her form of spiritual activism.[22]

Movidas of Spiritual Activism: Intergenerational Spiritual Knowledge Transmission

In the previous chapter, I used Inés Hernández-Ávila's metaphor of history as a "gran limpia" to show the ways in which Chicana feminist knowledge production yielded the feminist articulations of figures like Our Lady of Guadalupe as Tonantzin by Anzaldúa, Martha, and others. In this chapter, I focus on Guadalupe-Tonantzin as women's "'take' of reality," per Anzaldúa's discussion of spiritual activism: "By expanding your 'take' of reality, you make connections, not only to the physical, psychological and spiritual worlds via your symbology system, but also to political realities."[23] There is a politics to the spiritualities of the activists whose lives I discuss in this book. Their symbolic actions—the living and doing of their spirituality—are deeply intertwined with their feminist perspectives and are often reflected through Guadalupe-Tonantzin, who is, as I've emphasized, a central and constant presence in the lives of so many women.

Anzaldúa offers us a form of spiritual cleansing through her historical recovery work and revisions. She helps us re-member after generations of erasure and alienation by turning androcentric, colonized, and whitewashed histories on their heads. Through her philosophical explorations and theorizing, she does more than critique: She acts, delving into the complexities of the borderlands in ways that challenge, disrupt, and transform. It is, in the words of bell hooks, "theory as liberatory praxis."[24]

The Unconditional Love of Guadalupe-Tonantzin: An Offering

bell hooks says that "radical love is love that is evoked for the purpose of helping another grow spiritually."[25] This resonates deeply as I think about that love offering María Elena gifted me in the form of a spirit story on the phone all those years ago. She not only introduced me to Tonantzin, she explained her significance and invited me to think deeply about it, which I would do for years to come.

In this way, María Elena helped me—through Guadalupe-Tonantzin, and on many occasions thereafter—to grow spiritually. She guided me in reconnecting with my family, cultura, and, most importantly, myself. This act of reconnection is the essence of spiritual activism, the very work that María Elena and the other women in this book undertake by sharing their individual medicinas. Through movida praxis and spirit stories, they pass down this wisdom, ensuring its continuation and transformative impacts.

Through the stories shared in this chapter—women's relationships with Guadalupe-Tonantzin and the ways they invoke her in their feminism and activism—I am reminded of the familiar kind of love she evokes: unconditional and all-accepting. She is the torchbearer, lighting the path for each of us on our individual journeys and guiding us toward our own truths. Some of these paths, like mine and Meme's, intersect along the way. This is a love that allows truth to emerge without constraint—a radical form of unconditional acceptance. As a parent, I cannot help but reflect on this as I strive to support my own children in connecting with and living their truths. In doing so, I work to shed the scripts of my past that no longer serve me and write new ones from a place of love without conditions.

In the Interest of Liberation

I end this chapter with the following reflection, inspired by the women's stories shared here, as well as the work of Irene Lara and Inés Hernández-Ávila. It is inspired by the question "What do decolonial practices like invoking Tonantzin mean to us and do for us in these times that are upon us as we enter 2026?" As Inés says, "We don't have time for [inner group] *conflictos* and competition. We don't have time for that. . . . Every time we opt for . . . it again, . . . you have to ask yourself, whatever you're doing, is it [in the] interest of oppression or the interest [of] liberation?"

It is a question that Inés and the other women and this book overall invite us to reflect upon as we think about our own healing and liberation and those of others. What is our role? What can we learn from women's relationships to Guadalupe-Tonantzin? I believe that she can help us to remain connected to our roots and our individual truth at the same time. Her medicina becomes clear. She at once offers nepantleras caught between identities, beliefs, and ways of being both a grounding and the ability to soar. It is a loving medicina of acceptance and unconditional love. It is the ultimate gift.

This chapter puts forth another example of women's agency and cocreation of practices and places—within ourselves and outside of ourselves—that foster radical love, allowing us to show up in alignment with our truth, moving toward wholeness while remaining connected to a vital part of our past that colonization attempted, unsuccessfully, to sever us from. The gifts of the women discussed here are of ancestral knowledge and Chicana feminist praxis on the ground, in the everyday.

The next chapter explores Alma de Mujer Center for Social Change as a site of community gathering in the name of justice and for nourishment of the mind, body, and spirit. While Guadalupe-Tonantzin is an important guide and companion to women, Alma is a place where they gather in the natural environment, inspired by Indigenous philosophies and practices to express their true selves and embrace their medicina.

CHAPTER 4

ALMA DE MUJER CENTER FOR SOCIAL CHANGE

Embracing Our Medicina en Comunidad

Alma de Mujer is a sacred space, a wildlife sanctuary that provides a home to herbal medicine and animals, a place to pray with La Madre, *a consecrated ceremonial space, burial place for* Marsha Gomez *and* Bonnie Blackgoat, *a spiritual center with a consecrated* Medicine Wheel Garden, *a beautiful place in* Nature *that can teach us to be quiet and be in a state of gratitude, love, peace, tranquility. It is a place to connect deeply with* Mother Earth. *The spiritual community that is gathering around* Alma de Mujer *is important to the education and spiritual guidance of future generations who will take care of* Mother Earth. *Alma de Mujer is in our hearts.*

—MARÍA ELENA MARTÍNEZ[1]

The body is rooted in the earth, la tierra itself. You meet ensoulment in trees, in woods, in streams. The roots del árbol de la vida of all planetary beings are nature, soul, body.

—GLORIA ANZALDÚA[2]

Our Earth *faces ecological disaster. People continue suffering from social injustices. Alienation from self and communities persists. In this era of capitalist globalization, there is a great necessity for relief from physical, spiritual, and social afflictions. So, many of us (re)turn to indigenous and mestiza spiritual knowledges for empowerment—knowledge powerful enough to survive despite patriarchal and colonial efforts at destruction.*

—IRENE LARA[3]

The land, the land itself is what speaks; the land itself is what has soul, and the spirits of all the many elders that have been there.

—MARY MARGARET NAVAR[4]

One only needs to spend a few minutes walking the land of Alma de Mujer Center for Social Change in Austin to notice the presence of Guadalupe-Tonantzin. From the altar in Alma's main lodge to a statue in the meadow, Guadalupe's presence is woven throughout the center: Inspired artworks, books about her in the library, and other sacred spaces honor her influence.

As the previous chapter showed, Guadalupe-Tonantzin is a loving, nonjudgmental companion who reflects and supports women in their lives and work as they carry out their commitments to justice and liberation. Her presence spans many realms, both inner and outer, offering support across spiritual, emotional, and physical spaces. This chapter explores how several of the women in this project have engaged in the work of spiritual activism, soul making, and community building at the Alma de Mujer Center for Social Change.

Alma is a space where one can commune with and be enveloped by nature and focus on the divine within it. People gather there in the name of justice and liberation, and for the nourishment and healing of the mind, body, and spirit. Even before it became Alma de Mujer, the space was a healing center. That came as no surprise to me, for since I first stepped foot on the land, I knew in my heart that Alma was, and remains, an offering. It continues to be a healing space, and people seek it out as such. The land lends itself to the earth-based and Indigenous knowledge that is shared and transmitted there, passed down from our ancestors—not only those of our families of origin, but also spiritual teachers, godmothers, comadres, and others we connect with at the soul level.

As both a student of and teacher at Alma—this space where nature, spirituality, feminism, environmental justice, traditional medicine, and activism merge with our souls, selves, and communities—I'll reflect on her impact on my students, as well as on myself and others, and the continuity of Alma as a place that nurtures the soul.

Across the past and present, and into the future, she remains a gathering place for souls—a space where creativity, love, and the sacred work of soul making converge. My intent with this chapter is to share stories and through them the possibilities that exist for communal care, soul and self-care, love, healing, and connection. May these stories of Alma de Mujer inspire you to seek out, claim, and create spaces for such spiritual activism—both within and outside of yourself.

On Making Soul: The Nonlinear, Cyclical Ways of Alma

Much in the way that processes of healing, liberation, and social change unfold nonlinearly, so too does the process of writing about Alma de Mujer. There is no singular way to tell her story. There is no one story. There is no one entry point to sharing experiences of Alma; rather, there are many of them. So many arrivals. So many departures. Joy and pain, both. Entries into new identities, into new questions, into new connections with self and others. So, rather than an opening story to begin this chapter, I start with what feels right. I write guided by the energy within my heart. A heart touched by Alma and her community, an example of spaces and places where we can connect to our truth, medicina, and creative power and change ourselves, for, in the words of Anzaldúa, "by doing so, we change the world."[5]

Enter(ing) Alma

It was 2008, and María Elena invited me to join her and a small group of women at Alma for a women's weekend. The email invitation read:

> Date: January 19, 2008 9:34:46 AM CST
>
> Subject: circle of the queen/crones
>
> hola mujeres de belen,
>
> it is time for the queens to gather to relax, pray, meditate, do ceremony and hold each other to heal. February 1–2, 2008. Friday afternoon through Saturday.
>
> things to bring:
> -drum or rattle if you have one
> -2 blankets to work on the floor
> -votive candle
> -water to drink
> -object to place in the medicine cradle
> -yoga mat if you have one
> -journal for writing

tentative schedule:

Friday, Feb 1

1:30–3:00 P.M. arrive mid afternoon on friday to settle in and walk the land.

5:30 P.M. early dinner

7:30 P.M. Create a Sacred Circle

Walking Meditation

Healing Ceremony

Saturday, Feb 2

8:30 a.m. Breakfast

10:00 a.m. Gentle Yoga

10:30 a.m. Medicine Cradle Ceremony

12:00 noon Lunch

2:00 p.m. Fire Ceremony

6:00 p.m. dinner and closing circle

we will prepare our own meals and take our own food to save on cost. we will each make a love donation to alma de mujer for the use of the room and space.

tentative menu:

friday dinner: lentil soup, salad, bread or crackers, fruit (velia will prepare the lentil soup, maria elena will prepare a salad)

saturday breakfast: oatmeal, toast, juice, fruit

lunch: main dish, salad, vegetable, bread, fruit (modesta will prepare vegetarian lasagna)

dinner: stir fry of tofu and vegetables, brown rice, fruit

this is a tentative menu, and if you have any suggestions, please let me know. let me know what food items you want to contribute and bring to alma. i will then communicate to others what is needed.

looking forward to a wonderful and healing weekend.

love and many blessings, maría elena

The youngest of the group—the women lovingly referred to me as "the baby"—I was so honored that I had been invited to attend. That weekend, I received the gift of a refreshing departure from the pressures of my graduate studies at UT, just a few short miles away. The women's gathering was my introduction to Alma de Mujer. I was instantaneously drawn to the energy of the land and its rolling hills, the glistening stream that flowed below the crossing to Alma's entrance, and to the women gathered.

There, on my first trip to Alma, the women taught me about her history, the land, and her many *plantas* and creatures. I ate delicious, healthy food, bathed in nature, and participated in ceremony, meditative walks, and intense and healing bouts of laughter. I soaked in women's stories and accounts of times past and witnessed for the first time what I came to know as the spiritual activism of Alma de Mujer and her community. It marked the beginning of a lasting connection to the land and to a group of women who would usher in a new understanding of the power of community to support healing, growth, and my ability to tap into my soul wisdom and own my medicina.

Belonging as an Inside Job

> *I think that we best realize love in community.*
>
> —BELL HOOKS[6]

While the word is used often, *belonging* is not something that is easily attained in our society here in the U.S., particularly for those on the margins, such as the nepantleras in this book. In fact, their intimate knowledge of othering and alienation—shaped by lived experiences of racism and gender oppression in the Jim Crow South and being called vendidas, or sellouts, for enacting feminist principles during the movement, for their intuitive ability to recognize injustice, and for their early questioning of gender roles and power structures—inspired not only a movement, the Chicana movement, but also an academic field, Chicana/Latina studies, and a subfield of feminism, Chicana/Latina feminisms.

So the emphasis on community and the role of belonging at Alma de Mujer also comes from the embodied knowledge of knowing not belonging. These women created something different, something for others on the margins. Something other-wise.

The Role of Inner Work in Building Community at Alma de Mujer

The mujeres del alma have taught me/us to create community in ways that are intentional and rooted in a profound feminista praxis that encompasses soul/inner work. That is, María Elena and the others have taught me that this inner work is imperative to building community. It involves attuning to the individual, inviting and allowing them to be, to express their truth. It is healing work, in that it seeks to uncover and honor what has been buried: repressed truths, hidden stories, and minimized selves. This is liberation, medicina from the wounds.

When we commit to the inner work—as I've learned by integrating the women's teachings and ways into my own life and my practice as an educator—the outcomes can be powerful. This work has the potential to cultivate a deep sense of belonging. For as Tori, a former SU student, said, there is a distinction: It is one thing to feel welcomed but another thing to belong. So what does Alma teach us about building community? About facilitating belonging? The coming stories will convey insights about this. At the heart of these stories lies something this chapter, this book—this entire experience—has revealed to me. Belonging must come from within. Any community building and community connection we do are not complete without allowing space for one's full self to show up. We are all on different paths in terms of what that looks like for each of us. I am in awe that a space like Alma exists, as it has for me and so many others.

Memories of the women and their impact on my life and the lives of others flood my mind and spirit—my first interaction with the Mujeres de Belén; the community ceremony Meme led for Tommy and me; memories of Meme drumming away with my children as babies in the lodge; and day visits to Alma to be with and listen to the land and take students there. This is a place of refuge. A space where all people—the majority on the margins in our larger society—are welcomed. There, we can achieve a sense of connection to our truth and, hence, attain belonging. There we are free to be, and become, our full selves. In this way, in community, as bell hooks says, we realize love.

Like Our Lady of Guadalupe–Tonantzin, Alma is grounded in a feminist, communal ethic of care—an egalitarian consciousness rooted in deep respect for and commitment to Mother Earth and all her creatures.

The space and its community offer not just intellectual but spiritual nourishment. I provide numerous examples of how Alma, as a key space for spiritual activism in Central Texas, has also facilitated a sense of belonging for many women, gender-variant people, LGBTQIA+ individuals, and people of color who have faced exclusion, alienation, and marginalization in society and even their own families outside of Alma. Healing has taken place through the ongoing work of community building. Despite the challenges of COVID-19, economic instability, and persistent social and political violence—experienced both by the communities who gather at Alma and by Alma itself—the center has endured. Its persistence underscores just how vital these spaces, created and sustained by Chicanas and Indigenous women in Texas, continue to be today.

Mujeres del Alma

These are stories of people drawn to Alma. And of Alma, to them. They are mujeres del alma. They are women of Alma de Mujer—women involved with the space, land, and her community. And they are women of the soul. For in their own ways and through their own medicinas, their "souls speak and bodies act" as healers, creators, earth keepers, medicine women, educators, artists, and activists.

In the years since that first encuentro with María Elena, I came to know these women and Alma well. They included women from the movement era, such as María Elena, Cynthia Pérez, Modesta Treviño, Yvette Mendez, and Velia Sanchez. I came to know of Louisiana-born Chicana Choctaw artist Marsha Gomez, the original director of Alma de Mujer and early spiritual activist whose *Madre del Mundo* sculpture series has become the symbol of Alma. The Indigenous Women's Network (IWN) is also an important part of the Alma story, for so many Indigenous elders have visited and taken part in ceremony, conferences, and community gatherings on the land over the years.

Mary Margaret Navar, a fellow Tejana anthropologist, is another mujer del alma who continues to play a pivotal role in my life and that of my family. I also came into community with people of my generation, including Naya Jones, Gloria Quesada, Beth Ebbing, and mi hermana del alma, Alicia Enciso-Litschi. Alicia's vast knowledge of Alma, its history, and the women of Alma, as well as our shared connection to the land and love of the mujeres, positions her as someone whose vision, perspective, and medicina are so important to this chapter and this book. They are also much needed in this day and age as we think about extending and implementing the spiritual activism of the mujeres and their wisdom in our current times and into the future, for generations to come.

Soul Sisterhood

I feel called to write about soul sisterhood because it came to me so strongly when I began to write this chapter. There are two women connected to Alma whom I met years ago and have recently become reconnected with. I feel there is a purpose to this reconnection and its timing.

After numerous virtual, recorded, and live conversations with my dear (and patient) friend Alicia for this book, all of this became so much clearer. Alicia also worked with María Elena, Velia, and Cynthia. We have therefore bonded over a shared love of these women and Alma. Our relationship gives me a glimpse of the deep connection I've witnessed among las mujeres del alma. It reminds me that Alicia and I are part of Alma's lineage—a continuation of the legacy carried by the women who came before us. Now, it's our turn to carry that knowledge forward, to pass it down to future generations, just as they did. In this chapter, I'll share stories of Alicia and another hermana del alma, Naya Jones—two women who walk the intertwined path of spirituality and activism. I believe they carry the kind of heart-centered medicina we'll need in the years to come.

I've learned from las mujeres del alma how to live what they've taught my generation about how to come together in community and engage in feminist, justice-oriented healing through earth-based practices. They've shown us how to lift one another up, support one another, and stay connected to our truth. Women like María Elena, Cynthia Pérez, and others created space for and helped guide one another through their varied paths of conocimiento—spiritual, identity based, and more. They held each other through the sometimes arduous journey of venturing toward and embracing their truth. Arriving at their medicina. How can we continue this legacy?

FIGURE 17 The main lodge at Alma de Mujer Center for Social Change, Austin, Texas. Photo courtesy of Alma de Mujer Center for Social Change.

Mujeres del alma and other women in this book have reached a stage of life that feels like the final stage of conocimiento: spiritual activism. It is an inner state of self-acceptance, self-love, that they have attained alongside the outer work of sharing their medicina with the world. Alma is a place where this becomes clear. It is a pivotal site of women's journeys of conocimiento and arrival at their truth. I think we must honor the stages of life and the immense wisdom that comes with entering this particular stage. As I enter it myself, I am ever so grateful to have role models who share widely their knowledge, skills, wisdom, and consejos, for we need them now more than ever.

These people are the people of Alma that I have come to know. They are only a portion of the many people and lives that have been touched by the sacred land of Alma de Mujer, a site of Indigenous and Chicana spiritual activism in Central Texas, since its founding in 1988. In this chapter, I share a *mezcla* of cuentos, stories, to show how Alma de Mujer can serve as a model for tapping into and sharing our medicina, in community and through spiritual activism. Over the years, I experienced spiritual and other conocimientos that coincided with the writing of this book. A central lesson learned, and one deeply connected to my experiences at

Alma, is that the work of activism, community building, and community care is also about tapping into ourselves and our truth. It is about identifying and coming to express our soul and our purpose. It is about making soul, *haciendo alma*.

Alma de Mujer: History and Context

From its emergence and prevalence in the 1990s as a place where spirituality and activism converged to its resurgence in the early 2000s, Alma de Mujer is symbolic of Central Texas Chicanas' community-building efforts as spiritual activism. Alma is an important part of the Chicana feminist legacy in Texas in terms of how it served as a place to gather Indigenous ways, as well as the organization's ability to hold space for those on spiritual journeys.

Alma operates under the umbrella of the Indigenous Women's Network, a 501(c)(3) nonprofit organization. The mission of the IWN and

FIGURE 18 *Madre del Mundo* statue by Martha Gomez, Alma de Mujer Center for Social Change, Austin, Texas. Brenda Sendejo.

its leadership has been to "promote Indigenous knowledge systems and lifeways, especially by supporting the youth, women, environmental justice, and the cultural arts." Alma was envisioned by Indigenous elders on the IWN board as a space where "the North meets the South"—Indigenous ways of the North meet with those from the South—at this twenty-two-acre retreat space in the Texas hill country. As noted on the Alma website, "The mission of IWN with regard to Alma is expressed in this vision statement: To maintain Alma de Mujer as a spiritually based center which advocates for social change, working within the vision of our Elders for the future generations and fulfilling our role as Indigenous women leading social change in our communities and nations."[7]

This vision has manifested in women's circles, spiritual gatherings, ceremonies, youth camps, and other programming. I share how I learned about the healing potential of comunidad through the women in this project and how I have passed down the women's teachings, writings, and movidas to my students over the years. I began going to Alma in 2008 and served as an intern there during graduate school, working with then-director Ana Lara. I came to know the history and, importantly, the impact of Alma and its community.

In 1996, feminist philosopher Genevieve Vaughan gifted the land to the IWN. Under the founding leadership of world-renowned sculptor and Indigenous rights activist Marsha Gomez, Alma's first project director, Alma de Mujer was established as an important gathering place for IWN's international coalition of community leaders and the Foundation for a Compassionate Society, run by Genevieve. Together, these women were dedicated to promoting Indigenous values and knowledge in the service of resolving contemporary community problems.

Genevieve Vaughan first introduced the concept of the anticapitalist maternal gift economy,[8] and it has been a driving force at Alma de Mujer for decades. A feminist alternative to patriarchal capitalism, the maternal gift economy proposes a gift paradigm as a form of liberation from market capitalism, which Vaughn argues is at the root of an era of immense crisis for humanity and the planet. In this paradigm, gift giving is prioritized over exchange, with an emphasis on elevating the social value of mothering. This philosophy continues to be the cornerstone of Alma's mission today.

Environmental Justice

Alma de Mujer has served as a hub for spiritual activism through Chicana/Indigenous feminist community building, cultural arts, identity formation, and environmental justice in the Austin area since the 1990s. An important space of healing, where women, children, youth, men, and gender-fluid individuals have gathered in community, Alma de Mujer has been and continues to be a space for activists and community organizers.

Among these is Susana Almanza, whose environmental justice organization People Organized in Defense of Earth and Her Resources, has gathered at Alma to engage in the work of spiritual activism. In a documentary about Alma de Mujer[9] by Erika Gonzalez, Susana recollects that

> Alma de Mujer has been around for quite a while since the '90s, when a lot of the Indigenous women and activist Chicanas got together and said, "We really need a center, a place where we can go to have reflections, to have discussions, to talk about plants, and the medicinal healing plants, to have healers come in from other countries." . . . Alma de Mujer has played a major role in bringing Indigenous women from all over the world together to talk about our lives in general, our customs, our beliefs, our spirituality, our ceremonies, all of these things. . . . Alma has really focused on bringing us back to our Indigenous roots. It's played a major role in bringing the north and the south, the east and the west together to have those real deep discussions but also the sharing of knowledge.

Over the years, she says, she has gone to many healing and medicinal plant gatherings aimed at "healing the spirit out at Alma de Mujer." For her, the land itself is also a peaceful respite from the energy of the city; a place for healing:

> [Having] that place that is quiet and serene with the creek running through it . . . having a place to be able to do that [away] from the hustle and bustle of the urban city, it's like a blessing in itself . . . it's healing in itself just being there. It's a healing place, and PODER has always tried to hold a connection out there with Alma de Mujer. We've taken our Young Scholars for Justice out there so that they too can see the blessing out there, where they

can have a place of quiet, a place where they can still go into the creek and be with the water, where they can share knowledge with people out there.

Susana goes on to share that PODER has held healthy communities and climate justice classes at Alma de Mujer, in addition to classes on cooking, natural soap making, art, and tincture making. She notes that members of Alma de Mujer has have also gone out to the urban core in Austin to participate in the Festival de las Plantas, the event that PODER held for many years and which I cover in chapter 2. Alma community members and PODER staff and volunteers would attend one another's events and collaborate regularly.

Susana sums up the essence of Alma de Mujer:

I think Alma de Mujer is really that alma [soul] of everybody. . . . If we look at Mother Earth, she is a mother that embraces us and encourages us and protects us. Alma de Mujer is an extension of that. It's that spirit of Mother Earth that's out there—the connection back out there to the quietness . . . where you can hear the birds, and you can hear them singing and you can see the butterflies and you can see the toads. You can see the little fishes and all of the trees. All of these things that are out there, these are part of Mother Earth's soul. Her alma. Sometimes in the urban core you can't see it. You can't always recognize the alma de mujer, but when you go out there to Alma de Mujer Center, you feel it and you see it. And I think that that's so important—to have our Alma de Mujer social justice center out there so that we can [get away] from all the hustle and bustle, really experience the soul of Mother Earth.

Susana's reflections capture the essence of Alma. Fostering the well-being of the community occurs in conjunction with tending to the sustenance and preservation of the earth. It is a place to recharge our inner spirits so that we can do the outer work of social change.

Alma's community members, visitors, stewards, directors, and women's council have played an important part in creating and sustaining Alma as a space for the transmission of Indigenous knowledge. These people include elders from the south, such as Zapotec curandera, *hierbera* (herbalist), and *partera* (midwife) Doña Enriqueta Contreras Contreras, who visited Alma several times to share her traditional knowledge.

Through Doña Enriqueta, other Indigenous elders, and las mujeres del alma, Alma becomes a space where those who gather take part in the transmission and creation of transgenerational knowledge. This process reflects a decolonization of Western ways of knowing, made possible through the Indigenous and women of color feminist epistemologies and practices that have long thrived—and continue to evolve—at Alma. The presence of three generations, mujeres del alma, myself and Alicia, and my students attests to this continuity of knowledge production and spiritual activism.

As a site for contemplation and reflection, Alma shows us the power of such places to heal, liberate, and hold us as we seek connection to our soul's truth. The gift of Alma is a gift from Mother Earth. She beckons us to protect these spaces and sacred lands, as Guadalupe-Tonantzin does for us and our familias; it is imperative that we, as humankind, get it right. I am learning through Alma and its community that nature is where we can go to tap into ourselves, our truth, and our medicina. Then, we learn how to express it; as I was once reminded about my reluctance to put my gifts out into the world, "Aren't gifts meant to be given?"

FIGURE 19 Alma de Mujer Center for Social Change altar. Brenda Sendejo.

Nature is an expression of the divine—its flow, its cycles of life, death, and regeneration. Alma de Mujer stands as an active participant in las mujeres' sacred acts of soul making. Through their experiences with Alma, women learn to lean into and lead with their medicina. The inner and outer work are both embodied in the Alma community and its land, making them vital forces in the ongoing practice of spiritual activism.

In this way, Alma is a place where "ensoulment" happens.[10] That is, we connect with our inner selves, our souls, and our truth through nature, as many activists, artists, and creatives have done at Alma for decades. This chapter shows how mujeres have done so, while also drawing on and sharing their medicina to inspire healing, wholeness, and liberation.

We fortify our minds, bodies, and spirits at Alma. And it makes me realize how few places and spaces we have for doing so. At Alma, our unique forms of medicina are all welcome. What the land gives us when we are there, an offering, is the direction we are to follow. Otherwise, in this day and age, where do we learn what our medicine is?

Alma is an example of the kinds of energy that we can come into contact with and connect to and within. When we are guided by an energy of love and of being of service—much in the way that the women have been guided since the movement era—liberation and healing are possible, even imminent.

Intergenerational *Círculos*: Heeding the Call of the Soul, Listening to the Land

The soul speaks, the body acts.
The land speaks, the body acts.
Does the land have soul?
If we listen, what can we hear?
Whispers from the soul of the land to our own?

This chapter weaves stories of women's various relationships to Alma and the Alma community with an autohistoria of my own. I feel called to do so in order to show the possibilities of community as a space for both making face (constructing identities that are true to who we are, as the women taught me) and making soul (listening inwardly for guidance on how to live our truth and share our medicina with the world). For me this process was intergenerational, and that wisdom that I received, coupled with community, yielded self-love, healing, and empowerment—outcomes of spiritual activism. It is vital that we listen to the grandmothers, to our elders, our ancestors, and guides, and that we share such knowledges across generations, especially in the current moment.

Collective and communal care, soul wisdom, healing, belonging, and love signify the various energies and gifts that I both witnessed and received as women came together to organize, comfort, heal, nourish, and love one another and the land at Alma. A soul-filled place, gathering space, home in the soul sense, centered in the feminine divine, Alma exemplifies the coming together not just of people but of people with a purpose to hold space for their healing and that of others. A central player in all of this is the land, which holds space for us to do so—land and nature that embrace us through our experiences and the realities of conocimiento. Creating such spaces and opportunities feels urgent as we move forward in 2026 and in the years to come.

Making Soul at Alma de Mujer: A Testimonio

Sometimes my soul calls, and as happened today, I feel the urge to do certain things, like look for my emails about Alma. I found the invitation to a cradle ceremony María Elena hosted for my spouse, Tommy, and me to call in a child in 2013. We sought to become parents, and this beautiful offering would be an important part of our journey. I hadn't seen the email in several years. On this day, it made its way to me.

> Please join us for a Medicine Cradle Ceremony for
> Brenda Sendejo and Tommy Ademski
>
> You are invited to attend a Medicine Cradle Ceremony for Brenda and Tommy as they initiate a new beginning as parents of a newborn child and as they call to Circle an Austin family to support them. Alma de Mujer is a special place for Brenda, and Tommy and Brenda requested to have the ceremony at Alma because of her deep connection to the sacred land. The Medicine Cradle Ceremony, which is a gift of the Grandmothers, celebrates, restores, and enriches our lives as we move through our journeys

on Mother Earth. You are invited to bring an offering for the Medicine Cradle in the form of a small object that speaks to your loving intention for Brenda, Tommy, and the new baby. The offering will stay in the Medicine Cradle, which is honored each day in prayer with water and cornmeal. We will share food afterward. Please bring food or drink to share. Blessings. María Elena

The ceremony was a beautiful gathering of people from all aspects of our lives together. It represented the coming together of our worlds, with my Alma familia and my family of origin—my sister and nephew—in attendance. It was very symbolic of my journey. For even as I complete the writing of this book and venture out onto my new path, guiding others in matters of the spirit and living their truth, I am once again met with the calling to bring together worlds and people in community.

Amid the smudging, flowers, hugs, songs, and calling in of the directions, the beautiful energy and loving intentions for our new journey were palpable. I am reminded of the deep connection I have to Alma, having called in, not one, but two children with our community following

FIGURE 20 The author and her family at Alma de Mujer Center for Social Change, Austin, Texas, 2015. María Elena Martínez.

that ceremony. Even those not there in person were present in spirit, such as Mary Margaret, who captured the essence of this multigenerational ceremony and connection to Alma and her comunidad:

> Sweet Parents of Little Angel to come:
>
> Yes, I was with you in spirit and in love in this celebration in anticipation of this little soul that will find their way into your hearts and home, with all the smiling aunties surrounding the future crib. I could not be physically there, but my thoughts and prayers for you both were most present in my mind. I wish you joy, happiness, and lots of fortitude in becoming the guides and guardians of this little soul on their earth journey.
>
> Can't wait to meet them.
>
> Much much love,
> Margie

Alma Time

I have started this chapter time and time again. And I now know, of course, it's going to be written on Alma time, not Brenda time. No other time. Alma is a place where time feels suspended. It turns out writing about her feels similar. The process is not linear, not chronological, none of it. Even on a cold winter day, writing about Alma from miles away, I feel her presence in my spirit.

I have felt the rare feeling of the calling of my soul at Alma. And Alma taught me how to access it: how to listen without and listen within. When I go there, I am in communion with my soul. When I connect to the soul, I am connecting to my heart. And to my truth. I am making soul. Oh, the magic of nature. Alma de Mujer. The soul of the woman. That is the part of me that emerges like the fruit on the nopal, the bloom on the rose, when I go to Alma.

Alma as a Portal Back Home to Ourselves

I think of Alma as a portal back home to ourselves. She—like Guadalupe-Tonantzin—is a reflection of us. She calls those of us drawn to her to

FIGURE 21 Alicia Enciso-Litschi burning copal inside the lodge at Alma de Mujer Center for Social Change, Austin, Texas. Brenda Sendejo.

share our medicina—even if we had no intention of doing so. María Elena was called to heal, drum, sing, and teach youth, adults, students, families. Alicia, someone whose medicina includes weaving decolonial, feminista, and Indigenous perspectives into Western psychology and ways of knowing and healing—including listening to the land and ancestors—was called to conduct her doctoral research on Alma. I, too, had no intention of studying spirituality before meeting María Elena, and I, too, ended up at Alma, only to take students there years later. As Alicia said, "How much of it [the choice to write a dissertation on Alma] is my bright idea, and how much of it is the land, spirit, ancestors moving us? And we listen as well as we can. And a lot of it is showing up. To drop in, to be given the assignment . . . water the garden. Make a garden. And there are deeper forces. I think that Alma cultivates a potent container where these forces and relationships have been nourished."[11]

The Callings

Then, there are the callings. As Alicia recalls in an interview with Velia Sanchez, the Austin movement activist and longtime friend of María

Elena, it was a dream that called Velia to construct a medicine garden in the shape of a medicine wheel: "This garden is the coming together of the Medicine Wheel of the north and the nahui ollin of the south. They meet here at Alma. The vision for this garden came to me in a dream. I did not even know what a Medicine Wheel was until I dreamt it. I woke up from the dream and looked it up online and found out it was a real thing! Then María Elena—you'll get to meet her—told me, 'Velia, of course it's real!' Well, I didn't know, but I dreamt it."[12] And so the medicine garden was constructed, representing Alma—where Indigenous ways and people of the north meet those of the south—with the intention of supporting the cosmic balance of life, nature, and community.

Some carry deep plant knowledge and healing wisdom, like Velia and María Elena, who work with herbs and their many restorative properties. Then there is Mary Margaret, who met the Zapotec healer Doña Enriqueta Contreras Contreras at Alma through Marsha Gomez. That meeting marked the beginning of a long-standing relationship—Mary Margaret apprenticed with Doña Enriqueta for many years and eventually moved to Oaxaca to continue the work.[13] Others are firekeepers and conduct ceremony or temazcal on the land, such as Abuela Rosa Tupina Yaotonalcuauhtli. Others, such as former Alma women's council member Yvette Mendez, are drawn to Alma's waters. María Elena, called by the grandmothers to resurrect Alma in the early 2000s, is considered an elder maestra and leader in the Alma community. She led spiritual gatherings and ceremonies and worked to create a summer camp for youth on Alma's land.

FIGURE 22 María Elena Martínez (right) and Velia Sanchez (left). Courtesy of Alicia Enciso-Litschi.

As I've said, we each have our roles and unique medicina we are called to share with the world. The timing of this book is such that it culminates with me finally identifying mine—part of which involves supporting others in locating their own. And it is occurring over twenty years after having first met María Elena. Our medicina is the portal to our truth, the path to liberation for ourselves and others. I truly feel that I met María Elena in order to guide me to my current life path. And in some ways, I've been called to carry on the work through my own medicina—a path I came to recognize through María Elena, Alma, and the community that surrounds her.

Alma and Guadalupe-Tonantzin: Medicine Wisdom from the Heart

As I write about Alma de Mujer, I bask in the sunlight streaming through the trees outside my window and find myself thinking of the trees that grace the twenty-three acres of land at Alma. What is it about Alma de Mujer that gives me such a sense of connection, of belonging, of home? The memories of my time with the mujeres? How they embraced me after a devastating loss, seeing them together there in love, laugher, and comadrazgo? How they brought me into their circle? How they prayed for us to become parents? The return some years later with Meme, Tommy, and our babies, and memories of drumming, laughter, and love? Cynthia's welcoming of the students and their sense of belonging?

Then it came to me: Alma and Guadalupe-Tonantzin are connected.

Women's lives, their developing feminist consciousness, their paths of conocimiento, their search for their truth and purpose—all are reflected in their relationships to and resignification of Guadalupe and incorporation of Tonantzin, and their relationships to Alma de Mujer.

We can locate our medicina, connect to our truth, and listen more deeply to our hearts at Alma and through our own almas. As I have learned from María Elena and the other women, Guadalupe-Tonantzin can guide us on this path. She reminds us that we can fully accept ourselves, as she does—love ourselves unconditionally on our journeys of conocimiento. I often think, from having been at Alma, that we all possess portals to our souls, where we access our heart wisdom and our intuition. Accessing those forms of inner wisdom involves connecting to a deep sense of self. And I think, here, about our roots. Not the roots of who we are and where we come from in the biological or geographical sense—I am thinking of a connection beyond that. A soul connection.

The portal to our truths, our gifts, our medicina, our purpose. My time at Alma—and the lasting impact of those experiences—taught me to practice deep listening, both to the land and to my own alma. For as the ancient Nahua people whom Anzaldúa references said, the soul speaks and the body acts.[14]

Making Soul: Connecting to Our Truth at Alma

As I've said, making soul is a process of re-membering—of being put back together, again and again, in new ways as we express and live from our soul. Making soul is also about remembering in the sense of recalling who we truly are—our cultural roots, language, spiritual ancestry—but on our own terms and through the portal of our hearts, from our souls. We are being called, as the mujeres have shown me, to fully express our truths more in our lives. That may well be an inner sense of justice that has tugged at us since childhood, or a very strong intuition, or the gift of singing—we all have our individual truths, our individual songs that we must, must sing as part of the spiritual revolution that awaits us and that begins within.

So, as I reflect on my path and that of the women, I think that we engage in inner change—through self-awareness, spiritual conocimientos, and self-love—but perhaps it is less about changing from one thing to something different and, instead, about a reconnection. A reconnection to a place from which we have been distanced, or even severed, which results in depression, sadness, anxiety, and strife and requires re-membering. May these stories of movements and movement makers, movidas, and making soul support you in your re-membering. May you finish this book inspired to engage in your own process of reconnection—of linking your soul, your inner self, to the outward work you feel called to do in the world. When those aspects are aligned, it feels like exactly what we're being called to do in these times.

In this book that kind of reconnection is about connecting as well to our truth. How do we do that? Connect to, understand, know our truth? María Elena put it as such: "I get a real clear sense that we have not been told the whole truth—that there is another truth than what is in the Bible. And I think that is what we all wake up to find, what voice sounds true to us and resonates to what we are feeling, so I opened my heart to what I was feeling. . . . I feel very strongly connected to the earth—that makes a lot of sense to me, so my practice is very earth based."

María Elena offers a consejo of such massive proportions about listening to our hearts for guidance that I feel it bears repeating: That is where our truth resides, "what we all wake up to find, what voice sounds true to us and resonates to what we are feeling, so I opened my heart to what I was feeling." Connecting to our purpose, our truth, can happen through our hearts. What might "opening up our hearts" to what we are feeling connected to look like for each of us? To listen within and for guidance? It is hard. Likely because it is a decolonizing move, as much Western thought and teachings have pushed the idea that we should seek wisdom outside of us. I know this because it has been a very difficult thing for me—and many of my students—to do, given the West's binary ways of knowing and the focus on "objectivity."

Our World Today: The Urgency for Spiritual Activist Communities and "People Connected to Their Medicina"

As I noted in the opening pages of this book, the United States and the world are undergoing political, social, and cultural upheavals of massive proportions. According to astrologers, we are in a planetary pattern we haven't seen since the U.S. Civil War. A war is raging against many of the initiatives women fought for—and continue to fight for—around justice, liberation, healing, unsilencing erased histories and hence people, and embracing our full selves. Those projects under attack as I write include DEI, ethnic studies programs several women in this project helped found, feminist studies, intersectional pedagogies, and any forms of difference that don't align with an upper-middle-class/wealthy right-wing "Christian" heteropatriarchal whiteness. This is the antithesis of the Christlike values of love and acceptance to which women participants in this project who identify with Christ adhere. Lives and livelihoods are at risk like never before in my lifetime. It is an extraordinary time. Sentiments and messages about the dire need for collaboration and community care are rampant in networks of social change and racial and gender justice. Also simmering is the message at the core of this book:

that inner work and outer expressions of our souls—that is, love—are vitally necessary as part of our responses to such dehumanization and terror, and we must dig deep to learn what we are each called to do in this unprecedented moment. This chapter includes an invitation to the reader to explore what that means to and for you. For, as Anzaldúa proposes, as "I change myself, I change the world."

The outer world is beckoning us. It beckons us all to look within and bring forth our medicina because, as Alicia recently shared with me, "our world needs people connected to their medicina—whatever that is, their unique expression of the life force, the spreading of the wings. Our whole world needs to be able to be who we need to be." Doing so is not easy, but as Alma de Mujer has shown through the various groups, youth camps, and events held there over the years, community can play a vital role. For community nourishes. Alma de Mujer provides a model for the kinds of spaces and communities where this work can be done—and soul wisdom and our medicinas nurtured—as we enter this new era in our nation, world, and existence.

An Unexpected Message and Amazing Grace: Alma's Energía Extends Beyond the Land

It is March 24, 2025, and I begin to revise this section of the book. I go to my notes on a conversation about the garden with Cynthia Pérez, Alma de Mujer director and caretaker, movement activist and longtime Austin business and community member. I reflect on a day that she dropped consequential wisdom. Then, I glance over to my phone and see that she texted at that same moment. She told me to call her at La Peña, the Austin arts organization she runs with her sister Lidia, to let her know if Alicia and I want to go out to Alma this week, as her phone is on the blink. *The land speaks?*

I had emailed her about being called to use "making soul" in my offerings. In her text, she essentially expanded my thinking about it: "You have a soul so you're trying to embrace the connection with your soul."

"Yes, gotcha, thank you," I text back. "That's what I'm hoping to do with my practice of spiritual activism, what I'm calling Making Soul. And

I think that's what Alma de Mujer—and you—do for people: help them (re)connect to their souls."

She responds, "In this world it is the spiritual connection of love that endures across time." And I think to myself about the relationships with and between the mujeres, those lost, those still here, and about our children, our ancestors, and what really matters. Who really matters. Cynthia goes on, "You're a Mom, you want your children to lead a strong and happy life in a world of criminals. To not focus on the material—the title, the job—but on the day-to-day miracle of life; the abundance of light. Sun. The beauty. The Mother Earth. Life. Water (how good was the thunderstorm last night and wind? Clean, clear thinking). Late in life, we become worn out, lose our ability, become ill. We can't get out and around, we forget. We become angry or fearful. If we are living with Gratitude it is a harder Road."

I think to myself, *She's sharing the message of Alma*. It's so simple, and we complicate it. Focus on the children, gratitude for the day-to-day mir-

FIGURE 23 Cynthia Pérez (left) with María Elena Martínez in front of Marsha Gomez's art studio at Alma de Mujer Center for Social Change, Austin, Texas. Brenda Sendejo.

acles, blessings of Mother Earth and clear water and thinking. And live in gratitude. The song "Amazing Grace" comes in through my earbuds, and tears well up in my eyes, because I feel a beautiful vibration. I thought the last I would write on Alma would be about a visit from the past weekend. That didn't pan out. But sitting here in an East Austin coffee shop, I feel as if I'm at Alma through Cynthia's words, through appreciating the simplicity of life. We don't have to be there literally. Alma is a feeling. A soul connection, perhaps. A soul connection that then allows us to do the deeds—do the work of spiritual activism.

Cynthia often reminds me, through her consejos, of the important things in life. Her next text hits me at the soul level. "You know you have your children, your Elder María Elena, Gloria Anzaldúa. You don't forget them; their work, they are all still with you working." No doubt about it.

And in the next moment the song "Luna Lovers" comes through my earbuds. A song by Las Cafeteras that is special to me. It reminds me of my youngest child, Luna. The lyrics state, "So, the story goes that my heart met yours. You touched my soul . . ." I can't help but feel that Spirit is telling me to keep going, to write. Indeed, I am not alone.

So that story now becomes an unexpected preface for the next section, which I wrote in August 2022. I was still working as a faculty member. We were at the height of the COVID-19 pandemic, and we had no way to know the enormity of what would come in 2025. The following is a story about a spiritual connection, about love that endures over time, about remembering that our loved ones are always with us and that they offer us something very important. Our teachers and elders, are always reminding us of our purpose and our potential and guiding us on our paths toward our soul's work.

The Garden: A Metaphor for Personal Growth, Spiritual Expansion, and Love

I am coordinating a student visit for my Latinx Spiritualities class to visit Alma. When I inquire about visiting Alma with the students, as usual, Cynthia doesn't pause. She graciously agrees to have us whenever we'd like to go. I call Cynthia about logistics and dates and to ask if she still wants us to work on the garden. I had offered for our class to do a service project to support Alma as part of our visit. The thing is, I know close to nothing about gardening. I've always wanted to get close to gardening, and I so love nature—photographing and documenting spiritual metaphors I see in nature. But I just haven't gotten around to actually learning to garden. Nonetheless, I agree for the class to take on the garden, because it is what is needed.

Next, I ask if she will speak to my class. "I have nothing to share," she responds. "You should ask other people to visit." The thing about Cynthia is, I have been chasing her down for years now. I have yet to succeed in getting her to sit down for an interview. You just can't do that with Cynthia. But she has given of her wisdom in other ways—through consejos during my impromptu visits to La Peña,[15] at Alma, and at other instances over the years, like in the text exchange I shared earlier. They are unexpected morsels of wisdom, movidas of spiritual activism.

On this day, she gives me the most beautiful gift. It is more than I ever could have imagined, something greater than a formal interview could have provided. Rev. Virginia's words about platicando being our tradicíon resonate deeply. Cynthia shares her spiritual movidas and conocimientos through pláticas.

I ask her what we should do with the garden. I express nervousness at the fact that I'm not a gardener. She responds, "So this is the deal. What is the connection to the garden? What is it called?"

"Medicine Wheel Garden," I answer. She quizzes me further about its significance. I say that the garden is about our connection to Mother Earth, about honoring Mother Earth and calling in the ancestors. She responds, "C minus—no, D." We sharea a chuckle at my grade and she goes on, "So, OK, the idea behind a garden is this," noting that these are the things she wants me to teach my class, "and you already know all of this," which I am highly doubting at the moment, but she says, "Yes, you do. You're the teacher. The connection to the garden is this . . ."

Cynthia begins the metaphor—which reads like a life lesson—saying the garden shows us that we can become self-sustaining, that we can believe in ourselves and abilities. "You are the dirt. You have everything here. You decide what you want to grow. Start with medicine and your favorite food. Start with weed eating and cleaning." Then Cynthia says, "You will give them [the students] something they will take with them. They will remember the class, the professor that saw something in them."

And I think to myself, *Perhaps in that they will have the chance to grow further, into themselves, closer to their truth*—my greatest wish as a teacher.

Cynthia goes on to tell me about the importance of having a garden and about chemicals that are in plastics and our need to be self-sustaining. That we need to "keep life simple and easy and do the best we can." Then, she drops a *dicho*, a saying: "Which is the wolf that takes over? The one you feed the most." The first takeaway: We can have limiting beliefs about ourselves or others, or we can choose to believe in the possibilities to sustain ourselves and our communities. The depths of that consejo hit me in my heart.

The next takeaway is that we all have a connection to spirit and to each other. And to get there, we can ask, "What is the spirit in everyone?" Whatever we see on the outside, whatever is happening in society, how can we look for the spirit that exists in everyone? *A connection to an enduring love that we all carry, perhaps?* I think to myself.

We are back to the garden. "Get two to three yards of dirt delivered to Alma," Cynthia tells me. She says to get some of the traditional medicine plants that I was taught about by Meme. "Have each student bring a plant," she says. "Eighteen plants is good."

Then she uses a metaphor: "Turn over the dirt, reveal myself to myself—where are my tendencies and where are my weeds?" Students will need to decide what they want to grow, and I think to myself, *Within and literally, perhaps?* "Start where people are. They will self-reveal. Then," she says, "you'll know where to work with them." I think we are getting away from the garden, but I love the idea of the metaphor, so I go with it.

I express my concern about "not getting it right" regarding the garden. She says, "Nothing is perfect, nobody is an expert. Fumble your way through it. It's perfect." She tells me that I'm the child of the most high and I have everything I need. "That's your gift, and that's what you give these [students]. Your most important job is to connect [with the students]. Take your power!" Cynthia tells me I was sent to Alma for a reason, that I am connected there. I think of the ways that María Elena and the other women connected with me, and how that is the legacy of Alma that I am to pass along. First to my students, then to others in the years to come. Both on and off of the land.

Later, Cynthia shows me a photo of a giant pig she had to bribe with her taco just to get it to move so she could drive her truck onto the land at Alma. I have a good laugh. Such is the medicina of Alma, of Cynthia Pérez, of the souls of women.

"This Is Always Here for You": An Invitation to Alma, an Invitation to Belong

And so the visit with my students to Alma is set for spring 2023. That semester, I introduced students in my Latinx Spiritualities course to Alma through photos, its history, and my own experiences there. I prepped them with Alicia's writings on Alma. Our band of queer, mostly BIPOC folks of varying gender expressions arrived to the land on a beautiful day in March. The students carpooled, and one by one the cars pulled up to the main lodge. I'll never forget the look of wonderment on sof's face when they walked up to meet me and the others at the lodge. "Dr. Sendejo, you didn't say it was like this!" Indeed, there is an energy to Alma that sof picked up on, one that cannot be described but, rather, must be felt.

We made our way into the main lodge and Cynthia greeted us. She then led us through the field to the Alma garden and introduced us to the land and her history. She wove in stories of women who had contributed to the mission of Alma de Mujer over the years and/or were associated with the Indigenous Women's Network's work with Alma de Mujer in some way. She took students into the main lodge and told them about the women's photos on the altar, which paid homage to those who had gone to the spirit world, including IWN members and Marsha Gomez.

I recall thinking, as I witnessed the students listening attentively to Cynthia, that it was an incredible juxtaposition. I knew from stories they had shared with me that the majority of these students had experiences in life in general and on our campus specifically that led them to feel alienated and othered. I could not help but think about my student Tori's reflection from years prior: "It is one thing to be welcomed and another to belong." So much of what Alma was to the students was the antithesis of the neoliberal university founded on and maintained in many ways

FIGURE 24 Cynthia Pérez under a trellis teaching students about the garden at Alma de Mujer Center for Social Change, Austin, Texas. Brenda Sendejo.

by white supremacy. Alma offered a respite from that almost instantly, as sof's response indicated. I sensed in students something I, too, had felt since the first time I stepped foot on the land: a sense of ease, of not having to brace myself or watch my back. It was about acceptance, best articulated through Cynthia's words to the students later that day: "This is always here for you."

Those words encompassed so much. They marked a continuity of Chicana feminist thought and practice taking place in the central Texas region, a model for intergenerational, inclusive, and healing pedagogies and activism.

That spring of 2023 was the last semester I would teach as a faculty member. Though I didn't know it at the time, it made sense that this would be where I would end that chapter in my life and begin a new one. That journey that culminated in something I always knew needed to happen: taking students to Alma de Mujer. What I didn't expect was that in addition to experiencing the land, students would also come into a deeper experience of themselves.

Integrating Alma's Lessons and Messages

I have come into myself and closer to my truth more than ever before over the course of writing this book. This book reflects my journey of conocimiento. Each stage has allowed me to see a version of women's lives and stories through my own lenses of transition, transformation, and healing. Alma always offers clarity. Perhaps it is the effect of being in nature, surrounded by animals and away from the city, and basking in the energy of the land, her rolling hills and creek. Things so often become so much more clear in my life when I am there. This was the case during my most recent visit, on February 10, 2025.

I planned to go to a hotel to focus on writing. For two hours, I looked for hotels all over the area, a bit away from town—San Marcos, Wimberley. Finally I honed in on where I needed to be: A hotel was available less than a mile from Alma. The ancestors were probably giggling. "Ay, Brendita, just listen . . ." At last, I did. The timing was not intentional—on my part, anyway. The ancestors may have had other ideas.

I drove in from Austin, arriving at the hotel in the late afternoon. After unpacking my things, I made my way out to Alma, just a short distance away.

Writing and Making Soul at Alma

I sit here in the lodge on Alma's land, having just arrived. I call in the ancestors of this land and my own and ask them what they wish for me to share about Alma. I think to myself, *How amazing is it that I ended up here? Writing here? This chapter? Here, the site of so much teaching and learning, loving and living, expanding and mourning?* María Elena, Mary Margaret, Alicia, and Cynthia taught me the most profound lesson I take away from writing this book and experiencing all I have in the past twenty years: to listen and learn. To listen within. To listen to the land. All the answers exist there. All the answers exist here.

Mujeres in this book are spiritual warriors in that they fight oppression and subjugation on the levels of the mind, body, and spirit. Their medicina is the spirit story, told through recovered histories, such as that of Alma, stories of the many borderlands, identities, and complexities of home we come to understand as we travel our paths of conocimiento.

Their medicine is seen in the renewed relationships to Guadalupe through Tonantzin that they practiced and how to be in the world outside Alma's gates amid laughs and through the tears. I have learned from these women that being vulnerable is part of my own medicina—one I had to give to myself before I could practice it outside of me. I am the recipient of the spirit stories of these mujeres, of their medicina. They have helped me to see the possibilities for liberation and transformation. For existing otherwise. Through love. Through story.

(*Re*)*writing* My *Story*

I'm supposed to be writing the book during this time, with the goal of turning the manuscript in to my editor this week. I didn't get as much of the book writing done as I had thought I would in the past few days. But I did something else, something meant to be, something quite profound: I rewrote my story. Alma had played a big part in that journey, my arrival; my story began here, in many ways. So it is a beautiful synchronicity that I ended up here, finishing up this chapter on Alma *at* Alma. My story of becoming a parent began here. The spiritual birthing of babies and rebirth of self are my Alma stories, my spirit stories. Becoming an academic and meeting María Elena, witnessing her spirit story, and allowing my truth to lead me to her and the other women and Alma for what started out as "research" changed my life. And again, it all happened on Alma time. You cannot force what happens to you with regard to the land and its community. Don't even try. The land speaks when our hearts are open enough to listen, as María Elena said.

I have been grappling for so long with the question of my purpose. This weekend, I learned that my purpose speaks to me through the ancestors and through my soul. The heart speaks the wisdom of the soul. So what does my heart tell me? It tells me what Cynthia said when I asked about doing things around Alma to help out: "Go write!" Alas, here I am. Writing. I pictured this moment so many times in my head. What would come through at Alma? What would I write? It was never up to me. And I can sense my way through the things that feel contrived and forced, like making my way through a dark forest, arriving to the flow—the clear waters of Alma's creek—as I hold my arms out through my windows in the ritualistic crossing over her waters that I do each time I arrive. This time, my arrival felt very different. And my departure would be the same.

This phrase just came to me: *I have arrived.* This visit is different from the others. I have this print by the Chilean artist Liliana Wilson, a longtime friend of many Austin Chicanas in this book and of Alma de Mujer, a gift she gave me for my master's graduation. It is called *I Have Arrived.* It is painting of a young woman with dark hair and eyes, and the powerful look in her eyes has always spoken to me. I have written many versions of this chapter—of many of this book's chapters. But this time it feels different. As if I have arrived. It is a homecoming of sorts. Because, while Alma has always welcomed me and felt like home, nothing on the outside can truly give us a sense of home or belonging. That kind of familiarity, I now know, can come only from within. That is why belonging is an inside job. But we can go places that will allow us to connect within. And nature is a powerful place for that. I even think, being among the trees, streams, *animalitos,* is where we were meant to be. Convening, connecting with the soul of nature, in an opening kind of energy, in expansion, away from the energy of the city, life, people, demands, traffic, and all the rest of it. But we must all find those places from which to (re)connect if we do not have Alma. Even a small, quiet space in a local park or backyard, wherever we feel connected to ourselves.

Alma and Stories That Emerge from Within

I'm thinking once again about portals. And how, as I look at the hilltop and trees, the skyline on a gray, cold February day in Central Texas, the creek crossing at Alma is a portal. It is as though I shed something when I cross. I am transported into another way of being. I do not mean to romanticize. But I truly am in awe of the trees, of the rock, the many Guadalupe-Tonantzins, the baby deer, and the occasional llama from the land next door. The stories that emerge out of Alma de Mujer are stories that exist within me. They are stories I don't even know are there. They just come out; they want to be expressed. For too long so much has been suppressed. It's like finding a portal to my truth, coming out here.

I listen. I am being told to share that Alma is a place where stories emerge. Being on the land allows our souls to breathe. Going into nature does that for us, and my experience with Alma is one example of how we can connect to Mother Earth and, in doing so, connect to ourselves. The environment in which we tell our stories is therefore very important. She is cared for and is sacred. She has been protected. If we open our souls and our hearts here, they will speak. We can listen to the wisdom of our hearts, the whispers of our innermost truth—the soul. Here. At Alma. Few places afford me such peace. Serenity. Safety. Calm. I feel grateful and protected as well. Like I belong here. As the caretaker of this land, Cynthia has also created the circumstances for me and others to be at Alma. Energetically, allowing me and others to step into our full selves, our power, and our light.

An Invitation to the Reader: Where Is Your Alma? What Is Your Medicina?

It feels as if Alma is urging me to step into the work I am needed to do at this time. I'm to tell stories and help others to tell stories. For me, that work will happen in many places and ways, including at Alma. I feel it in my soul. Whether through writing, creating art, or recovering our stories, Alma continues to be a place where the many forms of medicine that women used to serve future generations come together to bring about justice, healing, and liberation. Even if not intentionally, the mujeres del alma—their presence, their being, and their love—have countered oppressive forces and helped many usher in a self-love that empowers us to do the outer work we are brought here to do. To be of service. We need stories of that, especially now.

What I take away from Alma on this February day is the message that my medicina involves stories, spirit stories. And that my work is to bring people together at places like Alma, but also outside of it. To build communities and create Alma-type spaces and experiences, much like I did with my classes as a faculty member. I can create spaces where folks can work on their medicine, to help them to practice it on themselves so they can then go into the world and use it. The much needed medicina. The work is also to share the story of Alma so that others can imagine and create such spaces, both externally and internally. Where is your Alma? What is that space for you? What spaces exist, could exist that do that for you, your communities, your family? So I invite you to think about how you will do your work of making soul, of turning your medicina within and then sharing it outside of you. As San Antonio activist Rosie Castro shared with me in February 2025, "So we've known bad times. And you can always be assured that bad times will pass, provided there's action against those times. If there's no action—inaction—then it's prolonged. Evil is prolonged. And so for me, even though you're older, you know that there's less that you can do, but there's something that you can do, and it's just a matter of trying to figure out what that is."[16]

Rebirth: A *Testimonio*

I just realized that the place where I sit right now is the same place where our medicine cradle ceremony took place all of those years ago. Where people prayed for our children to be birthed into this world. And it is here that I am experiencing my own rebirth. Through the tears and with a soft smile, I think to myself that these past two days away have been a rebirthing ceremony. And this time I was surrounded by the ancestors. And all of what just flowed out of me—I don't know if it's for the book or not, but I know I needed to get it out. I needed to have that limpia I had last night, and today I finished off the sacred release with a cleansing from the land of Alma de Mujer. I can't keep this gift. I must give it away. Why

FIGURE 25 María Elena Martínez (far left) drums with the author's children, Jude and Luna, in the same space where María Elena led ceremonies to call in the children's arrival at Alma de Mujer Center for Social Change, Austin, Texas. Brenda Sendejo.

even have gifts? Why would spirit give them to us if we weren't meant to use them? I trust myself. It is time. And yes, it happened on Alma time.

What does it mean to integrate the lessons I learned from the women of all generations, both in terms of documenting their stories for this book and also in terms of how I have grown so deeply, expanded spiritually and intellectually? The two happened simultaneously. There was a making of soul that happened to me as I wrote this book, as I expanded as well in my understanding of my own purpose. Why do I bring this up in a chapter about Alma de Mujer and community? Because that land, named for the soul of the woman, represents the coming together of minds, bodies, spirits, and hearts, and the coming together of people with their medicine, on land that held space for them to do so. Whether the work of mujeres of Alma is continuing inside us, on the land, or beyond, the work is, I believe, resurrecting community. Soul communities.

Spiritual activism is not solely a human endeavor. It is about humans in communion with land, nature, the earth, and our ensoulment with it as well as with the ancestors. The land of Alma de Mujer draws those of us who have come to know her glistening creek and expansive acres and, in the process, ourselves. She's like a valley of conocimiento. María Elena, Mary Margaret, Cynthia, and others introduced me to the land, and I received it in much the same way as I did when I was first introduced to María Elena at UT in 2004.

And, like my meeting María Elena and in various ways the other women in this book, Alma brought me home.

The Clarity of Alma: A Reflection

Thus far I have shared how Alma de Mujer is a space for, the site of, and a force that itself inspires spiritual activism by inviting us home. Alma is a place that brought into focus a glimpse of a part of myself I didn't know existed.

That first time I took students out to Alma, they were surprised about the land and its very existence, shocked at it, enchanted by it. Now I think that yes, it was the land that caused those effects, but also—maybe as much so—what the land reveals about us. About the parts of us that are dormant thirty miles away within the dorm or classroom walls of a university. Feeling even so very far away from Austin, a short five miles down the road, both of which felt like worlds away from Alma. We reconnect to ourselves, to our souls at Alma. Alma de Mujer shows the potential for the impact of land, nature, community, connection, belonging, and self-love on the souls of the women, including myself.

I now end this chapter with a reflection that brings us back to another, earlier time in Alma's history, one that resonates in the present.

The Oaxaca Connection: The Gift of Purpose, the Path Awaits

Oaxaca City, Oaxaca, has been in my heart since the 1990s, long before I knew about Alma de Mujer, but now—in this moment that I think of it—I realize that something was brewing at that same time. It was the period when Marsha Gomez and Doña Enriqueta Contreras Contreras met, the period when Alma would become connected to Oaxaca and the medicina of the south. Something drew me to Oaxaca for the first time in 1994, which overlapped with the Zapatista protest and teacher protest, an uprising in Chiapas, Mexico, that included demands around education, land, and health care. Thirty years later, I returned—not just to Oaxaca, but to a place within myself.

The context of the *retorno* to Oaxaca was the annual Mujeres Activas en Letras y Cambio Social/Women Active in Letters and Social Change (MALCS) conference in 2023. Mary Margaret had moved to Oaxaca thirteen years earlier, and I had been feeling called there for years. So it was a huge surprise to me when I learned that the conference would take place there that year, of all years.

Mary Margaret and I made a plan to connect while I was there. She offered to pick me up so we could spend time together before the conference started. She greeted me at the airport. It had been years since we'd seen each other. She had played such an important part in my Alma story and life story, connecting me and Tommy with Doña Enriqueta for a healing ceremony in our journey to become parents.

Back in Oaxaca, I learned something profound in the summer of 2023. I discovered, all these decades later, that I was supposed to end up

FIGURE 26 From left: Mary Margaret Navar, Zapotec curandera Doña Enriqueta Contreras Contreras, and Brenda Sendejo, after sharing in a ritual held for Brenda and her spouse, Tommy, Austin, Texas, 2009. Tommy Ademski.

there this whole time. And it would be, of all places, another place of the soul—an energetically powerful and spiritually nourishing space, land Mary Margaret and her Zapotec partner Val shared, which they call the rancho and named Rancho Aldea Celeste, intended to become a spiritual retreat center.

I learned so much from Mary Margaret and Val during that trip. My teachers, friends. Being on their land, in their home, and in their presence fed my soul and lit me up in ways I hadn't felt in a very long time. Being brought into that fold seemed like a blessing like no other I'd ever felt.—but as I am writing, it occurs to me that I have felt it before, at Alma de Mujer. It's funny, I was wondering how I would get to Alma in this story, and as usual, Alma came to me. The way I feel walking on the rancho is very similar to the feeling I had going to Alma for the first time and every time since. It's a kind of coming home that goes beyond place. I can only speak to how I've experienced it, but I know my students have felt something similar at Alma. I think some of them may have even felt it in my classes. It's the same feeling I had when I first met María Elena. I don't know that I can capture it here with words. What I do know is that it feels like a reconnection to self, to soul. My retorno to Oaxaca was significant. Mary Margaret essentially told me that now it's my turn to do the work. It's my turn to pass down the medicine, as María Elena passed it down to me.

Reconnecting to that feeling I had when I first met Meme—the same feeling my students describe when they hear these stories and I teach them—reminds me that this is inner work. It's about helping people reconnect with their truth, to experience joy, to find peace, and to remember who they are. Thank you, Great Spirit and Universe, for bringing me back to these beautiful, powerful messages.

So many messages, insights, consejos, and, mostly, realizations of my *sendero*, my path, emerged in the summer of 2023 in Oaxaca. Mary Margaret now calls me Brenda Sendero, since we talked about my path and its resonance with my last name, which likely originated from the word

FIGURE 27 The author (left) and Mary Margaret Navar near the foothills of the Sierra Norte, Oaxaca. Brenda Sendejo.

sendero. Oaxaca, Oaxaca, Mexico. The site of endings and new beginnings. The site of profound spiritual awakening and a reconciliation with an identity that never quite felt right. But it was never for the reasons I thought. I think that this camino ahead has the elements of all the things I'm writing about in this book.

Find Your Alma: Places Within and Places Outside of Ourselves

Alma de Mujer is the past, present, and future. She and her community have, do, and will offer sanctuary. Alma is a model for communal and individual healing, care, love, and self-acceptance. The story of Alma, like the land itself, allows us to imagine and then make possible the emergence of our soul wisdom, our truth, our medicina. Alma is a haven for it. When we are home and feel loved, we can truly come into ourselves.

This chapter and book offer ideas for those seeking to create space to express, to make soul in their inner and outer worlds. In the next chapter, I will share my vision for the path forward, by way of an experience that I call a limpia by my community. I was gifted this limpia in the context of a presentation I gave about Alma and mujeres del alma at the El Mundo Zurdo 2024 conference. As this book concludes, it is a story that marks my transition into this final state of conocimiento: spiritual activism.

CONCLUSION

INVOKING *SABIDURÍA*

Dreaming New Worlds into Being

> *We must build a practice of contemplation into the daily routines of academic and professional life. Contemplation allows us to process and sort out anger and frustration; it gives us time for the self, time to allow compassion to surface.... In short, we need a spiritual orientation to life. According to Aung San Suu Kyi, "The quintessential revolution is that of the spirit.... It is not enough merely to call for freedom, democracy, and human rights. Without a revolution of the spirit, the forces which produced the iniquities of the old order would continue to be operative, posing a constant threat to the process of reform and regeneration." By cultivating awareness, we minimize wounding.*
>
> —GLORIA ANZALDÚA[1]

I end this book much as the story began—rooted in Alma de Mujer, the place where my connection to these women first took shape. That connection traces back to Oaxaca, Mexico. Doña Enriqueta Contreras Contreras, a grandmother to Alma de Mujer, carried Zapotec spiritual knowledge there, planting seeds that would take root in all of us. And so, I begin this chapter with a return to Oaxaca—a homecoming in every sense. A return to myself. To the part of me bound to Oaxaca, to Alma de Mujer, and to the soul of this journey—the soul of this woman.

I look at the feathers resting in my bedroom and think about how they came into my hands. They carry the convergence of worlds—and my entry into a new one. Today is Mary Margaret's birthday, and I feel called to end this chapter, not with a neat conclusion, but rather with a turning toward a new path.

On my last visit to Oaxaca, in 2024, Mary Margaret gifted me owl feathers, harvested by María Elena on a trip to South Texas with Doña Enriqueta. Mary Margaret told me it was time to walk my path—the one

FIGURE 28 Owl feathers of María Elena's on the author's journal. Brenda Sendejo.

meant to help others find and walk theirs. Senderos. Paths. Sendejo. My name. In that moment, she passed along Meme's medicina in a way that touched the deepest part of my soul—the part that had been searching for my why. I had arrived. And in that arrival, I felt whole again. I knew what it meant: It was time to share these stories. To tell you about Meme and about the women who found their way back to themselves—as an offering, as an invitation—for you to come home to you.

This book has been about how the movement taught María Elena she could change the world, including and extending beyond what is traditionally considered "activism." The worlds she refers to include our inner worlds as well as the outer. That attending to the care of our—and our communities'—bodies, minds, hearts, and souls is the work. And it is imperative that we learn to do so and do so now. The time is upon us to go inward and to embrace the feminine divine. I learned through Meme and the mujeres that expressing and enacting our truth is our medicina, medicina that we can share to change the worlds of others as much as ourselves. What I took away from Oaxaca, from Mary Margaret and Val, was a gift of a word, a palabra to capture the essence of this. *Sabiduría*: wisdom of the soul.

Spiritual Revolutions and Revelations

As I write this final chapter, I have yet another revelation. Alma de Mujer and many other inner and outer sites offer us glimpses into the possibility for spiritual revolution. In my relationships with the women in this project, I have been afforded ways of knowing, new possibilities for being, and an expansion of my soul that I could have never anticipated. I grew as a result of learning from and writing about them. Applying their lessons has changed my life, and I share them here with readers who wish to apply their wisdom and incorporate it into their own movidas, lives, and spiritual activism. May you build upon and create new practices and communities that speak to the urgent needs of our time, both in the world outside of us and, more importantly, within.

It's time to use the histories, stories, wisdom, resources, and spaces afforded us as we move into a new era in our country and world. We must draw on our power but also listen and connect with and outside of ourselves. Irene Lara notes the emphasis Anzaldúa places on "developing a critical practice of listening to one's self and others," framing it as la Bruja's lesson, incredibly pertinent in the current moment:

> She [Anzaldúa] reminds us that in order to enact liberatory change one must also develop a critical practice of listening to one's self and others. This too is la Bruja's lesson: We need to listen to our hearts, intuitions, subconscious, bodies, bodymindspirits—whatever we want to call our faculties of knowledge that include but go beyond our rational minds. As spiritual activists we need to nurture our ability to hear each other, across differences. Talking back to each other will not get us far if we do not also listen back. Sure, there are those who may refuse to listen and may refuse to recognize our full humanity. As explored in [Anzaldúa's essay] "Speaking in Tongues" there are those who—in fear of our power to revolutionarily speak, create, transform, love, and enact other acts of magic—will try to shut us up and shut us out. However, others' fears cannot stop us from working toward being whole, as individuals and as a world community. To embrace a bruja positionality is to embrace our whole being and the whole beings of other women of color, in fact of all "others" who have been similarly other-ized and fragmented. Indeed, when I listen to my being, I know that we are all connected. With Anzaldúa and other brujanderas I implore us to use all of our powers—including our erotic powers—to work toward being whole and connected with our selves, each other, the earth, and the cosmos. For it is in this connecting that transformation is possible.[2]

This book—and the work of the women within it, along with those of us inspired and taught by them—honors and amplifies spiritual epistemologies that ground today's spiritual revolution. It's a revolution rooted in a soul-deep approach to change making, world making, and radical transformation. One that invites us to create, live, heal, and simply be, from the core of who we are—now more than ever.

Places and Spaces for Spiritual Activist Movidas

A profound takeaway from this project, one that will serve us in the days, months, and years ahead, is this: Creating spaces where spirituality meets activism can be impactful for the healing and the liberation of individuals' minds, bodies, and spirits at both the individual and the communal levels. Powerful healing happens when we tend to our relationship with self—the inner work—and when we allow that healing to unfold in community. The women participants in this project offer us a road map for doing so by attending to opportunities for the soul to speak. We only need to listen so that the body can act, as has been the case with the spirit stories created and disseminated through art, politics, spiritual healing, and pedagogies.

Such movidas of spiritual activism can promote radical love of self and others, care for oneself and community, and a deep connection to Mother Earth. This is the legacy of the women in this book. This final chapter explores ways to implement women's movidas, consejos, and conocimientos in the times ahead. We all have a role, as Rosie Castro says. It's our time. Our opportunity. Our right to create spaces and other opportunities to support one another in identifying our roles and carrying out our medicina. We need not do this alone. For decades, the women in this book have created communities, built institutions, curated bodies of scholarship, developed tools, and engaged in movida praxis and spiritual activism. They have taught us the power of connecting and leaning on one another—sharing the resources at our disposal, pushing past limitations, and viewing it all as part of the healing process.

Our Medicina Emerges from the Wounds

Another takeaway from my time with the mujeres is that we each have a path we are meant to walk, a purpose we are meant to fulfill. And we can do certain things to access these paths of conocimiento, where our truth and intuition guide us. Today, I apply their wisdom to my experience of clarifying and working to live my path and purpose. This project shows how the women have created—and continue to create—spaces where others can turn inward to explore, embrace, and love themselves. Spaces where they can rewrite and release the stories that no longer serve them. For—as was my experience and that of so many of the women—it is from that place of healing, self-love, and self-respect that we can identify our medicina. Always steadfast in their views on justice and liberation, during and since the movement women have embraced their medicina. The movement taught them they could change the world, and they taught me I could change mine.

In whatever format we choose to enact movidas of spiritual activism, we can be guided by the women's commitments and energía, by their love for comunidad, gente, familia, and one another. And by the reminder that as we heal our wounds, they are also sacred sites from which our medicina emerges. Importantly, these women also offer guidance for navigating difficult times—teaching us the power of inhabiting spaces of deep love, enacting movidas, and embracing the many forms of spiritual activism. Their wisdom points us toward purpose and transformation, both personal and collective. For me, this has become a commitment to nurturing the spiritual growth and well-being of changemakers. My wounds inspire me to do this work, which I desperately needed to engage in prior to my burnout/academic susto, or soul fright, and becoming ill. Hence, my life is also a road map that I use to think about what living a healthy and holistic life entails and what it is not. I know, deep in my body, that self-care and soul care are not separate from communal care—they are integral to it. I close this book with a story of my own transition into this new consciousness—a shift that makes visible the urgent need to do the inner work of love and liberation, both for ourselves and for those we serve.

Reclaiming Self- and Soul Care: Turning Our Medicina Back On Ourselves

> *Work on the physical body will actually improve everything about you as a person. And sometimes we exhaust ourselves almost to death without remembering that for ourselves. And so it's really, really necessary to remember that need for*

> *reflection, that is how the Zapatistas do it when they close their communities and they do not let strangers in because they're in a moment of contemplation.*
>
> —INÉS HERNÁNDEZ-ÁVILA[3]

In the final interview I conducted with her for this book, Inés Hernández-Ávila shared the sentiment above about the importance of caring for the body as well as the mind and spirit. Inés recounted an experience of speaking at the Color of Violence: Violence Against Women of Color conference at the University of California, Santa Cruz, in 2000, where she addressed the importance of self-care in relation to feminist activism. The talk didn't sit well with organizers. She shared with me an account of Anzaldúa giving a talk at the University of California, Berkeley, in 2002 on her new concept at the time, the path to conocimiento, and how it was not well received by the standing-room-only crowd. They were not impressed with Anzaldúa's incorporation of spirituality. They expected something different, very different, from Gloria Anzaldúa.

Anzaldúa and her feminist contemporaries, such as Inés, like their counterparts in the movimiento across the U.S., risked much for speaking out and embracing the calling of their souls, their sabiduría. For speaking out about feminism, self-care, self-love, spirituality, injustices such as sexual violence within the movement, and more.

One of their most enduring legacies—one that is at the heart of this book—is the reminder that while dismantling oppressive systems and remaking political, religious, and educational institutions are essential, so too is doing the inner work. Anzaldúa, Inés, and their Tejana colegas insisted on this dual focus: Transformation of the world must be rooted in transformation of the self. This wisdom is especially relevant today, as we witness the consequences of institutions robbing us, trying to convince us that they are more important than we are to one another, and all at the cost of self- and communal care.

Spiritual Activism as Self-Preservation, Self-Care, and Soul Care: Lessons from Mujeres del Alma

In *A Burst of Light: Essays,* Audre Lorde notes that self-preservation is a political act because it is a way to resist oppression. Self-care, for Lorde, was never just an individual act in and of itself but instead was inextricably linked to the health and well-being of others. She believed that self-care is a necessity, not an indulgence; it is a way to reclaim power, disrupt societal norms, and preserve oneself while the world often seeks to change or eradicate us. It is a way to love all the people you love and do as much as possible of the work you still have to do.

This project on spiritual activism has shown me that it's time to reclaim self-care—and to reject the pejorative narratives that dismiss it as indulgent or selfish. Tending to our health and well-being is not a distraction; it's a necessary part of the work. Too many of us have suffered. The women in this book and their contemporaries paid great prices for the wisdom they share here and in other outlets. They have courageously countered colonial legacies of mind, body, and spirit fragmentation and contemporary forms of structural oppression and institutional violence. Their unwavering dedication has spanned decades, illuminating a path toward holistic restoration and empowerment, one that they have carved for themselves and generations that follow. In honor of their sacrifices and legacy, in acknowledgment of their bold acts of self-love, is time for us to add self, soul, and communal care to our list of survival strategies and recognize that we can and will move beyond simple survival. Spiritual activism offers us a model for that, as does Lorde's work on self-preservation, with both including communal implications of care.[4] Whether it be by finding a place in nature to connect to ourselves and rejuvenate our spirits, prioritizing sharing a meal and laughs with loved ones, setting firm boundaries on what we will or will not allow into our lives, minds, and spirits, or implementing movidas for ourselves and others—and often—these women taught me that I could change the world, and that the work must begin within.

The Final Send-Off

The words read:

> I choose to resign.
>
> Sincerely,
> Brenda

And with the sending of that email, something shifts within me. In the days since, it feels as if my soul has taken a deep breath. There is a lightness to my being. People notice it in my eyes and in my energy at the El Mundo Zurdo conference and afterward. It is the taste of liberation.

I actually scheduled that email to go out on Friday, May 18, 2024, at 8 a.m. That morning, I looked down at the clock on my phone as I sat at the desk in my hotel room, preparing for my conference presentation. Right at 8 on the dot, I thought to myself, *It's out; it's done.* And then came relief. It felt right; I felt strong. I felt all kinds of things, unable to concentrate on the final preparations for my talk. The notes I had written up the night before didn't feel aligned with me. Something was off. They were fine from an intellectual standpoint, but I was nervous about the presentation. And then, I had this moment of release. Something came to me, and what followed flowed. I reworked the presentation, not from my academic ego/intellectual self, but from my heart. What flowed during the subsequent minutes was the essence of what I ended up sharing later that afternoon. It was my spirit story, and it was my truth.

Much to my surprise, I wept during most of my presentation.

I wept out of anger for the years I'd felt alienated, traumatized, excluded, exploited, made invisible, and more. I wept for the mujer who gave away her power because she just didn't know how not to. Yet.

Then, the energy of the tears shifted.

And I wept because I was in the presence of my people.

I wept because I talked about María Elena, Martha Cotera, Mary Margaret Navar, and Cynthia Pérez, about my love for them.

I wept because I looked out into the audience and I saw my comadre Jackie, Alejandra, Inés, Irene, María, Liliana, and others. These people represented the first time I entered graduate school, the first time I published on spirituality, the first time I saw myself, really saw Brenda, and many more firsts—firsts connected to my truth.

I wept because I needed to.

The presentation felt choppy at times and rushed. While I loved the content and the people I knew in the audience, my face turned hot and a feeling of embarrassment came over me after it ended. In retrospect, I was evaluating my presentation from my ego.

After I finished, the final slide remained projected on the screen. It was a photo of Meme and Martha hugging and kissing each other at Alma de Mujer during Meme's eightieth birthday party. That photo spoke volumes about deep love, shared struggle, loss, and mutual respeto. It also symbolized something about the spiritual and the political. They aren't stringent categories. There exists a borderland where the spiritual and political meet, where they are porous.

There was something so symbolic in that photo that remained unintentionally projected. It represented Meme leaving the Raza Unida Party and her political life for a spiritually informed path. It stayed on the screen, large and present, on that day that I turned in my resignation from academia—and in many senses, the political life—stepping more fully into the spiritual life, into making soul.

During their reunion at Alma, Martha had spoken of missing María Elena when she left political life, something I have heard her echo many times over the years. Yet even though they had parted ways in the political sphere when Meme turned her focus toward the spiritual life and her

FIGURE 29 María Elena Martínez (left) and Martha Cotera share a *beso* at María Elena's eightieth birthday party at Alma de Mujer Center for Social Change, Austin, Texas, 2021. Brenda Sendejo.

own form of spiritual activism, they remained connected and always will be through a mutual love, shared struggle, and strong feminist principles. As spiritual activists.

Following my presentation at the conference, something very unexpected happened. As I sat among my gente in an academic environment, with Meme and Martha projected behind me, and we started sharing, I felt a sense of ease. Of being held. Of belonging. As it had all those years prior, academia shifted with that initial encuentro with María Elena, and I felt something otherwise. I had spoken my truth, and not even an academic space could rob me of that. It was an unfamiliar sensation—something I never once experienced in my fourteen years at the institution from which I had just resigned. Was it the power of speaking my truth, from my soul? Of ripping off the cara/mask and revealing myself? Something I did not feel safe about before that moment and that I now know I was just not ready to do? What I learned, as I reflect back on my years with this project, the mujeres, and since that presentation, is that certain times and places are there to teach us lessons. Some are meant to teach us hard lessons that will become part of our medicina, and others help us learn how to come into our true selves.

But in that moment in San Antonio, Texas, in 2024, I was on a university campus where I experienced something transformational, thanks in large part to the people in attendance. It was a space where I could fully, vulnerably, messily cry and be myself. This has helped me to become more whole—closer to myself—and to usher in the final stage of conocimiento.

A Going-Away Limpia

On that Friday afternoon in May, the people in that room, my community, engaged in communal care. And in my heart, I will always feel it as a limpia. This, however, was far from what I thought after I finished, hanging my head, asking myself, *What did I just do?* I had presented through tears and felt scattered, unorganized. Yet what I'd done came from my heart. It was a true reflection of me and of what matters to me.

The exchanges that followed were like salve on my wounds. It felt as if I had shed the skin of white supremacy, self-doubt, and trauma. Marivel

Danielson, a scholar I had met in my early years of graduate school, applauded my vulnerability and said that we don't allow ourselves to cry enough, to express our emotions as part of this journey. Others chimed in. Irene Lara said that we need to be able to speak our truth. We had a peaceful and powerful plática. It was not the response I expected.

Later that week I emailed Inés and Irene to send them photos from the session they presented at the conference. I told them:

> I also wish to express my deep gratitude to you both for attending my presentation. I had submitted my resignation to Southwestern that morning and the energía around that move has been heavy and liberating both. The experience in the session felt like a limpia, with my tears shedding the old energy I've been carrying around from Southwestern and the beautiful and supportive words of audience members acting like rosemary brushing up against my soul and skin. Seeing you both in the audience—two mujeres who have deeply inspired me as an academic, spiritual seeker and being, mother and mujer—meant so much to me in this particular time in my life and on this path of conocimiento. So, mil gracias to you both!

I received an email response from Inés: "I was happy to be in your session. I'm so glad you felt the limpia from all the love and appreciation for your work!" She followed up by telling me to, yes, "release, release, release" all of the toxic energy from my space, that indeed it was a liberatory

FIGURE 30 From left: Irene Lara, Inés Hernández-Ávila, and Brenda Sendejo at El Mundo Zurdo conference, Trinity University, San Antonio, Texas, 2024.

move and "qué bueno!"[5] Coming from a participant in this project, Inés's response was a poignant example of how spiritual activism extends beyond our physical interactions with one another.

My 2024 El Mundo Zurdo conference presentation felt like a Chicana coming-of-age ceremony. In the coming days and months I would feel a sense of renewal and healing—what ceremony is said to inspire.[6] With multiple generations gathered, the room was a container for the transition that would mark my transformation from one identity into the next. My community helped usher me through conocimiento. I didn't have to do it alone, far from it. Who would've guessed that the day I submitted my resignation was the day that my gente would embrace me for being me? Unapologetically and fully me. As Jackie said in her text after the presentation, speaking my truth spoke to the audience.

In the several months since that time and this writing, I have grown exponentially into my skin and soul. I now know my wounds are my medicina. And I hope that through this story, others may see in themselves and in their communities the potential for healing—within or outside of academia, but always, always, within themselves.

Arriving at the Final Stage of Conocimiento: Expressing Our Medicinas on the Camino Ahead

The women in this project taught me that we are here—on this earth, at this time—to turn inward and connect with our souls. From that place of deep knowing, we are called to share our gifts and live out our medicina. It is what we are here for: to live our purpose, guided by the wisdom of our souls.

Within the pages of spirit stories, encuentros, moments of struggle, and moments of collective healing—and within each of us—there exist strategies for finding joy, love, and justice in the medicine we share with the world. These times offer us an invitation to act in the way each of us is called to. To look deeply within. To contemplate. To listen to the calling of the soul. And then, when it is time, to act. For when we make soul like this, we create and we change ourselves. And when we change ourselves, well, you know by now that . . . we change the world.[7]

Because María Elena shared her gifts, I am here. I am here because Martha, Mary Margaret, Carmen, Inés, Norma, Santa, Rosie, Sister Te-

FIGURE 31 The author's child, Luna (right), handing María Elena Martínez a copy of *Voices from the Ancestors*. This photo is symbolic of passing down of wisdom and spirit stories between generations, as María Elena would—along with Martha, Modesta, Gloria Quesada, Jackie, Alicia, Naya, and other wise women—write offerings of soul wisdom to my children Jude and Luna, to be shared with all children.

resa, Susana, Alicia, Velia, and *las dos* Glorias—Gloria Anzaldúa and my dear mother, who gave me gifts only a mother could—shared *their* gifts. It is now time for me to do the same. May this book offer you medicina on your camino. May it remind you that protecting your light and keeping it sacred is your birthright. And that when you shine, you allow others to do so.[8]

Permiso

October 18, 2005
Today I met with María Elena. We had a wonderful talk. She says her purpose on earth is to give—to offer comfort. Today, we talked, and she really helped me see some things very clearly. I asked her if she would work with

FIGURE 32 María Elena Martínez (left) and the author, 2019. Brenda Sendejo.

> me on my doctoral research, to which she responded, "Yes, mi'jita, I'll work with you. I trust you. Not everyone I would, but I trust you."

I located the above journal entry in the final weeks of completing this manuscript. As I think about its divine timing, I am reminded of the gift I was given, a gift to treasure and honor, to handle with respeto and care. I have intended with all of my heart to do justice to the stories I humbly share here. I know these stories are gifts to give, to put out into the world. And the time is now.

Later in the journal entry, I reflect on how María Elena helped me see the PhD for what it is. And that if I desire it, I should strive for it, but to remember not to put everything into it. The gift of that first encuentro has stayed with me and at different times in my life lands differently and more deeply. Today those words signify, *Don't get caught up in the need for external validation, competitiveness, and hyperindividualism of the academy or any other institution. Don't give everything and allow external forces to crush your spirit.*

Being Bold in Changing the World

I could not have arrived here, at the place of spiritual activism, without each and every encounter in my life that preceded the writing of this final section of the book. What are the moments in our lives that we need to "be bold," as Inés told me? What moments do we take hold of and not waver before, but choose to express? With the feathers she gave me in Oaxaca, Mary Margaret also gave me permiso to express my true self. To share my medicina with her blessing and that of Meme. To listen to my heart, and to take action. To embrace my medicine and to share it out with the world. For it is from that place that we can dream new ones into being.

The feathers remind me to be bold—to show up as my whole self, just like María Elena modeled. They call me to be a guide for others on their journeys within, just as Mary Margaret was for me when she named me Brenda Sendero.

The feathers remind me to tell stories from the pains, sorrows, realities, and contradictions of my lived experiences and always, always, from the depth of my soul, without apology, as the mujeres del alma and so many of their contemporaries have done. They remind me—all of us—to sing the songs only we can sing and use our voices to make change.

Their souls spoke, and their bodies acted. This book is my attempt at doing so with the gifts I was given. May you find peace on your sendero guided by the wisdom of your soul, these mujeres del alma, and your own ancestors, spirit guides, and light. These women taught me I could change the world with my medicina in the ways only I was put here on this earth to do. And you can, too.

NOTES

Preface

1. I use *medicina* and *medicine* interchangeably throughout the book. The context is in terms of the gifts and healing we each possess within us—both spiritual healing and knowledge. I am inspired by Patrisia Gonzales's work in *Red Medicine* and her assertion that birthing and "the attendant ceremonies" along with Indigenous knowledge are medicinal in that they "address soul loss, land loss, and cultural and spiritual fragmentation." I propose that the women in this project do work that addresses such soul loss brought on by the lingering effects of colonization, such as the mind-body-spirit split, a gender binary, and loss of ancestral and Indigenous ways of knowing and being. See Patrisia Gonzales, *Red Medicine: Traditional Indigenous Rites of Birthing and Healing* (University of Arizona Press, 2012), xvii.
2. María Elena Martínez, informal conversation with Brenda Sendejo, Austin, Texas, 2015.
3. Gloria, Anzaldúa, ed. *Making Face, Making Soul/Haciendo Caras: Creative and Critical Perspectives by Feminists of Color* (Aunt Lute Books, 1990), xxiv.
4. See the work of Valarie Kaur on revolutionary love: *See No Stranger: A Memoir and Manifesto of Revolutionary Love* (One World, 2021) and *Sage Warrior: Wake to Oneness, Practical Pleasure, Choose Courage, Become Victory* (One World, 2024). Kaur, an activist, author, and attorney, advocates for love in the face of hate and terror, a particularly important stance in this historical moment. However, the idea of love as revolutionary and as a vital aspect of any movement was also embedded in the feminist activism of the women in this book—love for one another, their communities, their families and *cultura*, and the causes for which they fought, sacrificed, and struggled, in some cases even resulting in death threats.

5. See Brenda Sendejo, "The Space in Between: Exploring the Development of Chicana Feminist Thought in Central Texas," in *Chicana Movidas: New Narratives of Activism and Feminism in the Movement Era*, ed. Dionne Espinoza, María Eugenia Cotera, and Maylei Blackwell (University of Texas Press, 2018), 189–211. As I state in "The Space In Between": "Cotera notes that the CRLC was inspired by the work of feminists in California such as Anna Nieto Gomez and others. Print materials developed and disseminated by Chicanas in California proved valuable to Tejana feminists, and they in return drew on the materials created by Cotera and the CRLC—another illustration of the collaborative model of women of color and Chicana feminist thought" (194). Also see María Eugenia Cotera, *Fleshing the Archive: An Intimate Genealogy of Chicana Knowledge Praxis* (University of Texas Press, 2026). Drawing on the substantial archives of the Chicana por mi Raza Digital Memory Project and Archive, Cotera offers an extensive analysis of Chicana feminist knowledge production and memory work across the United States in the late 1960s and early 1970s.
6. Inés Hernández-Ávila shared that, in terms of transformation, "hope is active, hope is not passive," leading me to think about hope as possibility, expansion, and connected to becoming. Inés Hernández-Ávila, virtual interview by Brenda Sendejo, February 9, 2025.
7. The Raza Unida Party Women's Oral History Project Interviews are housed in the Center for Mexican American Studies Records, Nettie Lee Benson Latin American Collection, University of Texas Libraries, the University of Texas at Austin. The students who contributed to the oral history project by conducting interviews and organizing public roundtables included Amelia Abreau, Rachel Carreon, Betty Harrison, Linda Ho, Hortensia Palomares, Sara Schueneman-Ayala, Rebecca Snow, and Teresa Taylor.
8. Emilio Zamora, "Raza Unida Party Women in Texas: Oral History, Pedagogy, and Historical Interpretation." *U.S. Latina & Latino Oral History Journal* 1 (2017): 30.
9. A huipil is a woven blouse created and worn by Latin American Indigenous groups such as the Maya of Guatemala, Southern Mexico, and Belize. The patterns on these textiles are known to have symbolic meaning and oftentimes tell stories about that particular group's history or worldviews.
10. As of this writing, there are concerted efforts and legislation across Texas to dismantle women's and gender studies, feminist studies, and ethnic studies programs and centers, as well as to surveil curricula of classes associated with these fields at numerous schools, including UT Austin. Women in this book, including Norma Cantú, Inés Hernández-Ávila, Martha Cotera, and Yolanda Chávez Leyva, struggled and sacrificed much to build and sustain such programs and bodies of scholarship since the 1960s.
11. See Jody A. Marín and Norma E. Cantú (eds.), *¡Somos Tejanas! Chicana Identity and Culture in Texas* (University of Texas Press, 2025), for an expansive collection of creative and scholarly works on Tejanx lived experiences and historical

contexts out of which they emerged, which include important historical recovery projects that counter historical silences and erasures. As Marín and Cantú note, "Being Tejanx means we are part of the majority in Texas but we are not part of the ruling class. In short, being Tejanx means having the cultural and linguistic hybridity and fluidity of our working-class Chicanx identity within the milieu of a constructed and historically oppressive US-Mexico borderland that is home" (18).

12. María Cotera, "Unpacking Our Mothers' Libraries: Practices of Chicana Memory Before and After the Digital Turn," in *Chicana Movidas: New Narratives of Activism and Feminism in the Movement Era*, ed. Dionne Espinoza, María Eugenia Cotera, and Maylei Blackwell (University of Texas Press, 2018), 299–316. My use of *encuentro* is inspired by María Cotera's discussion of Chicana memory praxis and the power of the encuentro: "A praxis of collecting and re-collecting, of membering and re-membering, Chicana practices of memory involve an active encuentro with the past to create knowledges that engage the present in critical ways. Neither memorializing nor overly wedded to an idealized notion of historical facticity, Chicana memory practice deploys the past to theorize the present and to move its practitioners through what Anzaldúa has called the path to *conocimiento*" (302).

13. María Elena Martínez, interview by Rebecca Snow, April 7, 2004, box 158, item 13–17, Center for Mexican American Studies Records, Nettie Lee Benson Latin American Collection, University of Texas Libraries, University of Texas at Austin. All subsequent quotes from María Elena are from this interview, unless otherwise noted. María Elena told us of her experience as the first woman to lead a political party in Texas as RUP's last state chair, from 1976 to 1978. In regard to her election to chair, she told us that the male contingent of the party originally approached her to run for vice chair. In her oral history interview she stated, "I said, 'Well, I really don't think we should automatically just say that we can only run for vice chair, I want to run for state chairperson.'" She said that until then, neither men nor women considered that women could take the RUP chairmanship.

14. In addition to María Elena Martínez, other women who took part in the oral history project who were in Mujeres por la Raza include Rosie Castro, Evey Chapa, Martha Cotera, and Luz Bazán Gutiérrez. Within the political spaces that gave rise to Mujeres por la Raza, feminist consciousness often met resistance. Chicana feminists were sometimes labeled *vendidas*, or "sell-outs," by men and women who argued that feminist critiques aligned Chicanas with the Anglo women's movement and threatened Chicano unity. As Alma García notes in *Chicana Feminist Thought: The Basic Historical Writings* (Routledge, 1997), these tensions were commonly framed as a divide between loyalists *and* feminists. Loyalists—often married women with families—maintained that the movement should prioritize Mexican American communities and family well-being over the individual woman. Feminists within Mujeres countered that

feminism was fundamentally about family and collective liberation, insisting that sexism weakened the movement itself. Martha Cotera, also married with a family, exemplified this stance through a feminist praxis that challenged patriarchy while remaining deeply committed to the movement's broader political aims. María Eugenia Cotera notes that her father, movement activist Juan Cotera, supported her mother Martha's work "back in the day, even in the face of machistas who questioned his manhood for doing so." María Cotera, *Fleshing the Archive*, 217.

15. María Elena also participated in organizing Teatro Chicano (a theater group for the people that explored movement-related themes) during her time at UT. After MAYO she went on to work with RUP and organized the party's first statewide convention. She was elected to be RUP Texas vice chair for the 1974–1976 term and served as chair in 1976–1987. She also participated in the Action for Better Citizens Committee in activities such as voter registration, immigration causes, and volunteer legal aid work as an interpreter. See "Cotera and Martínez, María Elena Martínez: State Chairwoman; Raza Unida Party, Austin, Texas," undated, box 1, folder 14, María Elena Martínez Papers, Nettie Lee Benson Latin American Collection, University of Texas at Austin.

16. The spring 2004 course was called Memory, History, and Oral Narratives: Mexican American Politics in Texas History. As part of the course, Professor Emilio Zamora, himself a former Raza Unida Party member and movement activist, as well as a friend to and contemporary of the women, initiated the Women of La Raza Unida Party Oral History Project and served as its director. He also supported the creation of UT Austin's Center for Mexican American Studies and was on the first advisory board of the Chicana Research and Learning Center; see María Cotera, *Fleshing the Archive*. Martha Cotera assisted in a number of class activities and is credited by Zamora with proposing the idea of an oral history project on RUP women. According to Cotera, women were the "backbone" of the party (as quoted and elaborated upon in Zamora, "Raza Unida Party Women in Texas"). The course involved graduate students assisting with the research and collection of oral history interviews. Professor Zamora arranged for the women to be interviewed by my classmates and me about their political involvement in RUP during the Chicana and Chicano movement. The purpose of the course was to expose students to the methodology and theory of oral history through hands-on experiences in collecting and analyzing oral narratives from women who achieved prominence in the Mexican American civil rights movement from the 1960s to the present. In addition to offering us the opportunity to learn about and conduct interviews with participants in the historic third-party politics of the 1970s and 1980s, the course hosted three public testimonio fora. During the round table discussions the nine former RUP members from various parts of the state offered testimonies on their lives and political histories as community activists. The women included Evey Chapa (Corpus Christi), María Elena Martínez (Austin), Luz Bazán Gutiérrez (Yakima,

Washington), María Jiménez (Houston), Linda del Toro (Austin), Alma Canales (Waco), Angelita Mendoza Waterhouse (Austin), Elvia Rios (McAllen), and Martha Cotera (Austin). See Zamora, "Raza Unida Party Women in Texas"; see also Dionne Espinoza, "'The Partido Belongs to Those Who Will Work for It': Chicana Organizing and Leadership in the Texas Raza Unida Party, 1970–1980," *Aztlán* 36, no. 1 (Spring 2011): 191–210.

17. María Elena has acquired knowledge on the use of herbs through her own study, by attending herb symposiums and workshops, and by apprenticing with Zapotec *curandera* (healer) and *partera* (midwife) Doña Enriqueta Contreras Contreras. María Elena has also studied with other Mexican Indigenous curanderas: Doña Modesta Lavana, a curandera from Hueyapan, Morelos, and Doña Julieta Casimiro Estrada from Huautla de Jiménez, Oaxaca. All three teachers have gone to Austin to teach and do healing sessions in the community. María Elena studies homeopathic remedies and lives an earth-friendly and environmentally conscious lifestyle. She identifies herself as "a shamanic practitioner who uses shamanic techniques which can be found in many shamanic cultures throughout the world." She is an active member of the Foundation for Shamanic Studies and the Society for Shamanic Practice, as well as a minister with the Circle of the Sacred Earth, a church of animism fostering shamanic principles and practice. She began her studies of shamanism in the early 1990s, and many of her teachers taught with the Foundation for Shamanic Studies, including Dana Kilgore, Sandra Ingerman, and Hank Wesselman.
18. See Aída Hurtado, *Intersectional Chicana Feminisms* (University of Arizona Press, 2020) for more on the life and work of Chicana scholar Martha P. Cotera.
19. These are prolific scholars. For a selection of their scholarship, please see their works listed in the bibliography.
20. Gloria Anzaldúa, *Borderlands/La Frontera: The New Mestiza*, 4th ed. (Aunt Lute Books, 2012), 19.
21. Cherríe Moraga and Gloria Anzaldúa (eds.), *This Bridge Called My Back: Writings by Radical Women of Color* (SUNY Press, 2021).

Introduction

1. Gloria Anzaldúa (ed.), *Making Face, Making Soul/Haciendo Caras: Creative and Critical Perspectives by Feminists of Color* (Aunt Lute Books, 1990), xvi. Anzaldúa also cites Inés Hernández-Ávila, "'Triumph Is a Sweet Song—the One You Know': The Voices of Gloria Anzaldúa, Wendy Rose, and Joy Harjo," presentation at the Modern Language Association Conference, New Orleans, December 1988.
2. AnaLouise Keating, "'I'm a Citizen of the Universe': Gloria Anzaldúa's Spiritual Activism as Catalyst for Social Change," *Feminist Studies* 34, nos. 1–2 (Spring/Summer 2008): 53–69. Keating offers deep insight into what she names as Anzaldúa's "politics of spirit" (54)—that is, as she notes, the bridging of seemingly opposing ideas of spirituality and activism. Rather, Keating proposes that

for Anzaldúa, "these very different worlds and worldviews are inseparable (although not identical). She embraces the apparent contradiction and insists that the spiritual/material, inner/outer, individual/collective dimensions of life are parts of a larger whole, joined in a complex, interwoven pattern. Anzaldúa's spiritual activism offers a visionary yet experientially based epistemology and ethics. Spiritual activism is spirituality for social change, spirituality that posits a relational worldview and uses this holistic worldview to transform one's self and one's worlds" (54). Also see Keating, "Perspectives: Spiritual Activism, Social Transformation, and the Politics of Spirit," in *Entre Mundos/Among Worlds: New Perspectives on Gloria Anzaldúa*, ed. AnaLouise Keating (Palgrave Macmillan, 2005).

3. The impact of that initial encounter with María Elena was so profound that it led me to shift my research focus toward the very subject of this book: Chicana spiritual activism in Texas since the movement era. Delving into spirituality, or the work of connecting with one's inner truth—including my own—was never on my radar as a subject for "research." Back then, such an idea seemed far-fetched. I had been conditioned to view certain kinds of research as more "valid." And Chicana spirituality and activism were just beginning to emerge as a subfield; the literature was at its very early stages. My use of radical inclusivity describes María Elena's acceptance of all people. Her home and the ceremonies and healing circles she hosted and led were open to anyone and everyone regardless of their identities or positionalities.
4. "Linguistic terrorism" is a term coined by Gloria Anzaldúa. It describes the violence of having one's native language denied them and being forced to adopt the dominant language, as was practiced in South Texas during the Jim Crow era. Corporal punishment was used against children for speaking Spanish in school. See Gloria Anzaldúa and AnaLouise Keating, *Borderlands/La Frontera: The New Mestiza*, 4th ed. (Aunt Lute Books, 2012).
5. Kazu Haga, Bernard LaFayette, and David C. Jehnsen, *Healing Resistance: A Radically Different Response to Harm* (Parallax Press, 2020).
6. The activism of movement participants like Martha, María Elena, and Emilio Zamora not only resulted in the creation of a Chicano studies program at the University of Texas at Austin but also, as Chicana historian and former student of Zamora Lilia Rosas has observed, "created the conditions" for future cohorts of Chicanx graduate students to find mentorship and support, to pursue doctoral research topics like those that inspired this book, and to succeed as scholars across numerous disciplines within Chicana and Chicano studies nationwide.
7. Brenda Sendejo, "Methodologies of the Spirit: Reclaiming Our Lady of Guadalupe and Discovering Tonantzin Within and Beyond the Nepantla of Academia," in *Fleshing the Spirit: Spirituality and Activism in Chicana, Latina, and Indigenous Women's Lives*, ed. Elisa Facio and Irene Lara (University of Arizona Press, 2014), 95–113.

8. Teresa Palomo Acosta and Ruthe Winegarden, *Las Tejanas: 300 Years of History* (University of Texas Press, 2020); Teresa Palomo Acosta, *Tejanaland: A Writing Life in Four Acts* (Texas A&M University Press, 2021).
9. I would interview Mrs. Orozco for the Voces Oral History Project at UT Austin, where I was also able to access her previous interview, conducted by Desirée Mata, and other World War II–era Tejana oral histories. Mrs. Orozco had a significant influence on the educational trajectory and feminist development of her daughters, including Tejana historian Cynthia Orozco as well as Sylvia Orozco. Both Cynthia and Sylvia allowed me to interview them for an essay I would write featuring their mother. See Brenda Sendejo, "Mother's Legacy: Cultivating Chicana Consciousness During the War Years," in *Beyond the Latino World War II Hero: The Social and Political Legacy of a Generation*, ed. Maggie Rivas-Rodriguez and Emilio Zamora (University of Texas Press, 2009), 156–77. Also see Aurora Orozco, "Dejar Mi Idioma Jamás (Never Abandon My Language)," The Latina History Project, https://latinahistoryproject.southwestern.edu/items/show/12.
10. Samantha Rodriguez and Stalina Emmanuelle Villarreal, "María Jiménez: Reflexiones on Traversing Multiple Fronteras in the South," in *Chicana Movidas: New Narratives of Activism and Feminism in the Movement Era*, ed. Dionne Espinoza, María Eugenia Cotera, and Maylei Blackwell (University of Texas Press, 2018), 276–89. Zamora would write in "Raza Unida Party Women in Texas" about Jiménez, "She explained that while her authoritarian father had taught her to speak boldly for social justice, her mother had shown her how to speak to power, a skill that she now uses when advocating for immigrant rights" (40).
11. See the "Main Building: Chicanos Protest UT Administration's Unwillingness to Create New Degree at the Main Building" on the "Rocking the Status Quo": Racial Justice Struggles in Austin website, https://storymaps.arcgis.com/stories/ff1e660665584c6ba2d15916a93c165e, which notes, "On Friday, January 28, 1972, members of MAYO respectfully disturbed the Board of Regents' meeting occurring inside the Tower. Students made loud noises and gathered a rowdy crowd to gain the board's attention. Finally, a few students went inside the meeting to negotiate directly with UT's Board of Regents. The students ultimately pressured the Administration into establishing a Mexican American Studies degree-granting program within the Ethnic Studies Department. One such student, Hortensia Palomares, said that 'everyone is enriched when it's not just one-sided history' and she beamed with pride as she recalled declaring her major as Mexican American Studies."
12. For documentary footage of Austin's Chicano civil rights participants, including María Elena Martínez, see the *Austin Revealed* episode "Chicano Civil Rights: Chicano Identity," March 23, 2016, PBS, https://www.pbs.org/video/austin-revealed-austin-revealed-chicano-civil-rights-chicano-identity.
13. Mujeres Activas en Letras y Cambio Social/Women Active in Letters and Social Change (MALCS) is a national professional organization of Chicanas, Latinas,

and Native American women and gender nonconforming activists, academics, and community members. The MALCS mission is "to work toward the support, education and dissemination of Chicana/Latina and Native American women's issues" (see https://malcs.org/about). MALCS hosts an annual Summer Institute where Chicanas/Latinas and Native American women from a variety of institutions come together to network, share information, offer support, and reenergize.

14. Brenda Sendejo, "The Cultural Production of Spiritual Activisms: Gender, Social Justice, and the Remaking of Religion in the Borderlands," *Chicana/Latina Studies* 12, no. 2 (Spring 2013): 59–109.
15. See Center for the Study of the Southwest, "East Austin Brown Berets Geography," Texas State University, https://www.txst.edu/cssw/news-events/cssw-projects-archive/brown-beret.html.
16. The SSGA hosts a conference every eighteen months, gathering scholars, artists, activists, and community members to explore the vast impact of Anzaldúa, her work, and its relevance in contemporary times. The space offers an energy distinct from that of a typical academic conference in its inclusion of and connection to the local community and various artistic, literary, and spiritual expressions and research.
17. See Sendejo, "The Cultural Production of Spiritual Activisms."
18. María Elena Martínez would reference Inés as "one of the major leaders in the Houston area—a major leader in RUP in Houston." Personal communication with Brenda Sendejo, 2018.
19. "Sister Teresa" is a pseudonym used at the request of this participant.
20. I credit Dr. Inés Hernández-Ávila for pointing out the immense variation in women's involvement in the movement.
21. As Yolanda Chávez Leyva notes, she was a friend and student of Anzaldúa in the 1970s. See Leyva, "Gloria Anzaldúa's Legacy Will Continue to Inspire Generations." *The Progressive Magazine*, June 9, 2004, https://progressive.org/op-eds/gloria-anzaldua-s-legacy-will-continue-inspire-generations/.
22. Mary Margaret knew many of the women mentioned above but was not active in the RUP era. She is a cultural anthropologist and spiritual activist, and she coined María Elena's nickname "Meme" as a loving gesture.
23. Here Santa references a social division between Mexican Americans and Anglos and a hostile racial climate in Kingsville. It was due in part to the opening of the King Ranch in 1953 and the shift from agriculture to a ranching economy in South Texas, which altered the social order by placing Mexicans as laborers rather than landowners on the ranch. Santa Barraza, interview by Brenda Sendejo, Kingsville, Texas, March 2009.
24. Mujeres Artistas del Suroeste (MAS) was a Latina arts network established in Austin by Santa Barraza and Nora González Dodson in 1977. The primary goal of the organization was to promote professional opportunities for Latina artists, as well as to educate local communities through their exhibitions and

special functions. The collective organized several important exhibitions, both in and outside of Texas, of photography, sculpture, and visual arts. The work of artists who showed under the banner of MAS represented numerous styles and themes, ranging from the political to the supernatural. The majority of MAS members lived in San Antonio, Austin, or Laredo. Its members included Santa Barraza, Carolina Flores, Sylvia Orozco, Carmen Rodríguez, and Modesta Barbina Treviño, among others. In the mid-1980s several MAS members left Texas for career opportunities elsewhere, and the organization folded. See María-Christina García, "Mujeres Artistas del Suroeste," *Handbook of Texas Online*, Texas State Historical Association, https://www.tshaonline.org/handbook/entries/mujeres-artistas-del-suroeste.

25. For some, reclaiming their Indigenous heritage during the Chicano movement involved reclaiming a spiritual heritage as well. See Elisa Diana Huerta, "Embodied Recuperations: Performance, Indigeneity, and Danza Azteca," in *Dancing Across Borders: Danzas y Bailes Mexicanos*, ed. Olga Nájera-Ramírez, Norma E. Cantú, and Brenda M. Romero (University of Illinois Press, 2009), 3–18. The dance form *danza azteca* is inspired by "pre-Columbian choreographies and pedagogies" that can be found in contemporary Mexico. These folk dances, or danzas, meld pre-Columbian and Catholic influences whose format generally relies on a group formation. They are ceremonial and have spiritual or religious connotations. The practice of danza in the United States, while less present than in Mexico, is said to have emerged during the Chicano movement as part of the act of self-determination and recovery of their ethnic heritage by Chicanos (8). As Huerta notes, however, it is important to state that while danza azteca is associated with emerging during this time period, it and other Indigenous dance and cultural traditions were practiced long before the 1960s in the United States. In addition to the danza azteca tradition there is also the *danza conchera* tradition, "marked by significant political and spiritual differences" (9). One key difference is that *concheros* have a more distinct Catholic influence, as indicated by the naming of their groups after Catholic saints.

26. Inés Hernández-Ávila, "Foreword: A Meditation," in Elisa Facio and Irene Lara, *Fleshing the Spirit: Spirituality and Activism in Chicana, Latina, and Indigenous Women's Lives* (University of Arizona Press, 2014), xiv–xv. With "sabor a rebeldía," Hernández-Ávila cites Berenice Dimas's piece "Queerandermiso," 76–80. *Sabor a rebeldía* translates to "flavor of rebellion." It is noteworthy that this anthology—the first to examine spirituality and activism in Chicana, Latina, and Indigenous women's lives—would be the first time I published on spirituality and activism, and contributors include Norma Cantú along with Hernández-Ávila.

27. Enciso-Litschi, Alicia. "Con Alma: Dialogues in Decolonizing Counseling—Reciprocal Ethnographic Explorations in Indigenous Spaces for Community Healing," PhD diss., University of Texas at Austin, 2014, 123–24, https://www.zlibrary.to/dl/con-alma-dialogues-in-decolonizing-counseling.

28. Gloria Anzaldúa, "now let us shift . . . the path of conocimiento . . . inner works, public acts," in *This Bridge We Call Home: Radical Visions for Transformation*, ed. Gloria E. Anzaldúa and AnaLouise Keating (Routledge, 2002), 544.
29. Emma Pérez, *The Decolonial Imaginary: Writing Chicanas into History* (Indiana University Press, 1999). Pérez challenges the regimes of power associated with the "colonial imaginary" by proposing the "decolonial imaginary," which offers opportunities for the negotiation and decolonization of identities, historiographies, and epistemologies and disputes the partiality of historical narratives and archives. She argues, "There is no pure, authentic, original history. There are only stories—many stories" (xv).
30. Anzaldúa, "now let us shift . . . ," 574.
31. Keating, "'I'm a Citizen of the Universe,'" 57.
32. Anzaldúa herself wrote many a spirit story, though her theories on spirituality were pushed to the margins until recently; mainstream, disciplinary-specific scholars were most focused on her borderlands theories.
33. Sendejo, "Methodologies of the Spirit."
34. Anzaldúa, "now let us shift . . ."
35. Brenda Sendejo, "The Face of God Has Changed: Tejana Spiritual Cultural Production and the Politics of Spirituality," PhD diss., University of Texas at Austin, 2011.
36. Gloria Anzaldúa and AnaLouise Keating, *Light in the Dark/Luz en lo Oscuro: Rewriting Identity, Spirituality, Reality* (Duke University Press, 2015).
37. Dionne Espinoza, María Eugenia Cotera, and Maylei Blackwell (eds.), *Chicana Movidas: New Narratives of Activism and Feminism in the Movement Era* (University of Texas Press, 2018); Chicana por Mi Raza Digital Memory Project and Archive, founded in 2009 by María Cotera and Linda García Merchant, https://www.chicanapormiraza.org/. According to the website, "The Chicana por mi Raza Digital Memory Collective is a group of researchers, educators, students, archivists, and technologists dedicated to preserving imperiled Chicanx and Latinx histories of the long civil rights era. Started by María Cotera and Linda Garcia Merchant in 2009, CPMR has traveled to over one dozen states to collect hundreds of hours of oral histories with notable Chicanas, Latinas, and allies. The project has also scanned personal archives for preservation and access. Using largely volunteer and student labor, CPMR offers a model for grassroots digital history that encourages further research into understudied aspects of the American experience. The overarching objective of the project is to provide broad-based public access to oral histories, material culture, correspondence, and rare out-of-print publications for use in both scholarly research and the classroom."
38. The seminal works of scholars who precede me inform this project by demonstrating that, as Cynthia Orozco states, "we [Tejanas] had a past that is specific to our ethnicity, race, region, and gender." Orozco quoted in Teresa Palomo Acosta and Ruthe Winegarten, *Las Tejanas: 300 Years of History* (University of

Texas Press, 2003), x. In addition to art and creative writing, this growing body of work on Tejana life and culture by Tejanas includes the foundational scholarship of Martha Cotera on Chicana history and heritage; testimonio and historical writings by historian Yolanda Chávez Leyva; works by scholar and poet Inés Hernández-Ávila; literature and folklore by scholar and poet Norma E. Cantú; and literature by author-poet Carmen Tafolla. Martha Cotera and María Cotera have also been instrumental in bringing to light the contributions of folklorist Jovita González de Mireles, an early Tejana scholar whose examination of Tejana life was likely the first anthropological account of Tejana experiences.

39. Facio and Lara's *Fleshing the Spirit* helped propel my own work on spiritual activism and my conception of "methodologies of the spirit." The volume was instrumental for raising critical awareness about spirituality and activism as formidable areas for scholarly inquiry. Lara Medina and Martha R. Gonzales (eds.), *Voices from the Ancestors* (University of Arizona Press, 2019), to which I also contributed, is a more recent compilation of great importance in the field, in particular because of its vast array of multigenre pieces, including prose, ceremony, poetry, and instructional works such as on *limpias,* or spiritual cleansings. My work in *Voices from the Ancestors* allowed me to bring multiple generations of Chicanas and their spiritual consejos and blessings to my children. Both anthologies promote a feminist, decolonial, and spiritual editorial praxis and represent vital contributions to the field of Chicana, Latina, and Indigenous spirituality, activism, spiritual identities and expressions, and healing practices.
40. Anzaldúa, "now let us shift . . . ," 540.
41. My intention is to do justice to the stories and lives of las mujeres with this humble offering. All oversights and errors are mine and mine alone.

Chapter 1

1. Patrisia Gonzales, *Red Medicine: Traditional Indigenous Rites of Birthing and Healing* (University of Arizona Press, 2012), xvii.
2. Per Patrisia Gonzales's image of the needle of the maguey as a needle weaving together stories, I see in the artwork on the cover of this book, Santa Barraza's *Guadalupe Cuando Joven,* a symbol of this book as the "medicine of stories" in the weaving together of women's stories with one another, nature, and spirit.
3. I borrow "survival knowledges" from María Eugenia Cotera, "Nuestra Autohistoria," panel presentation, Recovering the U.S. Hispanic Literary Heritage Conference, University of Houston, February 20–22, 2020.
4. María Elena Martínez, interview by Rebecca Snow, April 7, 2004, box 158, item 13–17, Center for Mexican American Studies Records, Nettie Lee Benson Latin American Collection, University of Texas Libraries, University of Texas at Austin.
5. As a bilingual educator of thirty years, María Elena has also changed the inner worlds of thousands of children and families.

6. I find it interesting that María Elena said the movement taught her she could change the world and that Anzaldúa writes about how changing ourselves can change the world in her work on spiritual activism. María Elena read Anzaldúa but had rarely referenced her work to me. It is a fascinating alignment in these spiritual activists' lives and perspectives on activism.
7. Gloria Anzaldúa (ed.), *Making Face, Making Soul/Haciendo Caras: Creative and Critical Perspectives by Feminists of Color* (Aunt Lute Books, 1990).
8. Anzaldúa, *Making Face, Making Soul.*
9. Anzaldúa, *Making Face, Making Soul,* xvi.
10. Anzaldúa quoting Rosario Castellaños's poem "El Mar," from *Poesia No Eres Tu,* in *Making Face, Making Soul,* 92.
11. Anzaldúa quoting Inés Hernández-Ávila, "'Triumph Is a Sweet Song—the One You Know': The Voices of Gloria Anzaldúa, Wendy Rose, and Joy Harjo," presentation at Modern Language Association Conference, New Orleans, December 1988, in *Making Face, Making Soul.*
12. Anzaldúa, *Making Face, Making Soul,* xxiv.
13. Anzaldúa, *Making Face, Making Soul,* xxiv.
14. Gloria Anzaldúa and AnaLouise Keating, *Light In the Dark/Luz en lo Oscuro: Rewriting Identity, Spirituality, Reality* (Duke University Press, 2015), 138.
15. Gonzales, *Red Medicine,* xvii.
16. Carmen Lomas Garza, phone interview by Brenda Sendejo, August 2008.
17. Anzaldúa, "now let us shift . . . ," 542.
18. Anzaldúa, "now let us shift . . . ," 542; Anzaldúa, *Light in the Dark,* 242.
19. Anzaldúa, "now let us shift . . . ," 574.
20. Gonzales, *Red Medicine,* xvii.
21. Brenda Sendejo, "Methodologies of the Spirit: Reclaiming Our Lady of Guadalupe and Discovering Tonantzin Within and Beyond the Nepantla of Academia," in *Fleshing the Spirit: Spirituality and Activism in Chicana, Latina, and Indigenous Women's Lives,* ed. Elisa Facio and Irene Lara (University of Arizona Press, 2014), 95–113.
22. Chimamanda Ngozi Adichie, "The Danger of a Single Story," TEDTalk, YouTube, October 7, 2009, https://www.youtube.com/watch?v=D9Ihs241zeg.
23. Alma M. García (ed.), *Chicana Feminist Thought: The Basic Historical Writings* (Routledge, 1997).
24. Anzaldúa, "now let us shift . . . ," 544.
25. Conversation with Nancy "Rusty" Barceló, MALCS Conference, University of Utah, Salt Lake City, 2008.
26. Anzaldúa, "now let us shift . . . ," 562.
27. "Gloria Anzaldúa," February 1, 1994, The Latina History Project, Southwestern University, https://latinahistoryproject.southwestern.edu/items/show/128.
28. Alicia Enciso-Litschi reminded me of the teachings and relationships that go into learning to "become an elder," as she rightfully pointed out the women are preparing me/us to do.

29. Irene Lara proposes the term *bodymindspirit* in order to emphasize the body as a central locus of oppression, a site of social struggle. She notes, "I slowly began to heal my fragmented self and move toward wholeness and balance. I think and feel at once. Unlearning the western mind/body split and learning to listen to the wisdom of my whole self, my bodymindspirit, is a perpetual process." See Irene Lara, "Healing Sueños for Academia," in *This Bridge We Call Home: Radical Visions for Transformation*, ed. Gloria E. Anzaldúa and AnaLouise Keating (Routledge, 2002), 433–38.
30. Used with permission of reflection author Laura Hoelter.
31. Anzaldúa, "now let us shift . . ."
32. Anzaldúa, "now let us shift . . . ," 542.
33. Cindy O. Fierros and Dolores Delgado Bernal's essay "Vamos a Platicar: The Contours of Pláticas as Chicana/Latina Feminist Methodology," which would become a seminal work in Chicana/Latina studies as one of its central methodologies, provided me with an important framework to further understand Rev. Virginia's use of *plática,* which Cierros and Delgado Bernal acknowledge emerges in our families and traditions. See Cindy O. Fierros and Dolores Delgado Bernal, "Vamos a Platicar: The Contours of Pláticas as Chicana/Latina Feminist Methodology," *Chicana/Latina Studies* 15, no. 2 (Spring 2016): 98–121.
34. María Cotera, "Unpacking Our Mothers' Libraries: Practices of Chicana Memory Before and After the Digital Turn," in *Chicana Movidas: New Narratives of Activism and Feminism in the Movement Era,* ed. Dionne Espinoza, María Eugenia Cotera, and Maylei Blackwell (University of Texas Press, 2018), 304.
35. Gloria Anzaldúa, *Borderlands/La Frontera: The New Mestiza,* 4th ed. (Aunt Lute Books, 2012).

Chapter 2

Portions of this chapter were published in Jody A. Marín and Norma E. Cantú (eds.), *¡Somos Tejanas! Chicana Identity and Culture in Texas* (University of Texas Press, 2025).

1. Inés Hernández-Ávila, quoted in Yolanda Chávez Leyva, "The Revisioning of History Es una Gran Limpia," *La Voz de Esperanza* 15, no. 7 (September 2002): 10–11.
2. Leyva, "The Revisioning of History Es una Gran Limpia," 10.
3. María Cotera, "Unpacking Our Mothers' Libraries: Practices of Chicana Memory Before and After the Digital Turn," in *Chicana Movidas: New Narratives of Activism and Feminism in the Movement Era,* ed. Dionne Espinoza, María Eugenia Cotera, and Maylei Blackwell (University of Texas Press, 2018), 302.
4. Anzaldúa describes border arte this way: "Chicana/Chicano artists currently are engaged in 'reading' that nepantla, that border, and that cenote—from which direction and renewal spring forth. Imagination, mundus imaginalis—the source of creativity, dreams, fantasies, intuitions, resides in el cenote and

symbolic events—resides in el cenote. For those of us who are receptive, el cenote offers the unconscious's resources for self-knowledge and transformation. Nepantla is the threshold of transformation. Art and la frontera intersect and a liminal space [is created] where border people, especially artists, live in a state of nepantla." Gloria Anzaldúa and AnaLouise Keating, *Light in the Dark/Luz en lo Oscuro: Rewriting Identity, Spirituality, Reality* (Duke University Press, 2015), 55–56.

5. Patrisia Gonzales, *Red Medicine: Traditional Indigenous Rites of Birthing and Healing* (University of Arizona Press, 2012), 39.
6. Inés Hernández-Ávila, as cited in Gonzales, *Red Medicine*, 39.
7. Brenda Sendejo, "Unsilencing the Past: The Spirit Work of Movement-Era Tejanas," in *¡Somos Tejanas! Chicana Identity and Culture in Texas*, ed. Jody Marín and Norma E. Cantú (University of Texas Press, 2025), 208–9.
8. Cotera, "Unpacking Our Mothers' Libraries."
9. A limpia is a spiritual cleansing. Of Latin American origin, the limpia can take many forms, often includes the use of particular herbs or resins such as sage or copal to cleanse energy, and is frequently performed by a curandera/o.
10. Michel-Rolph Trouillot, *Silencing the Past: Power and the Production of History* (Beacon Press, 1995).
11. Deep gratitude to Dr. Martha Menchaca. As my undergraduate professor, she suggested I pursue graduate studies, which inspired me to apply to my doctoral program.
12. I want to emphasize the importance of ethnic studies with this autoethnographic reflection—the power of knowing our history and its immeasurable impacts.
13. My reference to "unsilencing the past" is inspired by Haitian anthropologist Michel-Rolph Trouillot's 1995 work, *Silencing the Past: Power and the Production of History*. Trouillot examines power within the context of history and historical archives in terms of who has access to how history is created. He says that all histories comprise bundles of silences. I am concerned with the effects of historical narratives that erase and silence and the healing effects of historical recuperation efforts—that is, the power of history to both wound and heal.
14. I would choose to write my master's report and later publish on the influence of World War II–generation women on the Chicana consciousness of their daughters. It was not until after I turned in the report that I learned that my grandmother, María Balcazar Castañon Sendejo, who immigrated to the U.S. from Mexico, was also a World War II worker, like the women I had interviewed.
15. Leyva, "The Revisioning of History Es un Gran Limpia," 10.
16. My approach to "history" in this book is not something I take for granted; rather, it emerges as a central question within the context of women's histories and their potential to heal, as Leyva states. As a cultural anthropologist who deals in history, I know that historical narratives are dynamic and have effects.

I look at historical processes and the effects of histories; their making; the production of narratives and their power, holes, and symbols.

17. I co-founded the Latina History Project (LHP) with Dr. Alison Kafer. In addition to Tori, Adriana Romero, the other student who was among the first to join the LHP, made lasting and significant contributions to the LHP, setting the foundation for what would be powerful encuentros for many students who would follow in their paths, those working with the project and also those using the materials in their coursework and research. Charlotte Nunes, the digital humanities scholar in residence, lent the project her valuable expertise and commitment to unsilencing the past.
18. Tori Vasquez and Brenda Sendejo, "Unboxing the Buried Seeds of My Belonging," *Anthropology News*, May 2, 2017.
19. Tori shared an insight that has stayed with me for years, regarding the welcome she received upon coming to the university: "It's one thing to be welcomed, it's another to belong."
20. Gloria Anzaldúa, "now let us shift . . . the path of conocimiento . . . inner works, public acts," in *This Bridge We Call Home: Radical Visions for Transformation*, ed. Gloria E. Anzaldúa and AnaLouise Keating (Routledge, 2002), 562–63.
21. Espinoza, Cotera, and Blackwell, *Chicana Movidas,* 2.
22. Sendejo, "Unsilencing the Past."
23. Anzaldúa, "now let us shift . . . ," 541.
24. Espinoza, Cotera, and Blackwell, *Chicana Movidas,* 2.
25. See Sendejo, "Unsilencing the Past," for an account of Norma's feminist praxis and validating students' use of Spanglish as a sophisticated linguistic system.
26. Vicky Ruiz, *From Out of the Shadows: Mexican Women in Twentieth-Century America,*(Oxford University Press, 1998).
27. See Yolanda Chávez Leyva, "Listening to the Silences in Latina/Chicana Lesbian History," in *Living Chicana Theory*, ed. Carla Trujillo et al. (Third Woman Press, 1998), 429–34; and "'There Is Great Good in Returning': A Testimonio from the Borderlands," *Frontiers: A Journal of Women Studies* 24, nos. 2–3 (2003): 1–9, http://www.jstor.org/stable/3347343.
28. Olivia Evey Chapa (1946–2024) was a cofounder of Mujeres por La Raza Unida and a pivotal actor in La Raza Unida Party. Chapa earned a PhD in education from UT Austin and wrote numerous works on the Chicana movement, contributing to the efforts of the CRLC and getting material into the La Chicana course at UT, which she taught in addition to Gloria Anzaldúa and Inés Hernández-Ávila.
29. Brenda Sendejo, "The Space in Between: Exploring the Development of Chicana Feminist Thought in Central Texas," in *Chicana* Movidas*: New Narratives of Activism and Feminism in the Movement Era*, ed. Dionne Espinoza, María Eugenia Cotera, and Maylei Blackwell (University of Texas Press, 2018), 190. The work of the CRLC was collaborative and widespread in terms of audience and reach.

They worked with and contributed to universities, community-based groups, and Mujeres por La Raza Unida, the RUP women's caucus.

30. Cotera's feminism means liberation for the entire family. Her community activism extends decades, and she is still very active as a scholar, archivist, and feminist historian. Cotera helped to found Juárez-Lincoln University—the first Chicano university—in the state of Texas. She was a founding member of numerous organizations and was instrumental in creating the Center for Mexican American Studies and the Mexican American and Latina/o Studies Library Program housed in the Benson Latin American Collection, both at UT Austin.
31. Martha P. Cotera, *Diosa y Hembra: The History and Heritage of Chicanas in the U.S.* (Information Systems Development, 1976).
32. Martha Cotera, interview by Brenda Sendejo, Austin, Texas, 2016.
33. Sendejo, "The Space in Between." See also Sendejo, "The Cultural Production of Spiritual Activisms: Gender, Social Justice, and the Remaking of Religion in the Borderlands," *Chicana/Latina Studies* 12, no. 2 (Spring 2013): 59–109.
34. Sendejo, "The Space in Between."
35. Sendejo, "The Space in Between."
36. Levya, "The Revisioning of History Es una Gran Limpia."
37. See Sendejo, "Unsilencing the Past."
38. Patrisia Gonzales references Yolanda Levya's "The Revisioning of History Es una Gran Limpia" in her work on Indigenous stories and medicinal histories (where she also cites Aurora Levins Morales's work on medicine stories).
39. See Yolanda Chávez Leyva, "In Ixtli in Yóllotl/A Face and a Heart: Listening to the Ancestors," *Studies in American Indian Literatures* 15, nos. 3–4 (2003): 96–127; and Leyva, "If a Woman Stands at the Door You Can't Go In': Jovita's Story, April 1914," in *Entre Guadalupe y Malinche: Tejanas in Literature and Art*, ed. Inés Hernández-Ávila and Norma Elia Cantú (University of Texas Press, 2016), 126–31.
40. PODER was formed in 1991 to "increase Austin's residents' participation in corporate and government decisions related to economic development, environmental hazards and the impact on our neighborhoods." This nonprofit organization was established by a group of Chicana/o East Austin activists and community leaders to address the social, economic, and environmental impacts of such industries and the potential health hazards on East Austin's communities of color. PODER has shown that historically, communities of color—Latinos, African Americans, Asian Americans, and Native Americans—have been disproportionately affected by toxic contamination and that the surrounding communities have not benefited equitably from these industries. Within East Austin and in close proximity to residential neighborhoods and the PODER office, there is a power plant, fuel storage tank farms, lumber companies, and, most recently, high-tech industries that emit their pollutants into the air that communities and their families breathe, the water they drink, and the earth

that sustains them. PODER staff, volunteers, and supporters believe a safe and healthy environment is a fundamental right for all. See the PODER Austin website, https://www.poderaustin.org/.

41. Leyva, "There Is Great Good in Returning." Also see Aurora Levins Morales, *The Story of What Is Broken Is Whole: An Aurora Levins Morales Reader* (Duke University Press, 2024).
42. Leyva, "There Is Great Good in Returning."
43. *Temazcales* are common in parts of Mexico, including the Central Valley and Oaxaca. They have gained popularity among Chicanas and Chicanos in the United States, particularly among those who practice a Mexica spiritual path, reverting to the spiritual traditions of their Indigenous ancestors.
44. Hernández-Ávila is of Niimiipuu/Nez Percé heritage, enrolled in the Confederated Tribes of the Colville Reservation, Washington, on her mother's side, and Tejana (and Mexican Indigenous) on her father's side. She is recognized for her scholarship on cultural and linguistic revitalization movements among Indigenous peoples, as well as her work on contemporary Indigenous literature and Indigenous religious traditions in the Americas. As a Chicana and Nez Percé scholar, she has made and continues to make significant contributions to complex and critical discussions around indigeneity within and across Chicana/o studies and Native American studies.
45. Inés Hernández-Ávila, virtual interview by Brenda Sendejo, December 2024.
46. Mary Louise Pratt, "'Yo Soy La Malinche': Chicana Writers and the Poetics of Ethnonationalism," *Callaloo* 16, no. 4 (Autumn 1993): 859–73.
47. Gonzales, *Red Medicine*, 41.
48. Anzaldúa and Keating, *Light in the Dark*, 47.
49. Laura Elisa Pérez, *Chicana Art: The Politics of Spiritual and Aesthetic Altarities* (Duke University Press, 2007), 3.
50. See Carmen Lomas Garza, *In My Family/En mi familia* (Children's Book Press, 2000). Carmen Lomas Garza was born in 1948 in Kingsville, Texas, one of five children. Her father's family arrived in Texas during the Mexican Revolution, and her mother's family included vaqueros, railroad workers, and a chuck wagon cook. See Garza, *A Piece of My Heart/Pedacito de Mi Corazón: The Art of Carmen Lomas Garza* (The New Press, 1991). She earned two art education degrees in Texas and a studio art degree in California, becoming a renowned artist, children's book author, and illustrator. Through her artwork and family stories, she has chronicled the stories of Texas Mexicans and their history and cultural traditions. I came to know Carmen within the context of my job as an exhibit researcher for a children's exhibit called *In My Family/En mi familia*, based on Carmen's artwork and her children's book of the same name. The exhibition team would turn Carmen's paintings into three-dimensional, life-size environments. It was inspired by and incorporated images from the following works: *La Tamalada, Beds for Dreaming, The Birthday Party*, and *Conjunto*.

That exhibit is now on permanent display at the John E. Conner Museum at Texas A&M University, Kingsville.

51. Pérez, *Chicana Art*, 106.
52. Day of the Dead or Día de los Muertos originated in Mexico, where it is a widespread practice. Taking place on November 2, it is now celebrated in various parts of Latin America and the United States. People erect altars—ranging from small and intimate to large and elaborate—in honor of loved ones who have passed. It is typically celebrated in private, but public events, such as street parades, also take places in locations with strong Latinx communities, such as Austin, Los Angeles, and San Francisco. *Ofrendas* (offerings) are placed on the altars, including flowers, photos, and favorite foods and items of the departed. It is believed souls who have passed come back on the evening of November 2 to visit. See Garza, *A Piece of My Heart*.
53. Sendejo, "The Face of God Has Changed," 185.
54. Garza, *A Piece of My Heart*.
55. See Garza, *A Piece of My Heart*, 13.
56. Here Carmen references the nopal cactus that is often represented in her artwork as a symbol of South Texas, as in *Nopalitos* (1995) and other works.
57. This story on the Dia de los Muertos event is in my dissertation, "The Face of God Has Changed."
58. Sendejo, "The Face of God Has Changed," 193–97.
59. This story was taken from my dissertation, "The Face of God Has Changed."
60. Estella Garcia's daughter, Estella Cantú, shared with Santa that the tree is an olive tree and that it does not produce olives, but does produce golden flowers. This experience was part of my dissertation research, which I conducted with Santa in 2005.
61. Darin would later tell me that he believed the sound of the water flowing was actually that of the wind flowing through the leaves of the tree; because the tree is hollow, it allows for this sound to cascade down the trunk as if it were running water. I draw on this narrative to explain two things about my approach to studying spirituality in the borderlands. The first involves the experience of listening to the sound of the water running down the tree and later seeing the dozens of photos and supplications on the walls in the Healing Tree's small chapel. I have a deep interest in the *effects* of the Healing Tree and other such religious sites and rituals on people—how such rituals enable them to make sense of the world around them and the communal, spiritual, and emotional needs such rituals fulfill. Hence, there was no need to hear Darin's explanation for the sound of the running water. As an anthropologist, it is the impacts of religious and spiritual practices on practitioners that I am concerned with, not issues of "validity." This is a foundational approach to my feminist methodology and praxis and informs my concept of the spirit story and its effects.
62. Anzaldúa and Keating, *Light in the Dark*, 51.

63. Anzaldúa, *Light In the Dark,* 51. Anzaldúa cites Santa Barraza, who is quoted in Jennifer Heath, "Women Artists of Color Share World of Struggle," *Sunday Camera,* March 8, 1992, 9C.
64. Santa Barraza, *Santa Barraza: Artist of the Borderlands,* ed. María Herrera-Sobek (Texas A&M University Press, 2001), 48.
65. Anzaldúa, "now let us shift . . . ," 560. See also note 20 on page 207 in this volume.
66. Anzaldúa, "now let us shift . . . ," 562–63.
67. Leyva, "The Revisioning of History Es una Gran Limpia."

Chapter 3

1. María Elena Martinez, interview by Brenda Sendejo for *The Journey of María Elena Martínez,* student documentary produced and directed by Lynn Selby, Brenda Sendejo, and Clay Hawkins, University of Texas at Austin, 2005.
2. Gloria Anzaldúa, *Borderlands/La Frontera: The New Mestiza,* 4th ed. (Aunt Lute Books, 2012).
3. Inés Hernández-Ávila, interview by Brenda Sendejo, December 2024.
4. Hernández-Ávila, interview, December 2024.
5. This story was initially published in Brenda Sendejo, "Methodologies of the Spirit: Reclaiming Our Lady of Guadalupe and Discovering Tonantzin Within and Beyond the Nepantla of Academia," in *Fleshing the Spirit: Spirituality and Activism in Chicana, Latina, and Indigenous Women's Lives,* ed. Elisa Facio and Irene Lara (University of Arizona Press, 2014), 95–113.
6. Anzaldúa, *Borderlands.*
7. Anzaldúa, *Borderlands.*
8. See Irene Lara, "Tonanlupanisma: Re-Membering Tonantzin-Guadalupe in Chicana Visual Art," *Aztlán: A Journal of Chicano Studies* 33, no. 2 (Fall 2008): 61–90.
9. Irene Lara, "Goddess of the Américas in the Decolonial Imaginary: Beyond the Virtuous Virgen/Pagan Puta Dichotomy," *Feminist Studies* 34, nos. 1–2 (Spring/Summer 2008): 99–127.
10. Norma Cantú, interview by Brenda Sendejo, San Antonio, Texas, 2008. All subsequent quotes by Norma in this chapter are from this interview unless otherwise specified.
11. See Norma E. Cantú, *Fiestas in Laredo: Matachines, Quinceañeras, and George Washington's Birthday* (University of North Texas Press, 2024). Los Matachines de la Santa Cruz trace their origins to colonial-era celebrations of the Holy Cross in Real de Catorce, Mexico. Blending Indigneous and European ritual practices of dance, food, and music, they hold fiestas and practice devotion through celebrations on May 3 and December 12 (the Feast Day of the Virgen de Guadalupe), using a blend of Indigenous and European ritual practices.
12. Rosie Castro, interview by Brenda Sendejo, San Antonio, Texas, 2008.
13. Timothy Matovina and Gary Riebe-Estrella, *Horizons of the Sacred: Mexican Traditions in U.S. Catholicism* (Cornell University Press, 2002).

14. Founded in 1971, Las Hermanas was the first national religious-political organization of Chicana and Latina Roman Catholics in the United States. The mission of Las Hermanas was to create an alternative space for Latina Catholics to express a feminist spirituality and theology and to apply this to enhancing service to their communities. As agents of change, Las Hermanas transformed religious life so that it connected to the struggles of their ethnic and gendered communities. Their motto was "Unidas en accíon y oracíon" (United in prayer and action). Lara Medina, *Las Hermanas: Chicana/Latina Religious-Political Activism in the U.S. Catholic Church* (Temple University Press, 2004). From the early 1970s to the mid-1990s Hermanas chapters in Texas and other parts of the United States worked to increase awareness of the needs of their communities and to enact social change, bringing these issues to the attention of church hierarchy while also aiming to improve the role of women in the church. María Eva Flores, "Las Hermanas: Empowering Catholic Women Since 1970," *Handbook of Texas Online*, October 1, 1995, updated May 2, 2017, Texas State Historical Association, https://www.tshaonline.org/handbook/entries/las-hermanas.
15. Sandra Cisneros, "Guadalupe the Sex Goddess," in *Goddess of the Americas: Writings on the Virgin of Guadalupe*, ed. Ana Castillo (Riverhead Books, 1996), 46–51.
16. Alicia Gaspar de Alba and Alma López (eds.), *Our Lady of Controversy: Alma López's "Irreverent Apparition"* (University of Texas Press, 2011).
17. Padres Asociados para los Derechos Religiosos, Educativos y Sociales/Priests Associated for Religious, Educational, and Social Rights (PADRES) was an organization of priests founded in San Antonio in 1969 in order to serve the Mexican American population of San Antonio's Westside. Liberation theology and various other theological trends in Latin America informed the work of PADRES, which included involvement in settling local labor disputes, establishing grassroots organizations, and working with women's religious groups, like Las Hermanas, on various initiatives, such as the opening of the Mexican American Cultural Center. María Eva Flores, "History of Padres Asociados para los Derechos Religiosos, Educativos, y Sociales," *Handbook of Texas Online*, May 1, 1995, updated October 6, 2022, Texas State Historical Association, https://www.tshaonline.org/handbook/entries/padres.
18. Sendejo, "The Face of God Has Changed."
19. Anzaldúa, *Borderlands*, 27.
20. Martha Cotera, interview by Brenda Sendejo, Austin, Texas, 2012. All subsequent quotes by Martha in this chapter are taken from this interview.
21. Sendejo, "The Face of God Has Changed."
22. Portions of this story appeared in Brenda Sendejo, "The Cultural Production of Spiritual Activisms: Gender, Social Justice, and the Remaking of Religion in the Borderlands," *Chicana/Latina Studies* 12, no. 2 (Spring 2013).
23. Anzaldúa, "Spiritual Activism: Making Altares, Making Connections," 1996, 2, as quoted in Brenda Sendejo, "The Cultural Production of Spiritual Activisms."

24. bell hooks, “Theory as Liberatory Practice,” *Yale Journal of Law and Feminism* 4, no. 1 (1991): 1.
25. hooks, “Theory as Liberatory Practice.”

Chapter 4

1. Brenda Sendejo, “The Face of God Has Changed: Tejana Spiritual Cultural Production and the Politics of Spirituality,” PhD diss. (University of Texas at Austin, 2011), 145.
2. Quoted in AnaLouise Keating, “‘I’m a Citizen of the Universe’: Gloria Anzaldúa’s Spiritual Activism as Catalyst for Social Change,” *Feminist Studies* 34, nos. 1–2 (Spring/Summer 2008): 63.
3. Irene Lara, “Healing Suenos for Academia,” in *This Bridge We Call Home: Radical Visions for Transformation,* ed. Gloria E. Anzaldúa and AnaLouise Keating (Routledge, 2002), 433–38.
4. Mary Margaret Navar, phone conversation with Brenda Sendejo, June 2025.
5. Gloria Anzaldúa, “now let us shift . . . the path of conocimiento . . . inner works, public acts,” in *This Bridge We Call Home: Radical Visions for Transformation,* ed. Gloria E. Anzaldúa and AnaLouise Keating (Routledge, 2002), 540–87.
6 bell hooks, “Building a Community of Love: bell hooks and Thich Nhat Hanh,” *Lion’s Roar,* January 20, 2025, https://www.lionsroar.com/bell-hooks-thich-nhat-hanh-building-community-love.
7. Alma de Mujer Center for Social Change website, http://www.almademujer.org.
8. Genevieve Vaughan, *For-Giving: A Feminist Criticism of Exchange* (Plain View Press, 1997).
9. Susana Almanza, “Susana Almanza from PODER Shares the Importance of Alma de Mujer’s Center for Social Change,” YouTube, September 15, 2009, https://www.youtube.com/watch?v=5ZkfPJT6pk8.
10. Anzaldúa quoted in AnaLouise Keating, “‘I’m a Citizen of the Universe’: Gloria Anzaldúa’s Spiritual Activism as Catalyst for Social Change.” *Feminist Studies* 34, nos. 1–2 (Spring/Summer 2008): 63.
11. Alicia Enciso-Litschi, phone conversation with Brenda Sendejo, June 2025.
12. Alicia Enciso-Litschi, “Con Alma: Dialogues in Decolonizing Counseling—Reciprocal Ethnographic Explorations in Indigenous Spaces for Community Healing,” PhD diss. (University of Texas at Austin, 2014), https://www.zlibrary.to/dl/con-alma-dialogues-in-decolonizing-counseling.
13. Mary Margaret Navar, *Zapotec Woman of the Clouds: The Life of the Midwife-Healer Enriqueta Contreras Contreras* (Zapotec Press, 2011). This book, written by Mary Margaret with Doña Enriqueta, details Doña Enriqueta’s fascinating life as a curandera and partera and her expansive knowledge of traditional medicine.
14. Gloria Anzaldúa (ed.), *Making Face, Making Soul/Haciendo Caras: Creative and Critical Perspectives by Feminists of Color* (Aunt Lute Books, 1990), xvi. Anzaldúa also cites Inés Hernández-Ávila, “‘Triumph Is a Sweet Song—the

One You Know': The Voices of Gloria Anzaldúa, Wendy Rose, and Joy Harjo," presentation at the Modern Language Association Conference, New Orleans, December 1988.

15. La Peña is a Latino arts organization established to promote the arts and culture of Latin American and Latinx artists in Austin and across the region and country. It serves as a community gathering space in Austin.
16. Rosie Castro, phone conversation with Brenda Sendejo, February 11, 2025.

Conclusion

1. Gloria Anzalduá and AnaLouise Keating, *Light in the Dark/Luz en lo Oscuro: Rewriting Identity, Spirituality, Reality* (Duke University Press, 2015), 92.
2. Irene Lara, "Bruja Positionalities: Towards a Chicana/Latina Spiritual Activism," *Mujeres Activistas en Letras y Cambio Social* 4 (Spring 2005): 30.
3. Inés Hernández-Ávila, virtual interview by Brenda Sendejo, February 9, 2025.
4. Audre Lorde, *A Burst of Light: Essays* (Firebrand Books 1988), 131.
5. Inés Hernández-Àvila, email correspondence with Brenda Sendejo, May 25, 2024.
6. Patrisia Gonzales, *Red Medicine: Traditional Indigenous Rites of Birthing and Healing* (University of Arizona Press, 2012).
7. Gloria Anzaldúa, "now let us shift . . . the path of conocimiento . . . inner works, public acts," in *This Bridge We Call Home: Radical Visions for Transformation*, ed. Gloria E. Anzaldúa and AnaLouise Keating (Routledge, 2002), 540–87.
8. The photo caption references this essay: Brenda Sendejo, "Radical Mami Love: Chicana Consejos del Corazón," in *Voices from the Ancestors: Xicanx and Latinx Spiritual Expressions and Healing Practices*, ed. Lara Medina and Martha R. Gonzales (University of Arizona Press, 2019).

BIBLIOGRAPHY

Acosta, Teresa Palomo. *Tejanaland: A Writing Life in Four Acts*. Women in Texas History Series. Texas A&M University Press, 2022.

Acosta, Teresa Palomo, and Ruthe Winegarten. *Las Tejanas: 300 Years of History*. Jack and Doris Smothers Series in Texas History, Life, and Culture, no. 10. University of Texas Press, 2003.

Adichie, Chimamanda Ngozi. "The Danger of a Single Story." TEDTalk, YouTube, October 7, 2009. https://www.youtube.com/watch?v=D9Ihs241zeg.

Alma de Mujer Center for Social Change website. http://www.almademujer.org.

Almanza, Susana. Interview by Brenda Sendejo. Austin, Texas. March 2008.

———. "Susana Almanza from PODER Shares the Importance of Alma de Mujer's Center for Social Change." YouTube, September 15, 2009, https://www.youtube.com/watch?v=5ZkfPJT6pk8.

Anzalduá, Gloria. *Borderlands/La Frontera: The New Mestiza*, 4th ed. Aunt Lute Books, 2012.

———. "now let us shift . . . the path of conocimiento . . . inner works, public acts." In *This Bridge We Call Home: Radical Visions for Transformation*, edited by Gloria E. Anzaldúa and AnaLouise Keating. Routledge, 2002, 540–87.

Anzalduá, Gloria, ed. *Making Face, Making Soul/Haciendo Caras: Creative and Critical Perspectives by Feminists of Color*. Aunt Lute Books, 1990.

Anzalduá, Gloria, and AnaLouise Keating. *Light in the Dark: Luz en lo Oscuro: Rewriting Identity, Spirituality, Reality*. Latin America Otherwise Series. Duke University Press, 2015.

Barraza, Santa. Interview by Brenda Sendejo. Kingsville, Texas. March 2009.

———. *Santa Barraza, Artist of the Borderlands*, edited by María Herrera-Sobek. Rio Grande/Río Bravo: Borderlands Culture and Traditions. Texas A&M University Press, 2001.

Blackwell, Maylei. *¡Chicana Power! Contested Histories of Feminism in the Chicano Movement.* Chicana Matters Series. University of Texas Press, 2011.

Cantú, Norma E. *Cabañuelas.* University of New Mexico Press, 2019.

———. *Canícula: Snapshots of a Girlhood en la Frontera.* Updated ed. University of New Mexico Press, 2015.

———. *Fiestas in Laredo: Matachines, Quinceañeras, and George Washington's Birthday.* University of North Texas Press, 2024.

———. Interview by Brenda Sendejo. San Antonio, Texas. August 2008.

Cantú, Norma E., and Marta Sánchez. *Transcendental Train Yard: A Collaborative Suite of Serigraphs.* Wings Press, 2015.

Cantú, Norma E., and Raquel Valle-Sentíes, eds. *Chicana Portraits: Critical Biographies of Twelve Chicana Writers.* University of Arizona Press, 2023.

Cantú-Sánchez, Margaret, Candace de León-Zepeda, and Norma Elia Cantú, eds. *Teaching Gloria E. Anzaldúa: Pedagogy and Practice for Our Classrooms and Communities.* University of Arizona Press, 2020.

Castillo, Ana, ed. *Goddess of the Americas: Writings on the Virgin of Guadalupe.* Riverhead Books, 1996.

Castro, Rosie. Interview by Brenda Sendejo. San Antonio, Texas. July 2008.

———. Phone interview by Brenda Sendejo. February 11, 2025.

Center for the Study of the Southwest. "East Austin Brown Berets Geography." Texas State University. https://www.txst.edu/cssw/news-events/cssw-projects-archive/brown-beret.html.

Chicana por mi Raza Digital Memory Project and Archive. https://www.chicanapormiraza.org/.

Cisneros, Sandra. "Guadalupe the Sex Goddess." In *Goddess of the Americas: Writings on the Virgin of Guadalupe,* edited by Ana Castillo. Riverhead Books, 1996, 46–51.

"Cotera and Martínez, María Elena Martínez: State Chairwoman; Raza Unida Party, Austin, Texas," undated, box 1, folder 14, María Elena Martínez Papers. Nettie Lee Benson Latin American Collection, University of Texas at Austin.

Cotera, María Eugenia. *Fleshing the Archive: An Intimate Genealogy of Chicana Knowledge Praxis.* University of Texas Press, 2026.

———. "Nuestra Autohistoria: Toward a Chicana Digital Praxis." *American Quarterly* 70, no. 3 (2018): 483–504.

———. "Nuestra Autohistoria." Panel presentation, Recovering the U.S. Hispanic Literary Heritage Conference, University of Houston, February 20–22, 2020.

———. "Unpacking Our Mother's Libraries: Practices of Chicana Memory Before and After the Digital Turn." In *Chicana Movidas: New Narratives of Activism and Feminism in the Movement Era,* edited by Dionne Espinoza, María Eugenia Cotera, and Maylei Blackwell. University of Texas Press, 2018, 299–316.

Cotera, Martha P. *The Chicana Feminist.* Information Systems Development, 1977.

———. "Chingona Chones y Nuevas Generaciones: A Reflection on *Diosa y Hembra.*" *Chicana/Latina Studies* 19, no. 2 (Spring 2013): 32–49.

———. *Diosa y Hembra: The History and Heritage of Chicanas in the U.S.* Information Systems Development, 1976.

———. Interview by Brenda Sendejo. Austin, Texas, 2016.

———. Interview by Brenda Sendejo. Austin, Texas, 2012.

De la Portilla, Elizabeth. *"They All Want Magic": Curanderas and Folk Healing.* Texas A&M University Press, 2009.

Enciso-Litschi, Alicia. "Con Alma: Dialogues in Decolonizing Counseling—Reciprocal Ethnographic Explorations in Indigenous Spaces for Community Healing." PhD diss., University of Texas at Austin, 2014. https://www.zlibrary.to/dl/con-alma-dialogues-in-decolonizing-counseling.

———. Phone conversation with Brenda Sendejo. June 2025.

Espinoza, Dionne. "'The Partido Belongs to Those Who Will Work for It': Chicana Organizing and Leadership in the Texas Raza Unida Party, 1970–1980," Aztlán 36, no. 1 (Spring 2011): 191–210.

Espinoza, Dionne, María Eugenia Cotera, and Maylei Blackwell, eds. *Chicana Movidas: New Narratives of Activism and Feminism in the Movement Era.* University of Texas Press, 2018.

Facio, Elisa, and Irene Lara. *Fleshing the Spirit: Spirituality and Activism in Chicana, Latina, and Indigenous Women's Lives.* University of Arizona Press, 2014.

Fierros, Cindy O., and Dolores Delgado Bernal. "Vamos a Platicar: The Contours of Pláticas as Chicana/Latina Feminist Methodology." *Chicana/Latina Studies* 15, no. 2 (Spring 2016): 98–121.

Flores, María Eva. "Las Hermanas: Empowering Catholic Women Since 1970." *Handbook of Texas Online,* October 1, 1995, updated May 2, 2017, Texas State Historical Association. https://www.tshaonline.org/handbook/entries/las-hermanas.

———. "History of Padres Asociados para los Derechos Religiosos, Educativos, y Sociales." *Handbook of Texas Online,* May 1, 1995, updated October 6, 2022, Texas State Historical Association. https://www.tshaonline.org/handbook/entries/padres.

Garcia, Alma M., ed. *Chicana Feminist Thought: The Basic Historical Writings.* Routledge, 1997.

García, María-Cristina. "Mujeres Artistas del Suroeste." *Handbook of Texas Online.* Texas State Historical Association. https://www.tshaonline.org/handbook/entries/mujeres-artistas-del-suroeste.

Garza, Carmen Lomas. *In My Family/En Mi Familia.* Children's Book Press, 2000.

———. Phone interview by Brenda Sendejo. August 27, 2008.

———. *A Piece of My Heart/Pedacito de Mi Corazón: The Art of Carmen Lomas Garza.* The New Press, 1991.

Gaspar de Alba, Alicia, and Alma López, eds. *Our Lady of Controversy: Alma Lopez's "Irreverent Apparition."* Chicana Matters Series. University of Texas Press, 2011.

Gonzales, Patrisia. *Red Medicine: Traditional Indigenous Rites of Birthing and Healing.* First Peoples: New Directions in Indigenous Studies. University of Arizona Press, 2012.

Haga, Kazu, Bernard LaFayette, and David C. Jehnsen. *Healing Resistance: A Radically Different Response to Harm.* Parallax Press, 2020.

Heath, Jennifer. "Women Artists of Color Share World of Struggle." *Sunday Camera,* March 8, 1992.

Hernández-Ávila, Inés. "Dispelling the Sombras, Grito Mi Nombre con Rayos de Luz." In *Telling to Live: Latina Feminist Testimonios.* Duke University Press, 2001, 238–44.

———. Email correspondence with Brenda Sendejo. May 25, 2024.

———. "Foreword: A Meditation." In *Fleshing the Spirit: Spirituality and Activism in Chicana, Latina, and Indigenous Women's Lives.* University of Arizona Press, 2014, xiii–xix.

———. "Manifesto de Memoria: (Re)Living the Movement Without Blinking." In *Chicana Movidas: New Narratives of Activism and Feminism in the Movement Era,* edited by Dionne Espinoza, María Eugenia Cotera, and Maylei Blackwell. University of Texas Press, 2018.

———. "Sunrise Prayer." In *Voices from the Ancestors: Xicanx and Latinx Spiritual Expressions and Healing Practices.* University of Arizona Press, 2019.

———. "'Triumph Is a Sweet Song—the One You Know': The Voices of Gloria Anzaldúa, Wendy Rose, and Joy Harjo," Presentation at the Modern Language Association Conference, New Orleans, December 1988.

———. "That's Tejana." *Entre Guadalupe y Malinche: Tejanas in Literature and Art,* edited by Inés Hernández-Ávila and Norma E. Cantú. University of Texas Press, 2016.

———. Virtual interview by Brenda Sendejo. February 9, 2025.

———. Virtual interview by Brenda Sendejo. December 13, 2024.

hooks, bell. "Building a Community of Love: bell hooks and Thich Nhat Hanh." *Lion's Roar,* January 20, 2025. https://www.lionsroar.com/bell-hooks-thich-nhat-hanh-building-community-love.

———. "Theory as Liberatory Practice." *Yale Journal of Law and Feminism* 4, no. 1 (1991): 1–12.

Huerta, Elisa Diana. "Embodied Recuperations: Performance, Indigeneity, and Danza Azteca." In *Dancing Across Borders: Danzas y Bailes Mexicanos,* edited by Olga Nájera-Ramírez, Norma E. Cantú, and Brenda M. Romero. University of Illinois Press, 2009, 3–18.

Hurtado, Aída. *Intersectional Chicana Feminisms.* University of Arizona Press, 2020.

Hurtado, Aída, and Norma E. Cantú, eds. *MeXicana Fashions: Politics, Self-Adornment, and Identity Construction.* University of Texas Press, 2020.

Kaur, Valarie. *See No Stranger: A Memoir and Manifesto of Revolutionary Love.* One World, 2021.

Kaur, Valarie, and Keerat Kaur. *Sage Warrior: Wake to Oneness, Practice Pleasure, Choose Courage, Become Victory.* With Sonny Singh. One World, 2024.

Keating, AnaLouise. "'I'm a Citizen of the Universe': Gloria Anzaldúa's Spiritual Activism as Catalyst for Social Change." *Feminist Studies* 34, nos. 1–2 (Spring/Summer 2008): 53–69.

———. "Perspectives: Spiritual Activism, Social Transformation, and the Politics of Spirit." In *Entre Mundos/Among Worlds: New Perspectives on Gloria Anzaldúa*, edited by AnaLouise Keating. Palgrave Macmillan, 2005.

Lara, Irene. "Bruja Positionalities: Towards a Chicana/Latina Spiritual Activism." *Chicana/Latina Studies* 4, no. 2 (Spring 2005): 30.

———. "Goddess of the Américas in the Decolonial Imaginary: Beyond the Virtuous Virgen/Pagan Puta Dichotomy." *Feminist Studies* 34, nos. 1–2 (Spring/Summer 2008): 99–127.

———. "Healing Sueños for Academia." In *This Bridge We Call Home: Radical Visions for Transformation*, edited by Gloria E. Anzaldúa and AnaLouise Keating. Routledge, 2002, 433–38.

———. "Tonanlupanisma: Re-Membering Tonantzin-Guadalupe in Chicana Visual Art." *Aztlan: A Journal of Chicano Studies* 33, no. 2 (Fall 2008): 61–90.

Levins Morales, Aurora. *The Story of What Is Broken Is Whole: An Aurora Levins Morales Reader*. Duke University Press, 2024.

Leyva, Yolanda Chávez. "Gloria Anzaldúa's Legacy Will Continue to Inspire Generations." *The Progressive Magazine*, June 9, 2004. https://progressive.org/%3Fq%3Dnews/2004/06/758/gloria-anzald%C3%BAas-legacy-will-continue-inspire-generations/.

———. "'If a Woman Stands at the Door You Can't Go In': Jovita's Story, April 1914." In *Entre Guadalupe y Malinche: Tejanas in Literature and Art*, edited by Inés Hernández-Ávila and Norma Elia Cantú. University of Texas Press, 2016, 126–31.

———. "In Ixtli in Yóllotl/A Face and a Heart: Listening to the Ancestors." *Studies in American Indian Literatures* 15, nos. 3–4 (2003): 96–127. http://www.jstor.org/stable/20737216.

———. "Listening to the Silences in Latina/Chicana Lesbian History." In *Living Chicana Theory*, edited by Carla Trujillo, Teresa Córdova, Deena J González, et al. Third Woman Press, 1998.

———. "The Revisioning of History Es un Gran Limpia." *La Voz de Esperanza* 15, no. 7 (September 2002): 10–11.

———. "'There Is Great Good in Returning': A Testimonio from the Borderlands." *Frontiers: A Journal of Women Studies* 24, nos. 2–3 (2003): 1–9. http://www.jstor.org/stable/3347343.

Lorde, Audre. *A Burst of Light: Essays*. Firebrand Books, 1988.

"Main Building: Chicanos Protest UT Administration's Unwillingness to Create New Degree at the Main Building." "Rocking the Status Quo": Racial Justice Struggles in Austin website, December 7, 2021. https://storymaps.arcgis.com/stories/ff1e660665584c6ba2d15916a93c165e.

Marín, Jody A., and Norma E. Cantú, eds. *¡Somos Tejanas! Chicana Identity and Culture in Texas*. Joe R. and Teresa Lozano Long Series in Latin American and Latino Art and Culture. University of Texas Press, 2025.

Martínez, María Elena. Interview by Brenda Sendejo for *The Journey of María Elena Martínez*. Student documentary produced and directed by Lynn Selby, Brenda Sendejo, and Clay Hawkins. University of Texas at Austin, 2005.

———. Interview by Brenda Sendejo. 2008.

———. Interview by Rebecca Snow. April 7, 2004. Box 158, item 13–17, Center for Mexican American Studies Records. Nettie Lee Benson Latin American Collection, University of Texas Libraries, University of Texas at Austin.

———. "My Relations." In *Voices from the Ancestors: Xicanx and Latinx Spiritual Expressions and Healing Practices*, edited by Lara Medina and Martha R. Gonzales. University of Arizona Press, 2019.

———. Personal communication with Brenda Sendejo, 2018.

———. Personal conversation with Brenda Sendejo, 2015.

Matovina, Timothy, and Gary Riebe-Estrella. *Horizons of the Sacred: Mexican Traditions in U.S. Catholicism*. Cornell University Press, 2002.

Medina, Lara. *Las Hermanas: Chicana/Latina Religious-Political Activism in the U.S. Catholic Church*. Temple University Press, 2004.

Medina, Lara, and Martha R. Gonzales, eds. *Voices from the Ancestors: Xicanx and Latinx Spiritual Expressions and Healing Practices*. University of Arizona Press, 2019.

Moraga, Cherríe, and Gloria Anzaldúa, eds. *This Bridge Called My Back: Writings by Radical Women of Color*, 40th anniversary ed. SUNY Press, 2021.

Navar, Mary Margaret. Phone conversation with Brenda Sendejo. June 2025.

———. *Zapotec Woman of the Clouds: The Life of the Midwife-Healer Enriqueta Contreras Contreras*. Zapotec Press, 2011.

Orozco, Aurora. "Dejar Mi Idioma Jamás (Never Abandon My Language)." The Latina History Project. https://latinahistoryproject.southwestern.edu/items/show/12.

Orozco, Cynthia. "Mujeres por La Raza: Empowering Chicanas in the Raza Unida Party." *Handbook of Texas Online*, November 1, 1995, updated February 9, 2019, Texas State Historical Association. https://www.tshaonline.org/handbook/entries/mujeres-por-la-raza.

Pérez, Emma. *The Decolonial Imaginary: Writing Chicanas into History*. Theories of Representation and Difference. Indiana University Press, 1999.

Pérez, Laura Elisa. *Chicana Art: The Politics of Spiritual and Aesthetic Altarities*. Objects/Histories. Duke University Press, 2007.

Pratt, Mary Louise. "'Yo Soy La Malinche': Chicana Writers and the Poetics of Ethnonationalism." *Callaloo* 16, no. 4 (Autumn 1993): 859–73.

Rincon, Virginia Marie. Interview by Brenda Sendejo. Austin, Texas. July 2011.

Rodriguez, Samantha, and Stalina Emmanuelle Villarreal. "María Jiménez: Reflexiones on Traversing Multiple Fronteras in the South." In *Chicana Movidas: New Narratives of Activism and Feminism in the Movement Era*, edited by Dionne Espinoza, María Eugenia Cotera, and Maylei Blackwell. University of Texas Press, 2018, 276–89.

Ruiz, Vicky. *From Out of the Shadows: Mexican Women in Twentieth-Century America*. Oxford University Press, 1998.

Sendejo, Brenda. "The Cultural Production of Spiritual Activisms: Gender, Social Justice, and the Remaking of Religion in the Borderlands." *Chicana/Latina Studies* 12, no. 2 (Spring 2013): 59–109.

———. "The Face of God Has Changed: Tejana Spiritual Cultural Production and the Politics of Spirituality." PhD diss., University of Texas at Austin, 2011.

———. "Methodologies of the Spirit: Reclaiming Our Lady of Guadalupe and Discovering Tonantzin Within and Beyond the Nepantla of Academia." In *Fleshing the Spirit: Spirituality and Activism in Chicana, Latina, and Indigenous Women's Lives*, edited by Elisa Facio and Irene Lara. University of Arizona Press, 2014, 95–113.

———. "Mother's Legacy: Cultivating Chicana Consciousness During the War Years." In *Beyond the Latino World War II Hero: The Social and Political Legacy of a Generation*, edited by Maggie Rivas-Rodriguez and Emilio Zamora. University of Texas Press, 2009, 156–77.

———. "Radical Mami Love: Chicana Consejos del Corazón." In *Voices from the Ancestors: Xicanx and Latinx Spiritual Expressions and Healing Practices*, edited by Lara Medina and Martha R. Gonzales. University of Arizona Press, 2019.

———. "The Space in Between: Exploring the Development of Chicana Feminist Thought in Central Texas." In *Chicana Movidas: New Narratives of Activism and Feminism in the Movement Era*, edited by Dionne Espinoza, María Eugenia Cotera, and Maylei Blackwell. University of Texas Press, 2018, 189–211.

———. "Social Justice and the Remaking of Religion in the Borderlands." *Chicana/Latina Studies* 12, no. 2 (Spring 2013).

———. "Unsilencing the Past: The Spirit Work of Movement-Era Tejanas." In *Somos Tejanas: Chicana Identity and Culture in Texas*, edited by Jody Marín and Norma E. Cantú. University of Texas Press, 2025, 204–21.

Trouillot, Michel-Rolph. *Silencing the Past: Power and the Production of History*. Beacon Press, 1995.

Vasquez, Tori, and Brenda Sendejo. "Unboxing the Buried Seeds of My Belonging." *Anthropology News*, May 2, 2017.

Vaughan, Genevieve. *For-Giving: A Feminist Criticism of Exchange*. Plain View Press, 1997.

Zamora, Emilio. "Raza Unida Party Women in Texas: Oral History, Pedagogy, and Historical Interpretation." *U.S. Latina & Latino Oral History Journal* 1 (2017): 29–46.

INDEX

ABOUT THE AUTHOR

Brenda Sendejo is a cultural anthropologist, consultant, and scholar-practitioner of spiritual activism. For two decades, she has collaborated with movement-era Chicanas in Texas, documenting their spiritual activism and illuminating its continued relevance for contemporary struggles. Sendejo holds a PhD, MA, and BA in cultural anthropology from University of Texas at Austin and has contributed to anthologies including *Voices from the Ancestors, Chicana Movidas: New Narratives of Activism and Feminism in the Movement Era,* and *¡Somos Tejanas! Chicana Identity and Culture in Texas.*

Printed and bound by CPI Group (UK) Ltd, Croydon, CR0 4YY
14/10/2026
14981891-0001